RISKING INTIMACY

Overcoming

Fear,

Finding

Rest

NANCY GROOM

Baker Books

A Division of Baker Book House Co
Grand Rapids, Michigan 49516

Published by Baker Books
a division of Baker Book House Company
P.O. Box 6287, Grand Rapids, MI 49516-6287

Printed in the United States of America

Library of Congress Cataloging-in-Publication Data

Groom, Nancy.
    Risking intimacy : overcoming fear, finding rest / Nancy Groom.
       p.   cm.
    ISBN 0-8010-6158-X (pbk.)
       1. Intimacy (Psychology)—Religious aspects—Christianity. I. Title.
    BV4597.53.I55 G76 2000
    248.8′44—dc21
                                          99-087569

For current information about all releases from Baker Book House, visit our web site:
http://www.bakerbooks.com

To Steve and Lorraine Griffith
who know well how to risk
for the sake of intimacy

CONTENTS

ACKNOWLEDGMENTS

THE BOOK YOU ARE HOLDING has been long in gestation and almost as long in birthing. I am grateful to Steve Griffith and my colleagues at Baker Book House for their patience in my labor. For wisdom, encouragement, and prayer along the way I thank especially my good friends Jody Engel, Penny Freeman, Pat Landman, and Mary Ann Ulmer. Mary Suggs and Mary Wenger assisted the delivery with their kindness and their keen editing skills. And my husband, Bill, has been as always partner, participant, and coach in the bringing forth of new things from my heart: Thank you, my love, for your many risks in making our intimacy a place where I can rest.

Now to God our Savior, who alone gives life to any endeavor, even the writing of books, be endless praise for the unspeakable risks He takes in establishing and sustaining our intimacy with Him, for which He died and for which He yearns with the eagerness of a waiting bridegroom. Maranatha! Come soon, Lord Jesus!

INTRODUCTION

NOT LONG AGO, after I had returned from a speaking engagement in another city, my husband, Bill, admitted he felt more pressure having me home than he'd felt while I was away, though he was, as always, very glad to see me again. We talked at some length about why this was so but came to no definite conclusion beyond naming it "the friction of reentry." We obviously have more dialoging to do about this but we were reminded that the bright intimacy we have come to treasure is not without its shadows of ambivalence.

Intimacy is indeed a rainbow word, shining with irrepressible hope, though sometimes set against a darkened sky. Our times of closeness with God or with someone we love can bring us unspeakable joy, for we bear the image of a personal God whose very nature is glad intimacy within the threefold oneness of Father, Son, and Holy Spirit. Designed by God to image that oneness-in-diversity, we long for intimacy with Him and with others to nourish and enrich our lives. Being at rest in oneness is where we yearn to live.

But personal closeness can also be as disruptive as a storm in an otherwise sunny day, for sin has marred all aspects of our once perfect world, not least of all our relationships. Instead of finding rest in intimacy, we often find anxiety there, or perhaps deep fearfulness—the fear of conflict, disappointment, abandonment, death, even of love itself. Intimacy is an enigma, inviting us to both joy and chaos.

Because of culture and usage, *intimacy* is often thought to refer exclusively to sexual knowledge of another. But its meaning is far richer than that. According to the dictionary, *intimacy* refers to any relationship "marked by very close association, contact, or familiarity."[1] Under this umbrella will fall many relationships besides the sexual, including our oneness with God, and especially our connections with family and close friends.

However, a dictionary definition fails to capture the emotional nuances that the word *intimacy* evokes uniquely for each of us. I, for example, have struggled both relationally and spiritually with a kind of free-floating fear of intimacy, though I long to enter the relational rest into which God invites me. *Are rest and intimacy mutually exclusive?* I have sought to know. *If not, how can I learn to be at rest in my intimate relationships, especially with God and with my husband? I wonder what it would be like to live relationally off duty— not irresponsibly, but without striving.* Though sin has ruined the perfection of oneness God designed, I want to experience more and more the gospel's restoration of the connectedness I know God intends me to live in even now and until He takes me Home. Of particular concern in my struggle have been three questions, which form the framework of the book you now hold in your hands.

The first question is this: *What keeps us from resting in intimacy, human and divine?* Among the many casualties littering the landscape of our high-technology culture, perhaps none are so tragic as the loss of genuine connectedness in our relationships and the absence of tranquillity in ourselves. Even among Christians, where love and peace should abound, too often goal-driven agendas have taken precedence over people-centered interests. Nurturing a relationship takes time, and we have become a hurried and distracted—even disoriented—people. There is too much to do and not enough time to do it, for we have spread ourselves too thin and have said yes when we should have said no. Daily we face the danger of floating loose from the relational moorings that once secured us to God and connected us to each other, leaving us adrift in a sea of lonely activity. The first section of this book explores impediments to intimacy that diminish our fellowship with God and others, especially our spouses.

The second question then arises: *What would it take to bring us into the rest God offers, and what will it cost?* The real enemies of intimacy are more subtle—and more lethal—than mere busyness or distraction. What is it that provokes our busyness and energizes us to avoid being at rest with God and with ourselves? Will we allow the Holy Spirit to expose the motivation behind our sometimes frenzied striving, allowing us to rediscover inner quietude and to live in unhurried faith? God's promise of rest entices us, but to receive it requires much that is contrary to our old nature and to the habits we have formed. The middle section of this book examines the cost and process of yielding ourselves in an abandon of faith as God's sons and daughters.

Finally, then, we want to know: *What would it be like to live at rest in the relationships for which we are all created?* In what ways can the rainbow of quiet intimacy shelter us from the storms the enemy sends? How can we endure to the end without fainting in our relationships, bringing glory to our God and comfort to those we love? What would it look like to find in intimacy a place to genuinely rest? These are the issues addressed in the third and final section of this book.

TELLING STORIES

I love stories, as do most of us. In my previous books I have been an avid storyteller, for many men and women have honored me by telling me their stories, often giving me permission to share them with my readers. But God is a storyteller too and a number of His stories, told in His book, have shaped my thoughts about intimacy and our longing for rest.

Though the entirety of Scripture illuminates these concepts, I was drawn to consider in depth the narrative of God's deliverance of His people out of the bondage of Egypt and into the rest of the land of Canaan. Some of those stories may be familiar to the reader, but I wanted to probe the deeper meaning of the Israelites' movement from slavery to freedom, for it speaks to the journey we too must pursue in our quest for the alluring rest of intimacy.

I have also been captivated by Jesus' invitation to rest in Him (Matt. 11:28–30), and I was curious to explore how the people who met and lived with Him responded to that invitation. Of particular interest were the stories revealing how first-century men and women differed in their relating to Jesus, for I think it is relevant to our distinctiveness as male and female Christ-followers today.

And I have been eager as well to recount the more updated story of what God has been teaching my husband, Bill, and me about our own pursuit of marital intimacy. My earlier books revealed parts of our journey—especially the terrifying parts. And though we continue to face pockets of fear and confusion in our intimate walk with God and with each other, we are learning some important things about rest too and it seemed only fair to tell those stories as well.

That is why this book will tell many stories and examine their relevance to the struggles we face and the questions we ask about intimacy in our own lives. Each chapter begins with a brief scenario from the life of someone I know, though names and circumstances are modified to insure confidentiality. These opening vignettes are meant to provoke the reader to consider how contemporary situations intersect with the life stories told in Scripture, for relational conflict and spiritual struggle have always been part of the human experience, regardless of time or culture.

Each chapter then tells several Bible stories, beginning with a part of the narrative of the Israelites' exodus from Egypt and conquest of Canaan. This Old Testament story is followed by New Testament stories, some of which narrate the ongoing saga of Jesus' intimate relationship with the apostle Peter, and others exploring Jesus' interactions with several women important in His life and ministry. Finally, every chapter includes part of Bill's and my own journey into rest. Questions are also included as follow-up opportunities for individual or corporate reflection.

13

The deepest purpose of this book, however, the Story behind all other stories, is the revelation of the greatness of our God, the One whose story is the best of all, encompassing all of history as well as each of our own personal histories. For the glory of His Name, therefore, and for the edification of all His children, let the stories begin.

Part 1

FEAR

AND OTHER

UNQUIETNESS

CHAPTER ONE

AMBIVALENCE

The Seduction of Resignation

"MOM!" Annie called downstairs, a tinge of desperation in her voice. "Where is my pink sweater—the one with the blue and white flowers? I decided to take it with me and I can't find it!"

"Look in your closet," Shannon called back, "second shelf on the right. I think I saw it there a few days ago." Helping her second-born pack for college had become chaotic, and tomorrow was D Day—departure day. Saying good-bye to Annie would be a Velcro experience; Shannon's heart felt ripped apart already.

"I found it! Thanks, Mom!" came Annie's voice again, lilting this time.

Shannon would miss her daughter's chaos. In fact tomorrow's silence was what she dreaded most. Thinking back to four years ago when Tara had left for college, Shannon remembered the comfort she had taken in knowing Annie would still be home, bringing laughter and friends and delightful busyness into their home. This time the house would be empty, and even though Tara and her husband, Joey, would soon make her a grandmother, Shannon knew Annie's absence would leave a gaping hole in the fabric of her life. Listening to Annie singing upstairs as she packed, Shannon felt her eyes brimming in an ambivalence of pleasure and sorrow.

It's not just that Shannon would miss her daughter. She also knew that her "empty-nest" status would bring into bold relief the absence of intimacy in her relationship with her husband, David. Over the twenty-seven years of their marriage, Shannon's children and part-time job had gradually shifted David to the back burner of her life. At first he had complained of being neglected, but she had not taken him seriously, and eventually they had adjusted to fewer long talks and more hurried interactions, to diminished passion and more distractedness in their lovemaking, to less spiritual sharing and more television mindlessness, to shorter times of relaxation with each other and longer lists of commitments that kept them apart.

Shannon knew her home would be terribly lonely without Annie. Thinking back to her courtship and honeymoon years with David, she wondered what had happened to their once-but-no-longer spark of love. Slowly but surely the flame of their marital oneness—not just of body but of soul and of spirit too—had gone untended, and she was not at all sure it could be rekindled.

Fear suddenly caught at the back of Shannon's throat as she considered the changes she and David would have to make to deepen their intimacy. Both hated conflict, and their emotional distance had served them well for years. What would happen if they were to speak their true feelings to each other? Would David even want to change their functional but aloof relationship? Was it worth it to rock the boat? Maybe she should just resign herself to a tepid marriage and wait for grandchildren to fill the void in her relational life.

Yet, even as Shannon savored the sound of her daughter's singing, she realized that her longing to restore and deepen her intimacy with David was not going away. She yearned to rest her heart in him as she had once dared hope she could—before the children, before the job, before the deadening distance. There are some dreams that never seem to die. This, she knew, was one of them.

Intimacy—especially marital intimacy—is fraught with ambiguity. We long for it and simultaneously we fear it. It offers us our greatest joy yet it can also precipitate our deepest sorrow. Once we have tasted the sweetness of intimate connection with God and others, we are never the same, for our hearts call us back again and again. Like Shannon, we may vacillate between pursuing and fleeing the oneness we desire, but our need for intimacy is intrinsic to our humanness, however much we may dread its cost.

And so we are likely to be ambivalent about the relational closeness for which we long, willing to settle for the status quo (as Shannon is tempted to do) instead of taking the risks a deeper level of oneness would require. Designed to rest in intimacy, we nevertheless fall prey to the seduction of resigning ourselves to far less in our relationships than God wishes us to enjoy. It is a snare set for us all by the enemy of our souls.

The wilderness landscape was silent and wild but no longer foreign to the old man squinting against the early sun's relentless glare. In fact this desert and this mountain felt almost like home to him now, his early city life a fading shadow. Settled into the routine of his nomadic wandering, this refugee from civilization carried himself with the confidence born of nearly four decades of finding water and grazing land for his father-in-law's flocks.

But lately, during the long watches of the night, the weathered shepherd had begun pondering again the death of his former dreams. Born of enslaved parents but sent at an early age to be raised in the royal palace, the young man had grown up amidst sophisticated paganism and courtly splendor. Educated as a prince yet stripped of princely power, he had lived in a kind of no-man's-land—a stranger to his own people, an outsider in the court of the king. Yet he had never forgotten his roots nor the sense of personal destiny his parents had instilled in him: *Someday he would deliver his own people from their bondage.* "To this you are born," they had said, and he had embraced the vision, even as he had wondered how it could possibly come to pass.

Then had come the day and event that had changed everything. Seeing a taskmaster beating a slave—one of his own people—the adopted prince had murdered the abuser, burying his body in the sand. The next day, his crime exposed and denounced, he had fled for his life into the obscurity of anonymity, becoming at forty years of age an alien shepherd instead of an alien prince.

At least God had protected his life, but for what? To mourn the death of his destiny? To prove false the vision his parents had given him? Redeeming his people was no longer possible, and he had settled into a new life with a new family. Nevertheless, the memory of his long-ago yearning remained painfully alive as this man of the wilderness surveyed his sheep that solitary morning.

And then it caught his eye, a brightness to his right that was neither the sun nor the sun's reflection off a rock. Turning to look, he saw the blaze, a bush burning halfway up the hill. Satisfied that it posed no danger to his flock, he turned back to his musing, steadying himself against the slope with his familiar rod.

Soon after, the brightness caught his eye again, and again he twisted his body to see. It was the same bush, still burning, but not yet consumed. This called for a closer look. Such mysteries were not common to this region nor to this man.

ENCOUNTER WITH TERROR

So begins the oft-told story of God appearing to Moses in flames of fire from within a bush near Mount Horeb (see Exodus 3–4). Over four centuries had passed since God had spoken prophetically to Moses' ancestor Abraham, who was then living in Canaan. "Your descendants will be strangers in a country not their own," God had announced to Abraham, "and they will be enslaved and mistreated four hundred years" (Gen. 15:13). This had proved true, for Abraham's great-grandchildren had emigrated to Egypt, remaining there as aliens and growing more subjugated to the Egyptians from generation to generation. "But I will punish the nation they serve as slaves," God had also promised, "and afterward they will come out with great possessions" (Gen. 15:14). Both the prophecy of enslavement and the assurance of deliverance had been passed down through the centuries to all of Abraham's descendants.

But did they have the faith to embrace the promise? Given their increasing helplessness before the Egyptians, was anything but resignation to their grievous lot in life an option for them? Could they envision so massive a miracle as their release from the land of their bondage? Did even Moses, the man of destiny, really believe God was good enough to remember His ancient covenant with Abraham? Moses' own impetuous and unsuccessful attempt to intervene on his countrymen's behalf had rendered his leadership among them suspect, if not rejected altogether.

Yet here he stood on a desolate mountain slope before a flaming desert bush, hearing God call out his name, "Moses! Moses!" Instinctively he responded with the servant's reply, "Here I am," at which the Master instructed, "Do not come any closer. . . . Take off your sandals, for the place where you are standing is holy ground" (Exod. 3:4–5). Obediently drawing no closer to the wondrous burning, the ancient shepherd fearfully removed his sandals to honor the holy Presence that sanctified the desert space on which he stood.

Who can know the terror that Presence held for Moses as he hid his face, trembling and afraid to look at God? Had God come to pass belated sentence on his long-ago murder? Surely execution was imminent, for who could see the holy God and live? It's a wonder Moses' eighty-year-old heart didn't give out then and there.

Then God did the unexpected, speaking words not of judgment but of compassion, inviting this man of vision out from the relative comfort of resignation to the agony and responsibility of hope. "I have indeed seen the misery of my people in Egypt," God declared. "I have heard them crying out because of their slave drivers, and I am concerned about their suffering. So I have come down to rescue them from the hand of the Egyptians." God, the good and merciful Father, was moved to respond to the cries of His abused children, and it was time to initiate their deliverance. "I am sending you to Pharaoh to bring my people the Israelites out of Egypt," He announced to the barefoot shepherd.

Abruptly Moses found his voice. Dreams long dead are not easily revived. Moses was just a man, and his very human fear leaped up at God's words of commission. Startled out of reverence, he responded not with acquiescence but with a barely camouflaged, "I don't think so." Offered the lifelong desire of his heart, his first thought was to balk at it.

"Who am I, that I should go to Pharaoh and bring the Israelites out of Egypt?" he exclaimed. This was not the hesitation of a murderer humbled by his sin, but the cry of a man terrified of his own inadequacy. "O Lord," he protested, "I have never been eloquent. . . . I am slow of speech and tongue" (4:10). And though God assured Moses of His presence and His help, though He even gave him miraculous signs to substantiate his credibility, Moses ended up begging, "O Lord, please send someone else to do it." Terror of the responsibility of leadership came against Moses' lifelong passion to follow Yahweh's call on his life. Could he risk following an unpredictable, unmanageable God against the most powerful monarch in the then-known world?

At last God's patience ran out, and His anger burned against this man He had spent eighty years preparing for this very task—the parents' vision, the discovered basket in the Nile, the Egyptian language and education, the facility in reading and writing, the passionate homicide, the humbling lessons of the exile years, the hard-won knowledge of the desert's intricate secrets—and he wanted God to send someone else! What did this old rebel know of God's larger picture?

Yet even in the burning anger, the Father's patience with His child's frailty prevailed. "What about your brother, Aaron the Levite?" God asked. "I know he can speak well. He is already on his way to meet you, and his heart will be glad when he sees you. You shall speak to him and put words in his mouth; I will help both of you speak and will teach you what to do." Yahweh had incited Aaron to search for his long-lost brother so that Moses would not have to obey God in isolation. The brothers would bear the burden of ministry together, the old shepherd's vision complementing the older Levite's eloquence to accomplish God's intentions for His people. Aaron's gladness at seeing Moses would ignite their mutual passion to serve the God they could not see but had always longed to follow. Surely God was up to something very big.

Finally, at long last, came Moses' compliance. Perhaps the reverential awe of Yahweh had returned when God's anger had burned. Fear sometimes clears the head wonderfully. Obedience now seemed the only appropriate choice, though we have no record of Moses' acceptance speech. We do have, however, the story of his meeting with Aaron and of their return to Egypt. Evidently that was enough for God.

RESIGNATION VERSUS REST

Why is it so much easier for us to resign ourselves to "what is" than to risk pursuing the passionate living and loving for which we were created? Why would Shannon long for greater intimacy with David but settle for the safety of a hassle-free marriage? Why was Moses reluctant to embrace at eighty the passion that had consumed him at forty? Far too many of us have resigned ourselves to living the way we've always lived instead of embracing the risks of change.

There are, of course, times when circumstances call us to pray, "Lord, grant us the serenity to accept the things we cannot change, the courage to change the things we can, and the wisdom to know the difference." But acceptance is not the same as resignation. Abandoning our struggle against what cannot be undone—the death of a loved one, an irreversible loss of health, the hardening of someone else's heart—can eventually release us to rest in God's sovereign design for our lives if we turn to Him in our loss. Moses, for example, could not have undone his murderous revenge, and he was right to accept Yahweh's forty years of discipline in the desert of Midian.

But when Moses was offered the revival of his God-given dreams, he was invited to stop seeing himself as a throwaway man and to partner with God in redemption. Standing obediently barefoot on the mountain, his resignation to a life of failure battled against his awakened dream of emancipating his people. And rather than cling to the safety of regret and obscurity, he determined to risk returning to the scene of his crime, his life dependent on being intimately yoked to this dread Yahweh.

A similar invitation faces us all when God shows Himself to us (in burning bush or in empty-nest syndrome, for example) and urges us to something new. And the way we ultimately respond to God when confronted with His presence always reveals what is most deeply in our hearts toward Him. Moses' aroused terror gave way to his most fervent longing, which was to be connected to God in a way that would give purpose and satisfaction to his life. This is what we all most ardently desire, for our intimacy with Him is the source of profound and lasting joy. In communion with Him we find not only our true identity but also our truest rest. Moses' desire to be Yahweh's man made him obey God's call, and he went to Egypt because he wanted to, not without fear but in the face of his fear. He sacrificed the safety of Midian for the danger of Pharaoh's court because he had tasted intimacy with God and he longed more to do Yahweh's will than to settle for the desert's predictability.

The passion with which Moses lived the third forty-year span of his life flowed from his decision to reject the comfort of resignation and plunge himself into the chaos of hope and faith that God alone could quiet. It is a decision we all must face at one time or another in our own personal pilgrimages.

INVITED TO BELIEVE

Once Moses had chosen to follow God's call, he offered more than two million Israelite slaves a similar opportunity to trust and obey (see

Exod. 4:29–5:23). Returning to Goshen, where God's people lived in slavery, Moses and Aaron brought to their countrymen Yahweh's promise of deliverance from Pharaoh's slave drivers, and the Israelites responded gladly to God's words with faith and hope. Believing God would do what He had said, they bowed down and worshiped. In those joyous days, reverent fear of Yahweh and an expectation of salvation flowed like refreshing streams throughout the land of Goshen.

Unfortunately, however, the king of Egypt did not respond so reverently to Israel's God. The ancestors of this reigning Pharaoh had feared not God but Israel's growing numbers and they had subjugated God's people to keep them from prospering, thereby providing several generations of Pharaohs with the illusion of control over what they feared. It also supplied them with a huge cadre of unpaid workers for completing vast building projects to satisfy their egocentricity. Over the centuries the Israelites' bondage had increased in severity and cruelty.

Consequently when Moses and Aaron approached the reigning Pharaoh with the words, "This is what the LORD, the God of Israel, says: 'Let my people go, so that they may hold a festival to me in the desert,'" Pharaoh simply dismissed both them and their God. "Who is the LORD, that I should obey him and let Israel go?" he demanded. "I do not know the LORD and I will not let Israel go." Then, to flaunt his disdain for Yahweh, Pharaoh increased his brutality against the Israelites, no longer giving them straw for making bricks but forcing them to meet the same quotas as before.

This unexpected turn of events was faith-shattering for the hapless Hebrews. They had believed God was genuinely concerned for them, had worshiped Him in gratitude, had resurrected their faith in His goodness, and had allowed their hope to be rekindled. But when Pharaoh ordered them beaten for not meeting their quotas, they moved quickly from trust in Yahweh to a betrayed anger against Him. God now seemed more cruel than Pharaoh, and they flung their disillusionment at Moses and Aaron. "May the LORD look upon you and judge you!" they cried. "You have made us a stench to Pharaoh and his officials and have put a sword in their hand to kill us" (5:21).

Stung and shamed by this rejection of his leadership, Moses in turn flung his anger at God. "O Lord, why have you brought trouble upon this people? Is this why you sent me? Ever since I went to Pharaoh to speak in your name, he has brought trouble upon this people, and you have not rescued your people at all." Gone was Moses' hope for God's deliverance, deflated his trust that God had kind intentions toward His people. Supposedly seeing was believing, and though he had seen the bush and the miraculous signs, he had not seen a corresponding change in the Israelites' circumstances. This failure to experience an immediate shift in their bitter situation caused him and all Israel to disbelieve God's goodness. Their terror of Pharaoh's abuse was winning the day over their faith in Yahweh.

23

How shortsighted Moses' despair seems to us who have the advantage of hindsight, who know the end of the story. But we are no different. Does not our own hope often give way to fear, especially when our plans go awry and our expectations go unmet? When we face the decline of our health or the death of a loved one, does not terror leap up within us? When confronted with the loss of a job or of a significant relationship, are we not angry with the God who could have prevented that loss?

Moreover, the fear and rage that dominate our hearts when our circumstances disappoint or threaten us often dictate our perception of God's goodness. When our lives are going well, we say God is good. But when we encounter life's suffering and chaos, we ask, "Can God really be trusted?" Satan uses the evil he himself has incited in our world to make us question, "Can God make good on His promises? Will He help us? How long must we wait?" They are questions our integrity will not let us ignore.

GOD IN THE BOAT

The Israelites' discouragement in the face of their bitter bondage can perhaps be understood, if not excused. After all, their knowledge of God's character was limited to the ancient stories handed down through oral tradition from generation to generation. They also had, of course, the wonders of Moses' signs to inform them of Yahweh's power, but miraculous signs were no doubt far less convincing than the whips of their taskmasters.

In contrast, New Testament believers had fifteen more centuries of God's self-revelation than did the people of Moses' day, so one would expect their faith in Him to have come more easily. They knew the end of Moses' story—that Yahweh had been able to deliver their ancestors from Egypt and to bring them into rest in Canaan. They also knew about the exploits of the judges and the reign of the kings, as well as the many prophecies regarding the coming Messiah. New Testament Jews were far better informed regarding God's character and deeds than Old Testament Jews.

But genuine trust in God involves not merely true doctrine about Him but true relationship with Him. Old Testament believers may have had fewer theological concepts on which to build their understanding of Yahweh, but belief confined to knowledge is not the kind of faith that grows into a passionate abandon to God anyway. We must add to our theology a oneness with and an abiding rest in our heavenly Father, trusting Him with our hearts and lives. And trust, the doorway to rest, comes not from knowing *about* God but from knowing Him personally. Only then can we come to love Him passionately.

Whenever God reveals Himself to His image-bearers, He provides everything they need to take the step of faith to which He invites them, regardless of the extent of their theological experience. The journey into trusting God is made in increments, and no step is insignificant if it leads to greater trust. Consider, for example, the experience of the apostle Peter in his relationship with Jesus, God's Son. Peter's spiritual walk was as erratic as that of the ancient Israelites, but he kept taking small risks of faith until he came to trust Christ with his very life. The passion of trusting God enough to intimately connect our lives to Him comes to none of us without struggle.

At first, Simon Peter the fisherman knew Jesus only as a traveling rabbi, an itinerant teacher of God's truth. But things shifted dramatically one day when Jesus asked to use Peter's fishing boat as a pulpit from which to teach a crowd of followers who were pressing against Him on the shore of the Sea of Galilee near Capernaum, Peter's home village (Luke 5:1–11). After the sermon was over, Jesus told Peter to let down his fishing nets in deeper water, though this veteran of the sea had caught nothing at all the night before. Not hiding his skepticism, Peter nonetheless did as Jesus had instructed, and a huge haul of fish was drawn, almost swamping the boat.

Peter's terror was immediate—not of the boat's sinking but of Jesus' supernatural power over the fish of the sea; clearly He was a holy man. Impulsively Peter threw himself at Jesus' knees and pleaded, "Go away from me, Lord; I am a sinful man!"

Why would Peter fearfully beg his benefactor to leave? Perhaps it was because, like Moses' terror at the burning bush, Peter's experience of Jesus' divine power brought his own unholiness into sharp focus, and he wanted some distance between himself and that kind of righteousness. A God who interfered in a person's business life—even to his profit—was likely to interfere in other areas of his life too, and Peter was not at all sure whether this holy man would bless him or pass sentence on him. The ordinary fisherman was used to an ordinary religion with clear expectations and predictable rituals. Sharing a boat with God was not at all the same as traveling to Jerusalem once a year to offer an animal sacrifice to Him at the temple.

There is much we can learn from Jesus' response to Peter's fear, because He responds in similar ways to our own shrinking back from God. First Jesus encouraged Peter, "Don't be afraid." These are words Jesus would repeat time and again throughout His ministry, not just to Peter but to many others as well. Terror at suddenly finding oneself in God's presence is the appropriate and only sane response a mortal being could have. But Jesus' "Don't be afraid" reflects an important aspect of His mission on earth, which was to reveal His Father as a God of mercy and love, as well as a God of holiness and judgment. Amazingly, the God we are to worship with reverence does not want our awe of Him to keep us from drawing near to receive His grace. In fact just the opposite is true. God longs to bring us into reconciliation and renewed oneness with Himself, though it cost Him the death of His Son to bring us Home. This is the gospel, which is able to banish our deepest fear.

Moreover, after Jesus had told Peter not to be afraid, He went on to commission him, replacing his terror of God's holiness with a vision for his own transformed purpose in life. "From now on," Jesus told the fearful fisherman, "you will catch men." Surely this must have reminded Peter of the ancient story of the prophet Isaiah, who, when he saw a glorious vision of God in the temple, had cried out, "Woe to me! . . . I am ruined! For I am a man of unclean lips, and I live among a people of unclean lips, and my eyes have seen the King, the LORD Almighty" (see Isa. 6:1–8). For after God had cleansed Isaiah's lips with coals from the holy altar, He had commissioned him to preach to His hard-hearted people.

How like God! He had sent Moses, the murderer, to rescue the Israelites from their death-bound slavery in Egypt. He had sent Isaiah, the prophet of unclean lips, to speak true words to the liars and the disobedient among His own people. And now the same Yahweh in human likeness would send Peter, the sinful catcher of fish, to be a catcher of men for Christ's coming kingdom. God specializes in turning the hearts of the repentant toward Himself and preparing them to become His ambassadors. He has, after all, a far bigger plan in mind than any of us can possibly know.

There is also much we can learn from Peter's response to Jesus' invitation. We are not told what he and the others in the boat thought about becoming men-catchers. But we know they were willing to forsake the status quo altogether in favor of intimacy with Jesus, for "they pulled their boats up on shore, left everything and followed him." This first step of faith was huge—a forsaking of the only life they had known in order to go wherever Jesus led. Shrugging off Satan's seduction to resignation, they left their nets without looking back. One thing was sure: Life for them would never be the same again.

Peter, however, would have much to learn before he became a mature fisher of men. For him as for all of us, growing to trust God passionately is always a process, and sometimes the process is a long one. Nor was Peter always a ready learner. Impulsive and outspoken, he alternately delighted and frustrated the rabbi he finally came to love more than life itself.

So it was with all the men and women Jesus personally encountered as He revealed His Father's heart to those He taught, inviting them into oneness with Him. The New Testament stories of Jesus' interactions with His followers stand as an encouragement to us all. For not only do Christ's relationships with the men and women of first-century Palestine show us what God Himself is like, but they also teach us how Jesus even now continues to reach out to His Bride—to those of us who believe in His name—in the face of our fear, our love, our doubt, our longings, and our recurring failure. The stories of Scripture can instruct us by reminding us again and again of who and whose we are, out of which will flow the choices that make up our walk of faith.

INTIMIDATION BY OTHERS

The sun was high as the woman made her way to the town well. Drawing water in the evening was cooler and more social, but her reputation had distanced her from the other women, and she'd found the isolation of noon less hurtful. She pretended indifference but she knew her hunger for intimacy had not been satiated by her illicit liaisons with men. Hers was a lonely life, shrouded with shame and self-contempt, but there was no going back and doing things over a different way. She was sadly but stoically resigned to her fate.

She saw Him, a stranger and a Jew, sitting by the well as she approached. (This story is told in John 4:1–42.) Ignoring His presence, as was the custom, she was reaching to draw water when He spoke. "Will you give me a drink?" He asked, startling her. (*Jewish men did not speak to Samaritans, least of all female Samaritans. Certainly they didn't share drinking vessels with them lest they become ceremonially unclean—even she knew that!*)

Surprised but curious, she found herself responding with the obvious question, "How can you ask me for a drink?" (*What would the others say if they knew she was talking to a strange man—and a Jew at that? It would no doubt confirm their worst suspicions about her.*)

Then He spoke again, strange words, almost crazy. "If you knew the gift of God and who it is that asks you for a drink, you would have asked him and he would have given you living water." (*Living water? What was that? From this well? And without a jar? She'd better be wary of this one.*)

"Sir," she said as respectfully as she could, "you have nothing to draw with and the well is deep. Where can you get this living water? Are you greater than our father Jacob, who gave us the well and drank from it himself?" (*What was it about this man she somehow trusted against all reason? He had invited her, a stranger, a Samaritan, a woman, to connect with Him, showing her kindness, offering her a gift, engaging her in conversation. Social interaction had been scarce for her, and hope had long since died that she would ever be accepted, let alone treasured by anyone. She feared the intentions of men and the judgment of others and she had learned to shield herself against further rejection. Yet something was stirring in her at this man's kindness, crazy as His words seemed. Perhaps that something was the dawning of hope.*)

This opening scene in the drama of Jesus' interaction with an unnamed Samaritan woman is typical of Jesus' bold movement to penetrate the lives of those who needed God's love. Their social status mattered not at all to Him. It almost seems that the lower their perceived sense of their own

27

value, the more He desired to bring them the gospel of reconciliation, inviting them to embrace their truest identity and obligations as sons and daughters of the living God.

Moreover, we would do well to remember that restoring the physical body was not the only kind of healing Jesus offered those to whom He ministered. Equally important to Him—perhaps even more important—was the healing of their relationships (with God and with others) and their restoration to community, particularly for the outcast.

TERROR OF INTIMACY

This movement toward restoration into community seems to have been especially true in Jesus' relationships with women. Had He not in the beginning agreed with the Father and the Holy Spirit in saying, "Let us make man in our image" (Gen. 1:26)? And did He not know (better even than we) that women in their imaging of God are innately passionate for relational connection? More than that, did He not also recognize that relational disappointment often makes a woman feel unlovely and unworthy of the cherishing for which she yearns?

In fact, rather than risk being hurt again, a damaged woman is likely to guard herself against ever revealing or responding from her deepest heart, settling instead for much less in her intimate connections than God intended her to enjoy. Perhaps that is why in Jesus' personal interactions with women He consistently addressed both their longing for and their fear of being intimately seen and known, particularly by God and often by others as well, especially men. Jesus did not minimize women's disappointment nor justify their self-protective strategies. Instead, He invited them to interact with Him about what was really going on in their hearts. Then He told them how they could move into His rest so they could fulfill their design and offer kindness and refreshment to those around them.

Men, of course, also struggle in their relationships, for they too both desire and dread true intimacy. God's male image-bearers are designed for oneness with their Creator, for intimacy with a chosen beloved, for meaningful connection to their children, and for genuine openness with others, especially fellow believers. (This is what Jesus embodied in His incarnation as a man—oneness with His heavenly Father and intimate fellowship with the men, women, and children who would come to be known as the church, His betrothed Bride.) However, because of the fall, men often feel safer pursuing mastery over their world in their area of greatest competence, rather than surrendering to their desperate need for God to sustain their closest relationships. In a man's quest to prove himself adequate, developing a vulnerable connection (with God, with a woman, with his children,

28

or with other men) may be where he feels least adequate and thus most reluctant to proceed. This masculine tendency to not invest deeply in relationships usually stems more from a fear of failure than from an innate lack of desire for intimacy.

We all—men and women alike—struggle with fear in our relationships, particularly in our closest friendships and most especially within our marriages. The intimacy for which we were designed is continually being sabotaged by our fear, and we keep running away from what we long to be running toward. We desire oneness but we flee the closeness. Maintaining heart connection feels awkward and perilous—like speaking a foreign language in an alien culture. Who can be sure of knowing the right thing to say and the right way to say it without embarrassing or even endangering oneself? We wonder if we have what it takes to survive the risk without being destroyed.

Genuine intimacy requires openness, the reciprocal knowing and being known that characterizes deep friendship and marital love. But openness can be terrifying, compared to the relative security of hiding our true selves. We want intimacy but we dread it too. Our desire for love collides with our horror of vulnerability. We want closeness but we fear being consumed or ignored. We invite others in and then shut them out. Come here; go away. Here's your hat; what's your hurry? I hate you; don't leave me. Ambivalence abounds.

And in the face of our ambivalence, too often we retreat to the arena of the manageable instead of trusting God in the uncharted territory of our fear. Even in marriage, wives resign themselves to being uncherished and settle for being tolerated. Husbands stop pursuing heart intimacy and content themselves with hard work and obligatory sex. Resignation to a workable but passionless partnership characterizes countless marriages today, and Christian spouses are not immune.

THE RISK OF MARRIAGE

Sometimes we mistakenly think we have found rest when we resign ourselves to a safe marital dullness. The emotional cost of maintaining the status quo seems small compared to the price of longing for and pursuing intimacy. But though we may be seduced into resignation by hopelessness or fatigue, we will find there neither rest nor passion. Rather, we will encounter a recurring temptation to relieve our loneliness or boredom illicitly.

So many of today's marriages are mere shadows of the full-bodied, joyous reality God intended them to be—the yoking of two hearts, two bodies, two lives into one. Who can unravel the mystery of why so few unions reflect the anticipated oneness of Christ with His Bride? What we all most want we often most fear—we dread desiring love, because we can't control it.

29

Love cannot be demanded or earned but only freely given and received. Thus our longing for it puts us at the mercy of possible rejection, probable disappointment, and certain chaos. Relationships are complex, unmanageable, and messy. Someone has said there is always an easy solution to every human problem—neat, plausible, and wrong. How very true of the interaction between two imperfect human beings!

Marriage—being joined by covenant to another fallen person—asks more of us than we want to face, and sometimes shrinking back from it seems only reasonable. When we repeat the sacred vows of faithfulness, we bind ourselves until death to the life of another, and the covenant is, after all, so final, so all-encompassing, so emotionally expensive. Walter Wangerin reminds us that

> marriage is marvelous and holy; that's why we marry with a glad, nearly unspeakable excitement. . . . [Yet] grown men also tremble, don't they? And women lock themselves in bathrooms. We approach the wedding with fear, and it isn't just stage fright that weakens our knees. . . . If the commitment is to be timeless, if I'm bound no matter what the future brings, then my ignorance of that future may terrify me; for here at the wedding I stand peering into darkness, seeing nothing, yet depending for my life upon what is to be.[1]

No wonder we are afraid. Moreover, the committedness of our wedding promises only intensifies the fear.

And if at a marriage's beginning the unknown future terrifies us, as a marriage matures, another terror will likely grow—the fear that the openness that intimacy requires may be more costly than we have the resources or desire to pay. As a woman is more deeply known, she can be more deeply hurt and she may be reluctant to trust the one who can (and in fact certainly will) hurt her. Similarly, as a man is more deeply known, he fears he will be found inadequate, and moving toward his wife may seem overwhelming. Husbands and wives possess great power to do good or harm to one another, and though the prospect of that good holds the promise of life, the possibility of that harm feels like the threat of death. "Those who love us most are also most vulnerable to us," Walter Wangerin reminds us. "Daily we kill and are being killed" in our most intimate relationships.[2] Exemption from relational pain is nowhere included in the marriage contract, not even in the small print.

We who have voiced our vows know this best. My husband, Bill, and I, for example, have fought a difficult, often intense battle over the past decade to recognize and reconcile the dynamics that nearly destroyed our marriage. These dynamics most surely began long before we met each other, when he was thirty-four and I was twenty-seven. We both brought into our relationship a myriad of childhood fears and defenses of which we were for the most part totally unaware. The damage done to us many years earlier had gone unrecognized and undiscussed, but the consequences of that damage were being lived out in our marriage nonetheless. The next chapter will chronicle some of the early events that gave rise to the relational fears that haunted our hearts and sabotaged our oneness from the very beginning of our relationship.

But Bill and I came to a place in our marriage where we had to decide whether to continue the destructive patterns we had established and followed for fifteen years of married life or to risk changing those patterns, little by little and at great emotional cost. As is true in most relationships, the decision to change was not made by mutual consent. Though I had become desperate to "do something" to deepen our intimacy in spite of my fear, Bill was determined to maintain things as they were, because that is where he felt safest. He no less than I longed for more freedom in our love but he had lost hope it would ever happen and he was loathe to risk what we had for something we might never find. It is no little thing to engage the fears that have dominated our lives.

INKLINGS OF HOPE

For none of us is immune to the effects of our early fears. In fact the enemy of God and of our souls takes evil satisfaction in doing to all of us the kind of harm that even years later will keep us afraid, unwilling to rest in God or to risk genuine intimacy with others. This emotional and relational damage inevitably perpetuates itself unless and until somewhere grace breaks in.

For this also is true: Terror of intimacy, though learned young and reinforced often, can be changed by the redemptive work of the very One whose holy presence evokes our most fearful awe, even Yahweh, even Jesus. The atoning death of Christ and the inner presence of His Spirit not only can work our salvation but also can motivate and enable us to overcome our fears.

In Old Testament times, Yahweh invited His enslaved people to come to Him in the desert to rest and worship Him (see Exod. 5:1). Centuries later He again invited the Israelites through the prophet Isaiah, "Come, all you who are thirsty, come to the waters. . . . Give ear and come to me; hear me, that your soul may live" (Isa. 55:1, 3). And this same invitation was issued in the first century A.D. by God's Son, Jesus, when He urged His listeners, "Come to me, all you who are weary and burdened, and I will give you rest" (Matt. 11:28).

If we will respond by coming to the One who offers us life and inner rest, we can move beyond our dread of God's judgment and our fear of others' rejection. More than that, we can relinquish our resignation to relational

31

mediocrity and embrace instead a renewed passion for glorifying God and loving others well. Our terror of being hurt again need not be the ultimate motivator of our relational choices. We can know our fears transformed by God's power into a holy abandon of oneness with God, out of which can flow genuine intimacy with others, especially our spouses.

How can it be done? What must change in us? How do we move even in the midst of our deep fear into the rest Christ offers? In order to trace the path of this inner transformation, we must learn to see how our present behavior is often motivated by unacknowledged losses, the effects of which sabotage our intimacy with and our rest in the God who created us for oneness. To that end, the next chapter will examine how fear can leave its mark on our lives, and how the gospel can counteract it.

 ## QUESTIONS TO CONSIDER

1. Why is intimacy often frightening?

2. If you could change the *status quo* in one of your relationships, which one would it be and how would you want it changed?

3. Have you, like Moses, had dreams die that you would like to have revived?

4. How would your present relationships be affected if your dreams were to be revived?

5. Have you had experiences in which your fear threatened to undermine your faith? What was the outcome?

6. What in your present circumstances keeps you from resting in God?

Regarding the opening story:

Whether or not the Shannons of our world will stay resigned to their half-hearted marriages or enter with boldness, the terror of intimacy is far from certain. The hassles for Shannon and David are few right now, their conflicts infrequent, their energy less depleted than it will be if she steps into the risk of seeking to deepen their oneness. As Shannon's longing for renewed intimacy with David swells in her heart, anxiety about its cost will not be far behind.

7. What things would have to change for Shannon and David's relationship to deepen?

CHAPTER TWO

DAMAGE

The Ravages of Abuse

THE DIVORCE PAPERS *had been delivered to Jerry's office that morning, and he had told Lynda, his secretary, to cancel all appointments and hold all calls. Noon found him still alternating between sitting blank-eyed at his desk and pacing angrily back and forth, caught between despair and rage.*

What would he do now that Mona had left? He loved her—why had she gone? Didn't she realize how much he had sacrificed for her and the children? So what if he had lost his cool once in a while? Couldn't she understand that the yelling and the broken dishes and even his fist through the wall that one time were just his way of letting off steam?

Pacing now, Jerry told himself that Mona had no idea how stressful his work was and how irritating she and the children had been sometimes. Besides, he had always apologized and had even brought gifts to substantiate his sincerity about staying more calm next time. He was sorry when he saw their terror, especially in the eyes of the children. It reminded him of his own fear of his father's belt and raging words. That's why he'd vowed never to strike his own children—a vow he'd kept, though Mona had evidently failed to appreciate that too. He was a much better father than his own father had been!

And why was Mona always bugging him to "deal with the abuse"? How he hated that word and the sickening sense of helpless rage that erupted inside whenever Mona mentioned it! He was sorry he'd ever told her what the church janitor had done to him when he was ten. He had just wanted to justify himself for refusing to attend Sunday services with her and the girls. Besides, that was over two decades ago—what made Mona think it had anything to do with their marriage?

Jerry's anger surged at the thought that the monster who had haunted his adolescent dreams still haunted his thirty-something life. The sharp sound of his fist striking the polished hardwood of his desk startled even himself and brought Lynda to the office door.

"I'm okay," he lied. "And see if you can reschedule my afternoon appointments. I need to get back to work."

Abuse is a detestable word, calling to mind images of cruelty, betrayal, helplessness, pain, and emotional turmoil. It comes in many forms, some more subtle than others. But those who are its casualties are indelibly marked by its wickedness. Whether the abuse is physical, verbal, sexual, or spiritual, its damage is profound and long-lived. And any victim who does not find a safe place to grieve and come to terms with the damage (especially of childhood abuse) will experience difficulty establishing and maintaining intimate relationships as an adult. In today's culture, as in countless earlier cultures, the number of sufferers is legion.

And whenever mankind's inhumanity is exposed, whether toward individuals or toward groups, the character of God is inevitably called into question. For when Satan works his dirty work, he is quick to sabotage our intimacy with God by casting doubt on His concern for us. Can Jerry, for example, ever trust the God in whose house he was abused? The evil one always insinuates the worst about God. "Couldn't He have prevented the damage done to you by those who ought to have loved or at least protected you?" he reproaches. "Would your circumstances be what they are if God really cared?" And we begin to wonder ourselves, *"Does God really care?"*

We ask similar questions regarding our intimate relationships. Can we trust others when we have been damaged before? Would Mona ever be able to trust Jerry again, considering that his rage had harmed her and the children? Is it possible to rest in another person's love if one or both have been abused?

We all long for oneness, especially in our marriages, but often our fear blocks the way. What triggers our fear, and how is it keeping us from trust and intimacy in our present circumstances? Can we hope for genuine rest in our relationships without struggling about whether or not God is good? These are the issues explored in this chapter.

34

Panic presided in the desert camp. Recrimination was its second-in-command. No Israelite remembered the miracles in Egypt, nor were they delighting in the gifts the Egyptians had given them. Death was on their minds—their own deaths—and Moses was the target of their hostile terror. "Was it because there were no graves in Egypt that you brought us to the desert to die?" they shouted at him. "What have you done to us by bringing us out of Egypt? Didn't we say to you in Egypt, 'Leave us alone; let us serve the Egyptians'? It would have been better for us to serve the Egyptians than to die in the desert!" (This and the following stories can be found in Exodus 7–14.)

On the horizon were the chariots, wave after wave of them, advancing relentlessly in their direction. Many a time they had watched them clatter through the streets of Goshen, but today it was their own lives at stake, not the lives of some distant enemies of the Pharaoh. Their emancipation from Egypt had seemed accomplished at last. But now a vast sea of water lay in front of them, and a fearsome army of charioteers was bearing down on them from behind. The terrified Israelites were trapped, their learned helplessness as slaves reinforcing their despair. What could Moses say to encourage them now?

REDEMPTION BEWAILED

This was no time to recall for God's people the events of recent months. Of course, the early plagues Yahweh had visited on Egypt had been impressive, though they had done little to modify Pharaoh's animosity. In fact those plagues had only increased his rage toward the God who contended with him for the lives of His people. The Nile becoming a river of blood, frogs everywhere (even in the latrines), dust turned into gnats—these things had been irritatingly inconvenient. But Pharaoh's magicians could produce miracles almost as wondrous, and besides, set against the specter of losing hundreds of thousands of slaves, such nuisances could be endured. No minor-league god of a captive people was going to frighten *this* king into compliance.

Consequently, the plagues had increased, and Pharaoh's hatred of the Israelites and of their God had grown in proportion to the plagues' severity—flies, pestilence, boils, hail, locusts, and three days of the blackest darkness. Time and again Egypt's king would agree to God's terms in order to stop the plagues, and the Israelites' hopes would be revived. Then, each time the plagues were lifted, Pharaoh "hardened his heart and would not listen to Moses and Aaron, just as the LORD had said," and God's people would be disappointed again. Meanwhile, Egyptian citizens were being destroyed and their crops and animals ruined, until even Pharaoh's magicians and advisors pleaded for him to capitulate. Yet in spite of it all, this stubborn king maintained his intractable opposition to Yahweh.

Then had come the most terrible plague of all: the slaying of every firstborn of man and beast throughout the land. God's dire warning had been fulfilled: "Israel is my firstborn son," Yahweh had said to Pharaoh, "and I told you, 'Let my son go, so he may worship me.' But you refused to let him go; so I will kill your firstborn son" (4:22–23). The Israelites had miraculously been spared this bitter loss. Protected from the angel of death by a lamb's blood smeared on their doorposts in obedience to God's command, they rested secure in their homes while the death angel did his holy work.

The terror of Yahweh had finally prevailed in the land of the Israelites' bondage. Amidst loud wailing of grief over their dead, the Egyptians had "urged the people to hurry and leave the country. 'For otherwise,' they said, 'we will all die!'" Moreover, as the Israelites had hastened toward their freedom, they had "plundered the Egyptians," receiving from them the articles of silver, gold, and clothing they had asked for and would need on their arduous journey toward Canaan.

The impossible had happened. Pharaoh had let the Israelites go, and they had "come out with great possessions," as Abraham had been promised centuries earlier (Gen. 15:14). The Lord Himself went ahead of them in a pillar of cloud to guide them, and the pillar became fire at night so they could travel at any time.

But none of that could offset the Israelites' terror as they watched the chariots racing their way. Pharaoh had obviously changed his mind yet again and had sent the army of Egypt to reclaim his lost labor force. Any infantry of foot soldiers hearing the approaching thunder of horses and chariots would blanch in fear of their imminent death. How much more would they despair if this were not merely a battle against impossible odds but also their very first battle *and* their first taste of freedom from slavery in over four hundred years?

The Israelite army, though comprised of men now free, had more to overcome than a pursuing enemy. They had their own ingrained way of approaching life that would cripple their effectiveness as soldiers. Scripture tells us that earlier, "when Pharaoh let the people go, God did not lead them on the road [north] through the Philistine country, though that was shorter. For God said, 'If they face war, they might change their minds and return to Egypt.' So God led the people around by the desert road [south] toward the Red Sea" (Exod. 13:17–18). God knew these just-emancipated prisoners were not ready to defend themselves or their families.

In more ways than one, God's people were unprepared for warfare. Disaster was at hand, and they were wishing their deliverance undone. Standing exposed on the danger side of the Red Sea, they rued their freedom and called God homicidal.

It is a pattern they would repeat for forty years.

SLAVE MENTALITY

Why? Why would the pattern of hopelessness and terror be so often repeated in the life of God's people? Perhaps the answer lies at least partly in the legacy of their four hundred years of enslavement. It is said that goldfish raised in small bowls swim in small circles even when put into big ponds. The imprint of the Israelites' years of bondage was not suddenly erased just because they were no longer in Egypt. People who have never known imprisonment or abuse may find it difficult to understand its pervasive and damaging impact. But the Egyptians' cruel oppression of the Israelites over many, many decades certainly had left a profound mark on how God's people thought and acted, particularly as they encountered the dangers of warfare.

Any Israelite slave, for example, would likely have had to develop a certain inner discipline in order to survive subjugation. Three rules in particular would have governed the mentality necessary for someone to survive a life of enslavement: Don't trust. Don't risk. Don't hope. These guidelines would serve to make slavery endurable, but even one of them would jeopardize the effectiveness of an army's military mission. In fact a slave mentality would undermine the success of any enterprise, individual or corporate. Consider the long-term impact of each of these three survival "rules."

Don't Trust

There is perhaps nothing more crucial to the well-being of any team effort—of an army, an athletic team, certainly a marriage—than trust among and between its members. Distrust and dishonesty sabotage communication and mutual interdependence, dooming the team's efforts to failure. And nothing demolishes trust and breaks down oneness between people like forced subservience or any other form of abuse.

The habits of captivity, for example, had taught the Israelites to fear and distrust the Egyptians with whom they had once lived in peaceful coexistence. They were being abused; how could they trust their abusers or desire to work for the best interests of their taskmasters? Unable to act or speak freely, the Hebrews could never have been off duty with their captors.

No doubt God's people also observed a certain level of distrust even toward one another. After all, Pharaoh's slave drivers had chosen some of the Israelites to be foremen over the work of their own countrymen, and the "divided loyalty" of these foremen must surely have broken down trust even within the ranks of God's chosen people. Forty years earlier Moses had expected to find unity of spirit among the Israelites, at least in opposition to Pharaoh's cruelty. But it was an Israelite slave who had heard about Moses killing the Egyptian taskmaster and had turned against the Hebrew prince, berating him for his radical and misguided intervention in the affairs of his own people (Exod. 2:11–14).

Judith Herman, in her book *Trauma and Recovery*, writes that traumatized people "lose their trust in themselves, in other people, and in God."[1] So instead of reciprocal rest and openness among God's enslaved people in the land of their bondage, vigilance and secrecy and suspicion and betrayal were more likely the order of the day.

A similar dynamic is at work in the life of any person who has been abused or harmed as a child. In a healthy, loving family, trust flows naturally between the parents, between parents and children, and among siblings. But wherever there has been infidelity or abandonment, neglect or favoritism, trauma or abuse, trust is shattered and is difficult to reestablish. The affected parties learn to be inwardly wary, to obey the law of silence, and to confide their true hearts to no one. This pattern of guardedness in relationships continues unconsciously in the adult lives of children raised in those circumstances, spilling over into their relationship with God as well. Regardless of external appearances, the inner life of the enslaved or abused is characterized by anger, distrust, and deep loneliness. Can there possibly be rest where there is no trust?

Don't Risk

A second unspoken rule that slaves will observe is the refusal to risk. They seldom make waves, nor do they wish to draw attention to themselves. Better to blend in with everyone else, take no initiative, and learn to manipulate within rather than work against "the system." Fear of punishment becomes a paramount motivation behind behavioral choices, and predictability (even the expectation of mistreatment) is preferable to risking contrary behavior.

Especially after prolonged servitude, captives feel safest waiting to be told what to do. Judith Herman writes that "constriction [in initiative and planning] becomes most pronounced in chronically traumatized people, who are often described as passive or helpless."[2] One political prisoner describes what it was like when he was finally released:

> Once we got out, we were suddenly confronted with all these problems. . . .
> Ridiculous problems—doorknobs, for instance. I had no reflex any longer to
> reach for the knobs of doors. I hadn't had to—hadn't been *allowed* to—for

over thirteen years. I'd come to a closed door and find myself momentarily stymied—I couldn't remember what to do next.[3]

External controls had come to replace the inner cultivation of volition, let alone resistance, in this man. Obey the rules and don't let anyone know what you're thinking—that was how to survive.

Again, the similarities between enslavement and abuse are evident. A child who has been neglected or abused or abandoned clings to whatever is familiar in order to survive in his or her world. To risk the unknown is terrifying. It is far better to slavishly follow the rules, even if they are impractical or difficult, because the responsibility of free choice carries with it the frightening unpredictability of the outcome. Adjusting to one's place in the family system, even if that system is destructive, feels safer than losing connection with one's primary caregivers. Regrettably this pattern of running from risk becomes intrinsic to the child's adult behavior as well, and the no-risk rule will have an impact on all his or her relationships.

Don't Hope

Perhaps most damaging of all to the spirit of a person subjected to enslavement or mistreatment is the loss of hope, which deadens the soul. In the centuries during which the Israelites' freedom in Egypt had waned and finally disappeared, they had had to learn to accept "the inevitable." The status quo would not be changed, and they would be foolish to hope for any future relief or deliverance. Judith Herman explains the refusal to hope in these words: "Thinking of the future stirs up such intense yearning . . . that prisoners find it unbearable; they quickly learn that these emotions make them vulnerable to disappointment and that disappointment will make them desperate."[4]

Thus, even when God's people had believed Moses and Aaron's assertion of God's compassion for their plight and His promise to lead them out of bondage, their hope had been quickly and easily squelched by the additional work Pharaoh had heaped on them to punish them for their "laziness" in asking for a religious holiday. Given their mindset of hopelessness, is it any wonder that even after Moses reiterated God's promises to them again, "they did not listen to him because of their discouragement and cruel bondage"? Finally even Moses lost hope, complaining to the Lord: "If the Israelites will not listen to me, why would Pharaoh listen to me, since I speak with faltering lips?" (Exod. 6:9–12).

Hope, the expectation that good will come to us, is essential to the flourishing of the human spirit. Those who believe that *nothing* they can do will be able to improve their situation often end up thinking there is little to live for. Particularly for children caught in a family system that causes them to feel unloved or worthless, the loss of hope that they will ever be loved is devastating, though usually subconscious. In fact resignation and emotional deadness are less painful to such children than the anguish of hoping for what may never come. That is why even if abused children mature into adults whose hope for intimacy is revived by new, more reliable relationships, often the underlying dynamic of those relationships is a subtle expectation that disappointment rather than fulfillment will likely be the final result. Hope once dashed by fear is most difficult to resurrect.

DISAPPOINTMENT'S TRAIL

In our day it has become fashionable (though wrong) to justify our present faults by focusing on our past woundings. It is nonetheless true that childhood trauma does not simply disappear from our adult emotional landscape. As is obvious from the Israelites' recurring recrimination against Moses and against the God for whom he spoke, the impact of their four hundred years of bondage lingered long after their release. Even the astonishing miracle of Yahweh parting the Red Sea so they could escape Pharaoh's pursuing army on dry ground did not settle them into rest for very long. Neither did the drowning of Egypt's charioteers, which finally freed them for good from their wicked taskmasters. Joyfully they had danced before God and had sung their songs of Yahweh's triumph over Pharaoh's horses and riders. But their ecstasy was soon forgotten, for their freedom presented them with problems they had never faced as slaves.

Though we are image-bearers of God, we are all bound inextricably to our humanness. The frailty of flesh and bone is such that our physical needs preempt spiritual reality far too easily. It wasn't long after the miraculous crossing of the Red Sea that the Israelites had eaten all the food they'd carried with them out of Egypt, and drinkable water had become scarce. Then, instead of trusting the God who could make a dry pathway through the midst of the sea, they yielded to their fear and hunger, hurling their outrage at God again. Frustration and grumbling replaced tambourine and song, and Egyptian slavery in retrospect seemed better than their present freedom.

Instinctively God's people yielded to the slave mentality instilled in them by centuries of harsh treatment. Trust in God and in Moses gave way to pining for the predictability of their former oppressors. Unaccustomed to risk taking, their future seemed death-bound. Angry that their physical gratification was delayed, they raged against having hoped for a better life. Though God would once again meet their need by supplying them with sweet water and daily food (manna), the Israelites' pattern of living without trust, without courage, and without hope would continue causing brokenness in their relationship with God and with their leaders, and sin would always be sure to follow.

The golden calf fiasco was just around the corner.

TERROR IN THE BOAT AGAIN

Though it is seldom clear to us in the midst of crisis, fear inevitably sabotages our trust in God's commitment to our good. When terror clouds our conscious thoughts, faith is likely to be swallowed up by self-preservation, for our deepest terror is of death—primarily our own physical death, with its finality of separation from this world and its terrible silence about what awaits us beyond. The author of the Book of Hebrews declares that we are all in need of God's help against "him who holds the power of [physical] death—that is, the devil," because we are "those who all [our] lives [are] held in slavery by [our] fear of death," and only God can set us free (Heb. 2:14–15). Our bondage to the fear of dying can come on us with sudden force or with insidious nagging, but none of us is immune to its presence. It is our greatest terror.

This perennial death-dread of ours has the power to move us farther and farther away from the only One who can free us from its stranglehold on our lives. Far too often, fear for our physical well-being instinctively replaces our trust in God's kind intentions toward us. We question His sovereignty and His goodness—not theologically, for we know He is good and all-powerful, but experientially, for we want to see more evidence of those divine attributes applied to our immediate circumstances. Even orthodox believers can become practical atheists when they find their lives suddenly at risk, and then God may be put to the test of their own finite perceptions of what He is like and what He is up to.

Such was Simon Peter's experience when he and several other disciples faced extreme danger and ended up maligning Jesus' character. (This story is told in Mark 4:35–41; Matt. 8:23–27; Luke 8:22–25.) The scene of terror was the Sea of Galilee, known for its beauty, its bounty, and its unpredictable weather. Wind rushing in from the surrounding hill country often roiled the water with sudden squalls, and those who regularly fished its waters knew best its treacherous petulance.

Jesus Himself had initiated the boat trip to the opposite shore. Exhausted from His teaching and healing that day, Jesus had left the rowing and navigation to His disciples, while He took a nap on a cushion in the stern of the boat. Surely His sleep was deep, for the furious storm that arose had nearly swamped the boat before His friends finally decided to awaken Him.

Perhaps they had shot anxious—even angry—glances His way more than once, silently resenting that He wasn't helping out; an extra pair of hands was always welcome in a storm. But it was not until their straits were desperate that they finally voiced their wake-up call—and their misjudgment of Him.

"Master, Master, we're going to drown!" they cried out. This after Jesus had just evidenced His supernatural ability to heal the sick and demon-possessed. "Don't you care if we drown?" they demanded, doubting His goodness and His concern for them. At least someone had the right idea, begging Him, "Lord, save us!"

Jesus' reply to their panic is most enlightening, for it reaches to the core of the disciples' problem—and our own as well. He did not say, "Oh my, I had no idea things were this bad—no wonder you're terrified!" Nor did He offer them four steps for calming their terror and taking hold of the situation more confidently and aggressively. Instead, He rebuked them, asking, "Why are you so afraid? Do you still have no faith?" Evidently He had expected their faith to have been much larger, considering the company they were in and the power He had only recently revealed.

Jesus' questions are always instructive, though He never asked them because He lacked some necessary information. Rather, He intended by them to illumine the hidden places in the hearts of His listeners. "Why are you so afraid?" Jesus had asked the disciples, inviting them to an inward look. And when they did not answer (though they probably thought Him crazy for not thinking death a legitimate reason for fear), the Master offered a clue to the real reason for their fear by asking, "Do you still have no faith?" The implication is that the presence of the disciples' fear indicated the absence of their faith in Him. And indeed there is a direct correlation between much fear and little faith. Perhaps what Jesus had hoped to reveal to these men about their hearts was that their terror of death had blinded them to the deeper reality of Jesus' concern for and commitment to those He loved. It is a mistake we often make as well.

Jesus' question, "Where is your faith?" may seem harsh in the context of His disciples' terror. How could He have expected them to believe the impossible—that a raging wind and a nearly swamped boat would not deliver them to certain drowning? For that matter, how could Yahweh have expected the Israelites not to have panicked at Pharaoh's approaching chariots? What kind of God would ask His people to rest in Him so completely that even imminent death could not shake their faith in His goodness?

Surely the stories of God's sovereign power, displayed both to the Old Testament Hebrews and to the New Testament disciples by His absolute control over the physical world, are meant to assure them (and us) not merely of God's omnipotence but also of His love. "Lord, save us!" the disciples had cried out to Jesus. And He did. Having asked His penetrating questions, Jesus rebuked the weather, reining in wind and wave to sudden calm with the stern command, "Quiet! Be still!" It's a good thing He had not demanded greater faith from them before saving them from drowning.

However, the miracle of calm terrified the disciples as badly as had the raging storm. "Who is this?" they asked one another in amazement. What kind of man can command wind and water—and be obeyed? The very thing that should have put them at ease (Jesus' ability to save them) had instead caused commotion in their souls. Were they afraid that the "kind of man" able to control the elements could also use His power against them just as easily as He had so recently used it for them? Jesus had demonstrated His mighty power, but the disciples' faith in His goodness was yet small. So was their willingness to wholeheartedly throw in their lot with this One who had shown Himself worthy of their trust. They had left their fishing nets to follow Him but they would not rest securely in Him nor risk their lives for His sake until they were more confident of His love for them.

Other Deaths, Other Terror

There are other deaths that terrify us besides the loss of physical life. In the beginning, when God warned Adam not to eat from the tree of the knowledge of good and evil, He also announced to him the consequence of disobedience: "When you eat of it you will surely die" (Gen. 2:17). Later, as Adam relayed the divine directive to Eve, neither of them had any inkling what "die" meant, nor had they experienced relational terror, but only holy awe and joy in Yahweh's presence, and unreserved delight in one another.

However, when our first parents rebelled, though they did not immediately fall over dead, they learned at once what both terror and death were. For their unhindered love toward one another died in that moment, and they fearfully hid from each other behind fig leaves. Far worse than that (and intricately connected to it), their uncompromised intimacy with God died too, and they hid also from Him among the garden trees. Spiritual and relational brokenness was their first taste of death, and they were horrified at finding themselves in the presence of the one (and One) from whom their hearts had become estranged.

This terror of standing alone and exposed before another—not just physically naked but having our sinful hearts revealed—runs deep in every one of us. We fear the eyes of the person with whom we need or want relationship, the one whose love or respect we fear we cannot live without. What if those eyes see us and turn away? What if we are known and not wanted? What if we fail each other (and of course we will) and the other's disapproval is not just of what we have done but of who we are? What if we have experienced abuse at the hands of a parent and we conclude we are unlovable? What if we inherit the consequences of a spouse's ungrieved losses and lose respect for the one we genuinely love? The death of love, of respect, of acceptance—these deaths we encounter more frequently and fear as intensely as the threat of physical injury or death.

Often in fact, the loss or absence of intimate connection *feels* like death to us. Especially is this true in the marriage relationship, where seeing deep into each other's heart not only is likely to happen but is necessary for genuine oneness. The risk of honesty is enormous because the possibility of rejection feels deadly. In the face of such danger, we fashion our fig leaves and strategically arrange them to cover our greatest shame, hoping to fool even ourselves by maintaining a facade of respectability and a pretense of closeness.

But God, instead of legitimizing or rewarding our attempts to stay safe from our marriage partners, invites us to even greater marital risk. "Wives, submit to your husbands as to the Lord," the apostle Paul writes (Eph. 5:22), inviting women to the "death" of opening their hearts to their husbands and of relinquishing their attempts to control or change them. Does God really expect wives to trust Him enough to long for their husbands' leadership and love?

And to the men Paul says, "Husbands, love your wives, just as Christ loved the church and gave himself up for her to make her holy" (Eph. 5:25), inviting them to the "death" of sacrificing their self-protective withdrawal or attack. Does God really intend them to stop demanding their rights and start moving instead with understanding and kindness toward their wives, even when those wives don't deserve it?

What Paul admonishes will increasingly threaten to undo us the more we try to obey what he says. How can wives rise above their fear of being unloved and find the courage to respect their husbands according to God's plan? And how can husbands push past their terror of failure and find the commitment to love their wives utterly and sacrificially? Given the fallenness of us all, who would *not* tremble before such a task?

INVITED TO RECEIVE

The terror of intimacy, with its ever-present danger of betrayal, confronts each of us, and we each deal with the threat differently, though not always consciously. The Israelites feared Yahweh had led them into danger and they railed against His goodness. The disciples feared the storm and demanded of Jesus, "Don't you care?"

And the tainted, lonely woman at the Samaritan well had run from the threat of rejection and aloneness by pursuing illicit relationships with men. (This story is continued from John 4.) Perhaps that was why she was undone by the inexplicable kindness of the Jewish man who spoke to her that day.

"Living water" the stranger had offered to give her—what was living water? What was "the gift of God" He spoke of, and who was this man who offered it? Did He have delusions of grandeur? Was He saying He was superior to the patriarch Jacob, who had given them the well from which she intended to draw?

The man explained, "Everyone who drinks this water [from the well] will be thirsty again, but whoever drinks the water I give him will never thirst. Indeed, the water I give him will become in him a spring of water welling up to eternal life."

The Samaritan woman missed the words about an inner spring of water and eternal life. She had stopped listening after the part about never being thirsty again. What a relief *that* would be—never struggling again to evade her neighbors' eyes or to lug water from the well in the heat of the day. "Sir, give me this water so that I won't get thirsty and have to keep coming here to draw water." She would be glad to receive His gift.

However, Jesus was not referring to her physical thirst but to her spiritual and relational longings. Jesus was so in tune with His Father's purposes that He was able to take any circumstance in which He found Himself—even one so ordinary in that day as drawing water from a well—to illustrate spiritual truth. Of course, this immoral woman did not expect to be reminded of her lost hope for meaningful connection in her relationships, and so Jesus' next words drew her up sharply and brought fear to her heart. "Go, call your husband and come back," He instructed her.

Oh-oh. Now He would find out who she really was if she weren't careful. Then He would no doubt retract the gift; such things had happened to her before.

"I have no husband," she said, diligent to avoid His gaze.

"You are right when you say you have no husband," He replied. "The fact is, you have had five husbands, and the man you now have is not your husband. What you have just said is quite true."

How did He know that? Being divorced once or twice or even three times still allowed room for social acceptance. But five times marked her as clearly immoral, and she hadn't even bothered to marry her present lover. Then why didn't He react with scorn and condescension like the others?

Embarrassed at this exposure of her sin, she steered the conversation to more comfortable territory. "Sir," she said, "I can see that you are a prophet. Our fathers worshiped on this mountain, but you Jews claim that the place where we must worship is in Jerusalem."

Perhaps this theological question would divert Him from discussing her personal life. At the very least it would distance her from the ambivalence of feeling this surge of both shame for her history and longing for a cleaner, more genuine intimacy. Besides, maybe she could learn something about religion in the process—it couldn't hurt.

But Jesus' answer, instead of ignoring or mitigating her desire for connection, heightened it, for He spoke of God's own desire for *her.* "Believe me, woman, a time is coming when you will worship the Father neither on this mountain nor in Jerusalem. . . . The true worshipers will worship the Father in spirit and truth, for they are the kind of worshipers the Father seeks."

"Seeks"? God so desires men and women to worship Him that He will seek them out? And "Father"? What did she know of a good father's love and protection, though it was what she'd always wanted? How did this man know everything about her anyway? Who was He?

The Samaritan woman was confused. Jesus' connection with her was relentless in its candor, but not at all contemptuous. In fact she felt drawn to Him, even though He clearly saw her for who she really was. He had been kind to her, and His words had stirred her desire for relational connection in a cleaner way than she'd ever known—connection not just with Him but with the God He had named "Father." This was new for her, enticing yet uncomfortable. Despite her ambivalence, she found herself wanting to tell even her estranged neighbors about this new friend—though they probably wouldn't believe her anyway. She wondered if she could find the courage to risk their scorn.

ROOTS OF DREAD

What is the good of speculating about this immoral woman's inner dilemma as she stood talking with the Savior? Why wonder whether or not her past experiences were coloring her reactions to Jesus' words? Scripture doesn't say she was an abused woman, but five divorces and a live-in boyfriend are details that suggest deep damage done to her heart. Is it not legitimate to conclude that her history was profoundly influencing her?

The same dynamics apply to the connection between the Israelites' slave mentality and their later experience of rebellion in the wilderness of freedom. Their grumbling against God may have been more than simply the perversity of their nature. Perhaps their fear and disbelief, sinful as they were in God's eyes, had taken root during the decades of their captivity. Terror always leaves its mark.

Our dread regarding the risks required in our own intimate relationships also has many secret roots. Western culture, for example, with its worship of youth, beauty, success, and power, influences us (often unconsciously) to fear aging, financial loss, failure, and weakness of any kind. Men in particular struggle to maintain the image if not the reality of personal adequacy, and women strive to maintain a youthful appearance and to control relational uncertainty so they will not be abandoned.

But it is not only our culture that shapes and reinforces our fears. Our families too have modeled for us whom and what to fear—usually without words. We watched our parents' eyes, listened to what they said and did not say, and sensed their reluctance to open their hearts—to each other, to their children, to God, to certain kinds of people. We unquestioningly absorbed their often unspoken apprehensions as our own, because fear begets fear from one generation to the next.

Another source of the particular fears that shape our adult connections is any painful or abusive childhood experience we may have encountered. Abused little girls, for example, both desire and fear closeness with men, and as grown women they are baffled by their ambivalence regarding their relationships with the opposite sex. The little boy beaten by his father or shamed by a teacher learns to either cower or swagger as a grown man, and it inevitably complicates his intimacy with women. Some adults struggle to respond to God as "Father" because of negative experiences with their earthly fathers, and the gap in their souls has caused them to stay at arm's length from God and ultimately from others in their lives.

There are also those who distrust God because they were abandoned (physically or emotionally) by a parent and they decided to trust no one. Their learned isolation continues to keep them from God's rest as adults and it leaves them disappointed in people as well, especially those closest to them. They refuse to risk a holy abandon of love to Christ, giving their hands but not their hearts to God and others, and they end up being dutiful but seldom passionate. We all carry into our adult relationships something of what we learned to fear as children.

It may be that the Hebrews' experience in the desert and the Samaritan woman's response to Jesus at the well have something to teach us about ourselves and about our own relationships. Perhaps we are not as unlike them as we want to believe. Our early experiences of loss have left their mark on us as deeply as theirs had on them. We walk in the footsteps of the disillusioned Israelites and the lonely Samaritan woman more than we know, and our failure to love God and others, like theirs, is often the result.

FEAR'S LEGACY

This was what Bill and I experienced, though in different ways. My husband learned relational fear early in life. He remembers being beaten often as a child by a father given to alcohol abuse and violent outbursts of rage. When Bill was seven or eight, for example, his father became so infuriated at his desperate but unsuccessful attempts to do his spelling homework correctly that he backhanded him out of his chair. More than once Bill spent his childhood evenings going from bar to bar with his father, waiting alone outside for long hours until his father came out.

The alcohol eventually took its toll on Bill's dad. He lost his job, left his family, and died in an accident in another state when Bill was eleven. At the funeral Bill was inconsolable and had to be coaxed from the casket where he had flung himself to hug his daddy.

Bill has memories of good times with his father—sharing ice-cream sodas at the corner drugstore and going hunting with him. But deeply etched in his soul from an early age was a hatred of weakness, a fear of abandonment, and a terror of death. Those fears, born in the environment of abuse, intensified in his teen years. Uprooted when his childhood home was sold, forced to live without family when his mother moved out of state to find work, and vulnerable to emotional and sexual abuse, Bill's adolescent desperation soon hardened into a fierce and angry independence that deepened into defiance. He would keep everyone at arm's length and depend on no one but himself.

This defiance followed Bill sure as a shadow into adulthood as he developed strategies for running from his fear, deadening his pain, and trying to minimize further loss. For more than two decades he reaped the consequences of his hostility and chosen isolation: juvenile run-ins with the law, alcohol abuse in the military, and eventually a failed marriage. He also suffered the collapse of a business enterprise because of a relative's betrayal. Brought to a point of helpless fury and hopeless resignation at the age of thirty-four, Bill moved to Miami to escape the scene of his sorrow.

But he could not escape the effects of his abuse. Even in Miami his binge drinking and desperate partying threatened his new job, his health, and even his very life. His childhood fears had left a devastating mark on his life before God's grace intervened.

My own fear of relational loss had taken root in a less dramatic but no less damaging way. My father's alcoholism had advanced more slowly, but by my teen years my parents' preoccupation with his drinking had undermined the loving stability and attention my siblings and I needed from them. I had learned to fear not only the exposure of our family's secret (especially to our church community) but also my father's sometimes unpredictable behavior and absence, as well as my mother's distress and emotional distance.

I would not have described my childhood as miserable. In fact I have many wonderful memories of happy times with my family, including extended family connections, many of which remain to this day. But my learned vigilance and the uncertainty flowing from my fear of relational disconnection followed me too, far beyond my junior high days.

Compared with Bill's adolescence, my own teen years and early adulthood were externally far less tragic. No one knew, however, that my unfulfilled longing for emotional connection had left me, as a teenager, vulnerable to being abused by older men. Even I did not recognize how I had responded to the betrayal of trust by deadening my soul and isolating my inner life. I made profession of my faith in Christ when I was sixteen, graduated from high school and college, took a teaching position in a Christian school in Miami, and never acknowledged (even to myself) that I often felt I was standing on the outside watching myself live life, so different was my surface facade from the inner reality of my soul.

During those years, my worship of God was sincere and regular, but I seldom felt really connected to Him. I wanted to love Him but I couldn't make it happen, even though I worked at it diligently. My work and church involvement opened the door to many friendships, but I gave no one my true heart. Though I did my job faithfully and tried to help others, inwardly I held myself in contempt, determined to let no one know the dark secrets of my heart. The truth was that I was dying inside and had no idea what to do about it.

My unacknowledged fear of abandonment was in some ways self-fulfilling. Professionally a success at the age of twenty-seven, the legacy of my childhood fear nonetheless had left me secretly depressed and lonely. No one guessed my inner turmoil, for even I did not know how fearful I was deep within. So Bill was not the only one in dire need of God's intervening grace when we were finally brought together in the autumn of 1969.

AN INEVITABLE END

What Bill and I would both eventually discover to our mutual dismay is that our fears, though unspoken, had sprung up from the deep roots of our childhood experiences. Fear always has its reasons and it always seems reasonable to avoid further damage by protecting ourselves in even our most intimate relationships.

But we forget that running from fear instead of grieving the losses that occasioned it (and repenting of our strategies for staying safe) will inevitably result in our being unable to rest with God or others. Jesus' words of invitation, "Come to me, all you who are weary and burdened, and I will give you rest" (Matt. 11:28), were spoken in the context of His sorrow at His people's rejection, for the Galileans had not responded to His teaching with repentance and faith. Christ grieved at what the end result of their disbelief would be. "Woe to you!" He declared against the hill country cities in which He had preached, denouncing them "because they did not repent," even though He had performed many miracles there to substantiate His authority (see Matt. 11:20–24).

Woe is always the consequence for those who refuse to repent, for they are choosing death by clinging to their strategies for living life on their own. Jesus' deepest desire was that those to whom He ministered would respond with repentance for their sin and with faith in His forgiveness, for by His coming death they could be reconciled to their heavenly Father. To reject this invitation into Christ's rest is the worst kind of foolishness, for it always ends in woe.

Whatever our background, whatever our losses or disappointments, whatever our sinful strategies for dealing with those losses, we must admit that our fear of death in any of its insidious forms, and the sin we commit because of that fear, inevitably results in the woe of relational separation from God and other people. Usually we have not consciously sabotaged faith in God nor deliberately undermined our intimate relationships. But the particular style of fearful self-protection by which we personally strive to keep our terror at bay and our hearts safe from being hurt again will eventually destroy our oneness with God and others, whether we intend it to or not.

Surely the sins of the fathers are visited on succeeding generations, and few of us realize the extent to which, because of our childhood fears, we have forged self-protective links that strengthen the enslaving chain of sin. And to the degree we live at the mercy of our fears, to that degree we will fall again and again into the calamity of sin. Somehow our terror must give way to a power greater than ourselves, and we must yield our fear to a new and living hope in the grace and sufficiency of God in Christ. This will be the topic of chapter 3.

QUESTIONS TO CONSIDER

1. Which aspects, if any, of the "slave mentality" describe your own patterns in relating?

a. Don't trust. b. Don't risk. c. Don't hope.

2. How does the lack of trust damage a relationship?

3. What similarities are there between the Israelites' style of relating to God and your own experience of Him?

4. What kind of death (physical, spiritual, relational, etc.) do you fear most? Why?

5. What relationship or event from your childhood has had the greatest impact on your present way of relating to others?

Regarding the opening story:

Jerry had experienced the false intimacy of childhood abuse and repeatedly flew into rages as an adult. Mona was terrified of Jerry's rages and chose to abandon the marriage.

6. Why do you think Mona wanted Jerry to "deal with" the abuse from his childhood?

7. What might change if Jerry would decide to "deal with" his abuse?

CHAPTER THREE

DISOBEDIENCE

The Calamity of Unbelief

INSPECTING HER REFLECTION in the full-length mirror, Anne indulged herself an approving nod, a smile of satisfaction briefly lightening her face. At thirty-three she looked much younger, having been careful to keep her shape and attractiveness. After all, she'd lost so many other advantages. Her father, the pastor of a small Midwestern church, had always told her she should be glad to be pretty, because she wasn't good for much else. She guessed he was right after all.

With a pang, Anne thought about how desperately she had wanted to escape her father's house and make her own way in the world. But getting pregnant when she was only sixteen had derailed her dreams of freedom, trapping her in a different kind of bondage. Anne loved her son, Peter, but his conception had been not just wrong (as her father never failed to remind her) but inconvenient as well. Anne shook her head ruefully, remembering her shame at having had her sin exposed to the entire congregation. The pain of the memory had diminished very little over time.

51

At least Scott had "done the right thing," marrying her a week after his high school graduation. And, to his credit, he had continued to stand by her, even after her affair four years ago. Anne had given up her lover when Scott had discovered them together—the romance had begun to sour anyway, and she had not been prepared to survive on her own. Thankfully, Scott had never told anyone, not even her father.

"I suppose I should be grateful for Scott," Anne mentally scolded herself, though her image stared back at her with little sign of remorse for how she had wronged him. Scott had been a diligent Christian and faithful provider but his passivity had always left Anne deeply dissatisfied, and she was bored in her marriage. Gratitude could sustain a relationship only so long, and this time Anne was determined to flee for good. Her new lover promised to provide the freedom and excitement she'd always wanted.

Besides, Peter was now sixteen, old enough to manage without her. Anne hoped he would finish high school—something she had never been able to do. She had done her best with Peter, and though she would miss him, her own happiness seemed more important now.

Carrying her suitcase into the hallway, Anne passed her son's room one last time, glancing inside to be sure the envelope with his name on it was on his dresser where she'd left it. Then she descended the stairs, checked her hair in the front hall mirror, stepped out to the front porch, and locked the door of her old life firmly behind her.

How persistent is our longing for happiness, and how consistently we sin in our efforts to satisfy it! We will abandon duty, vows, scruples, and even faith in our search for relief from remembered or repressed pain. For it is often our own personal unhappiness that drives us to exchange one survival strategy for another, hoping the new tactic will work better than the old. This was Anne's expectation as she left her old life behind that fateful day.

But without an internal transformation of mind and heart, any external change of relationship or circumstance will provide only temporary relief for our heart sickness. Anne's dissatisfaction, for example, will resurface time and again unless and until God intervenes with His grace and she receives from Him the soul-rest for which she—and all of us—yearns so unrelentingly. It is a lesson some never learn.

The people trembled before the blazing mountain, this time fearing not Pharaoh but the Voice. (These stories are told in Exodus 19–20.) Above the roll of thunder and the crescendo of trumpet, out of billowing smoke and thick darkness, the Voice pierced their hearts and buckled their knees.

"I am the LORD your God, who brought you out of Egypt, out of the land of slavery," Yahweh sang out full-voiced in the hearing of them all. The Voice resounded across the sacred mountain space, which separated the holy from the profane, echoing and reverberating until the earth itself trembled at the coming of its Maker. The holy Word, not yet made flesh, not yet dwelling among us, revealed His own unapproachable splendor and required that His people obey Him in all things.

"You shall have no other gods before me," He thundered.

"You shall not make for yourself an idol in the form of anything in heaven above or on the earth beneath or in the waters below," they heard God command.

"You shall not misuse the name of the LORD your God," Yahweh warned.

"Remember the Sabbath day by keeping it holy," He ordered.

"Honor your father and your mother, so that you may live long in the land the LORD your God is giving you," He demanded and promised.

"You shall not murder.

"You shall not commit adultery.

"You shall not steal.

"You shall not give false testimony against your neighbor.

"You shall not covet."

Thunder and lightning and trumpet and smoke punctuated the voice of God, burning His commandments into heart and memory, until at last the Israelites could bear it no more. In terror they cried out to Moses, "This great fire will consume us, and we will die if we hear the voice of the LORD our God any longer. For what mortal man has ever heard the voice of the living God speaking out of fire, as we have, and survived? Go near and listen to all that the LORD our God says. Then tell us whatever the LORD our God tells you. We will listen and obey" (Deut. 5:25–27). God's people had come to the limit of what their terror could endure.

Yahweh was not displeased with their fear, for it was accomplishing its intended purpose of drawing His people to worshipful obedience. "I have heard what this people said to you," He told Moses. "Everything they said was good." Sorrow, however, no doubt tinged His voice as He added almost yearningly, "Oh, that their hearts would be inclined to fear me and keep all my commands always, so that it might go well with them and their children forever!" (vv. 28–29). He knew their hearts would all too soon be seduced away from Him.

Nonetheless, God's kindness prevailed. "Go, tell [the people] to return to their tents," He instructed Moses. "But you stay here with me so that I may give you all the commands, decrees and laws you are to teach them to follow in the land I am giving them to possess" (v. 31). So the people hurried thankfully back to their campsites, and Moses alone approached the thick darkness on Mount Sinai where Yahweh was.

What happened to Moses when he disappeared into that dread cloud? The Israelites, huddled fearfully in their tents, awoke each morning to the fire and smoke and glory of Yahweh hovering over Sinai. But what was going on with Moses?

VISION ON THE MOUNT

From within the cloud of terrifying glory God for forty days communicated to Moses the civil and ceremonial laws that would shape the Israelites' culture and direct their worship now that they were no longer subject to the authority of their abusers. There on the blazing mountain was forged the covenant that would yoke Yahweh to His people by strong bonds of sacred love. This covenant would mark the Israelites as no longer owned by the cruel Egyptians, but bound in intimate identity as "firstborn son" of the Almighty One. God Himself would lead them, not by whip or chain but by cloud and fire, by voice and love, and soon by written Word. Yahweh, not Pharaoh, would govern these people now, for Egyptian law was being replaced by Sinai's holy commands.

But what was most blessedly unique about this covenant was the provision made for God's people when they failed to keep it. Yoked to the Egyptians, the Israelites had received death for their disobedience. But intrinsic to Sinai's yoking was God's gracious offer of forgiveness for their disobedience if they would repent of their sin and in faith turn back to Him. This forgiveness and restoration, moreover, would be won not by their own efforts, nor by their own deaths as just payment for their sin, but by the death of a substitute taking their place. In this covenant between Yahweh and His people, law would be linked to grace, Yahweh's justice and mercy inextricably intertwined.

For of the many wonders God revealed to Moses within the glorious cloud cover, the most amazing was the vision of the holy place of infinite grace: the heavenly Holy of Holies, where the eternal death, which God's image-bearers deserved, would be atoned for through the shedding of substitute blood. The law Moses was given revealed God's perfect standard for obedience; the vision Moses was given revealed God's provision of grace for His people's disobedience.

In showing Moses this vision, Yahweh wished to establish for His people a physical, earthly replica of what existed in the celestial realm. Moses was told to build a portable worship center that would occupy an open area situated in the middle of the Israelites' desert campground. A holy tent, or tabernacle, would be the central feature of this worship area, precisely patterned after the vision Moses was shown of its heavenly, spiritual counter-part. (The tabernacle is described in Exodus 25–27.) Moses was warned, "See to it that you make everything according to the pattern shown you on the mountain" (Heb. 8:5), so that divine realities would not be mis-represented by the earthly copies the Israelites would make.

Moses was told to place in the courtyard in front of the tabernacle (the holy Tent of Meeting) a basin for ceremonial cleansing of the worship com-ponents and a bronze altar for shedding the blood of animal sacrifices. The inside of the tabernacle would contain furnishings fashioned from gold and splendid fabric "plundered" from the Egyptians, the furnishings to be arranged in this fashion:

> In [the tabernacle's] first room were the lampstand, the table and the con-secrated bread; this was called the Holy Place. Behind the second curtain was a room called the Most Holy Place, which had the golden altar of incense and the gold-covered ark of the covenant. . . . Above the ark were the cheru-bim of the Glory, overshadowing the atonement cover.
>
> HEBREWS 9:2–5

In this room behind the second curtain, above the golden ark with its atonement cover, Yahweh Himself would dwell among His chosen people. It was, indeed, a Most Holy Place.

SIN'S RELENTLESSNESS

Why did God give His servant Moses such careful instructions regard-ing holy things and blood sacrifices and priestly rituals? Why were these things significant, even indispensable? It was because of what was hap-pening at the foot of the mountain beneath the cloud at the very time Moses was receiving those instructions from God. It was because of the Israelites' sin and rebellion. (The following events are told in Exodus 32–34.)

For while Moses lingered forty days on Sinai, the Israelites grew accus-tomed to Yahweh's glory until it awed them no more. Their appropriate ter-ror of God's voice at the foot of Sinai had not given way to rest in Him. If it had, they would have waited as long as it took for Moses to receive Yahweh's instructions and they would have been eager to obey (as they had promised). Instead, they became restless and dissatisfied with God's covenant. Even their freedom no longer thrilled them, and the absence of productive work had become unsettling for these former slaves used to forced labor.

Finally, bored with resting and impatient with uncertainty, they decided on a new course of action. "Make us gods who will go before us," they demanded of Aaron. "As for this fellow Moses who brought us up out of

Egypt, we don't know what has happened to him" (32:1). They were familiar with taskmasters and preferred a leader they could see and hear. Influenced by the paganism of Egypt, they wanted to be able to look at their god, so they could ground the mystery of deity in the visible and the manageable. Doing something—*anything*—was better than waiting and resting in Yahweh.

And Aaron, who surely knew better, fashioned for them a calf made from Egyptian gold, a shining statue reminiscent of the familiar idols of Egypt. Without Moses' presence, Aaron fell prey to the power of fear—the fear of an insurrection among the people. He tried to integrate the Israelites' idolatry with the worship of Yahweh, calling for a "festival to the LORD," but his words contradicted the very words of Yahweh Himself, who had said in the hearing of them all, "You shall not make for yourself an idol in the form of anything."

Besides, the golden calf no doubt recalled to the people's minds the Egyptian worship orgies they had witnessed (and perhaps had entered into) in the past, and after Aaron had led them in bringing ceremonial burnt offerings and fellowship offerings to the "god" he had made for them, the Israelites "sat down to eat and drink and got up to indulge in revelry" in debauched imitation of those who had abused them. Thus can abuse pursue its victim into a repetition of his or her own violation. In the strength of the manna Yahweh had provided, Yahweh's children rebelled against Him.

Is it any wonder God's anger burned against His chosen people? Their former abuse at Pharaoh's hands was no justification for their idolatry. They had heard Yahweh's voice with their own ears and they had chosen to disobey, leaving them utterly without excuse. How could God, who is holy, *not* exact justice for the rebellion of His people? Can He be respected, let alone trusted, if His commands are ignored and He does nothing to enforce them?

GLIMPSES OF GRACE

Surely it goes without saying that Yahweh had every right to punish the Israelites for their blatant disobedience. He had drawn a clear line in the sand, and His children had stepped boldly across it. Now the Almighty One said to Moses from within the cloud of His dread glory, "Go down, because your people, whom you brought up out of Egypt, have become corrupt." Disclaiming His ownership of the Israelites by calling them "your people" when He spoke to Moses, Yahweh invited the shepherd prince to speak on behalf of the rebels.

In doing so, God gave Moses the option of intervening for the Israelites or stepping out of the way of God's wrath toward them. "Now leave me alone," Yahweh said, "so that my anger may burn against them and that I may destroy them." Since when does God need anyone to step out of the way of His intended action? Was this not rather an invitation for Moses to show his true heart not only toward the grumbling, mutinous rabble God had chosen but also toward God Himself? And to reveal Moses' loyalty even more clearly, God added, "Then I will make you into a great nation."

Which would Moses choose: The comfort of "no more hassle" and the pride of patriarchy or intercession for the disobedient? Surely he was stunned by what the Israelites had done. But he was also made courageous by his intimacy with this now angry God. Moses had been forty days close to God's heart, and God's love for His people now throbbed in Moses as well, diminishing the appeal of an easier life without these rebels and the honor of becoming the new progenitor of Yahweh's chosen nation.

Reflecting God's own passion, Moses chose to bend his energy toward intercession on behalf of the redeemed Israelites, who even then were carousing at the foot of Sinai. On his face before Yahweh, Moses confessed the sin of the Israelites and begged God to preserve His own reputation among the nations by honoring His covenant with Abraham. "Turn from your fierce anger; relent and do not bring disaster on your people," he pleaded.

In mercy God heard the prayer of His servant. He would slay many with sword and plague when Moses went down to the scene of the crime, for they had blatantly sinned against Him. But because of Moses' persistence in mediation, Yahweh would not altogether obliterate the Israelites. He said, however, that He wouldn't go with them to Canaan, either, explaining, "You are a stiff-necked people. If I were to go with you even for a moment, I might destroy you" (33:3).

When Moses announced this to the people, they were deeply distressed, wailing in grief while Moses pleaded with Yahweh yet again. "If your Presence does not go with us," he implored, "do not send us up from here. How will anyone know that you are pleased with me and with your people unless you go with us? What else will distinguish me and your people from all the other people on the face of the earth?" (33:15–16).

And again God relented, promising Moses, "My Presence will go with you, and I will give you rest" (v. 14). The fugitives would find refuge; the rebellious would not be cast aside; the repentant could still enter rest. Surely God was, as He declared of Himself to Moses, "the compassionate and gracious God, slow to anger, abounding in love and faithfulness, maintaining love to thousands, and forgiving wickedness, rebellion and sin" (34:6–7). The Israelites deserved death, but God was willing to give them rest.

How could this be? Had God's ten commandments been merely ten recommendations? Shouldn't the people have had to pay for their rebellion and idolatry? How could God forgive them when His holiness demanded justice? How can any of us straying sheep find forgiveness for our defiance of God's commands?

The answer is to be found in the spiritual significance of the tabernacle rituals designed by God Himself and revealed to Moses on Sinai. For by those rituals God's people would enact the spiritual reality of God's plan to deliver His people—not merely from Pharaoh (whom they had left behind) but from their sin (which they had carried with them out of Egypt).

SIN AND BLOODSHED

In fact ever since our first parents rebelled against God's prohibition regarding the fruit of the forbidden tree, all mankind has stood in need of redemption from sin. For disobedience against any of God's commands is always a capital offense, and when Adam and Eve disobeyed God, they became worthy of the death penalty.

Moreover, because of Adam's and Eve's sin, we all come into the world spiritually dead and prone to disobeying God's law, which demands perfect love toward Him and toward others. Self-centeredness is not learned but innate. Scripture reminds us that "all have sinned and fall short of the glory of God" (Rom. 3:23), though few of us can remember the first of our countless transgressions against God's glory. Jesus stands alone as the only human being who ever "was without sin" (Heb. 4:15). The rest of us stand condemned and deserving of not merely mortal death but eternal death as well.

Jesus Himself ranked spiritual death more terrible than its physical counterpart when He told His disciples, "Do not be afraid of those who kill the body but cannot kill the soul. Rather, be afraid of the One who can destroy both soul and body in hell" (Matt. 10:28). It is the holy God we are to fear, for His power to bring judgment against our sin reaches beyond the grave, and "it is a dreadful thing to fall into the hands of the living God" (Heb. 10:31). Fear is most appropriate when we are confronted with the altogether righteous One, who can sentence to eternal death those who refuse to repent and believe in His provision for forgiveness. Being separated forever from God, who is love, should be what we most fear.

But do we? Is not our fear more likely to flow from the possibility of economic loss or physical catastrophe or relational isolation than from the specter of eternity without God? How many of us have come to the kind of rest in God's love in which we are more afraid of living without God's presence than we are of losing our wealth or our happiness or even our lives? Our humanity often blinds us to the terrible ugliness of our sin, and we fear altogether the wrong kinds of things. We fear not separation from God but our own bad health or loneliness or incompetence. Our personal discomfort is harder to bear than the exercise of godliness, and our mortal circumstances preempt our immortal destiny. Even sin's punishment appears more calamitous than the sin that merited the punishment.

We have been deceived by the evil one, but like Eve and the Israelites of old, we persist in our self-deception until we find ourselves hopelessly enslaved to sin. We embrace the "virtual reality" of trying to compensate for past losses or to evade sin's consequences, but the calamity of our disobedience is real and will not go away. Deceived or not, we are death-bound because of our sin.

However, Yahweh, out of love for His fallen children, offers us hope by shedding blood to satisfy His justice against disobedience. In the Garden of Eden, for example, He killed one of the animals in which He had earlier delighted, then "made garments of skin for Adam and his wife and clothed them" (Gen. 3:21). This first blood-bought covering was not merely for their bodies. It also symbolized the covering of their sin so they could be forgiven and restored to God. From then on, the shedding of blood was required whenever God's image-bearers sought reconnection with the God they had alienated by their own sin.

Thus it was that Yahweh on Mount Sinai ordained explicit animal sacrifices to cover the sins of His people individually and corporately. As He commanded Moses, animal sacrifice was to become the centerpiece of the Israelites' worship in the tabernacle, the "sanctuary that is a copy and shadow of what is in heaven" (Heb. 8:5). The shedding of the blood of bulls, sheep, and goats was required as part of their worship experience, though God's people would not fully understand its meaning until Messiah Himself had come to fulfill its heavenly and eternal significance.

RITUAL OF BLOOD

The highlight of the Hebrew worship calendar was the annual Day of Atonement, Yom Kippur, when the entire congregation of God's people convened at the tabernacle to know their sins were covered by the sacrifice of blood. (The celebration of Yom Kippur is detailed in Leviticus 16.) On Yom Kippur the high priest would enter the open area in front of the tabernacle wearing his sacramental turban, sash, and the priestly blue robe hemmed with gold bells and embroidered pomegranates (Exod. 28:31–41). There he would slaughter first a young bull to atone for himself and his household, and then a goat to atone for the sins of the people.

Taking some of the animal blood, the high priest would approach the tabernacle itself, where a rope would be tied around his ankle. Because he would soon enter the Most Holy Place, into which only he could go—and that only on this day of the year—the rope would be used to retrieve his dead body if the bells on his robe stopped tinkling, indicating he had defiled

God's holiness and had died inside the holiest of sanctuaries.[1] With the rope in place, the high priest would then enter the tabernacle with a basin of blood and a censer of burning coals taken from the altar. Drawing back the heavy curtain that concealed the Most Holy Place, he would place two handfuls of fragrant incense on the coals in the censer so its smoke would obscure from his view the ark of the covenant where God dwelt in His glory, for no one could see God and live. Then he moved toward the sacred ark, and God alone saw him splash the life-saving blood against the mercy seat, first for his own sins and then for the sins of the people.

Outside the tabernacle the Israelites would wait in reverent fear for the high priest to emerge, for his appearance would indicate God had accepted the blood sacrifice and had forgiven their sins. With relief and joy they would greet the high priest's coming and would then watch him lay hands on the head of another sacramental goat, signifying the transfer of their sins to the goat. This sin-burdened animal (the scapegoat) would in turn be led outside the camp and driven far into the wilderness to perish, banishing forever the year of individual and corporate sins atoned for on the blood-spattered covering of God's holy ark.

Why this ritual, this perpetually recurring animal bloodshed? Could an animal's death ever pay for a person's sin? Scripture declares that "it is impossible for the blood of bulls and goats to take away sins" (Heb. 10:4). Why then did God ordain this elaborate system and insist that Moses teach it to the Israelites?

God's gracious plan for redeeming His fallen image-bearers was not made clear to His people all at once. Rather, it was cloaked in symbolic imagery and revealed to them in increments throughout the Old Testament. Beginning with the animal blood shed to clothe Adam and Eve, Yahweh established the principle that "without the shedding of blood there is no forgiveness" (Heb. 9:22). Moreover, God prepared our first parents to expect a coming Savior from their sin, promising them that a descendant of theirs would someday crush the life out of the enemy who had led them into sin (Gen. 3:15).

However, the calamity of their disobedience would require more than the substitution of animal blood for their own deserved death penalty. Only a perfect man could pay the price of mankind's sin, so the blood of God Himself would have to be shed through the freely chosen death of the promised Messiah, who would be both true God and true man.

This holy Anointed One would enter the Most Holy Place, but it would not be in tent or temple. Rather, He would approach the *heavenly* tabernacle, offering not "the blood of goats and calves" but "his own blood" to obtain "eternal redemption" for His people (Heb. 9:12). The blood of Old Testament sacrifices had covered the sins of God's people for centuries but it had never atoned for them. With the crucifixion of Messiah, however, sin was removed altogether, for Jesus was "the Lamb of God, who takes away the sin of the world" (John 1:29). The accumulated sin of all who believe in Messiah from the beginning to the end of time would be and has been taken away by Jesus when He died—the perfect sacrifice—on the cross of Calvary. Only Messiah's blood shed on the cross is able to save sinners, whether it is Old Testament sinners who believed He was going to come, or New Testament sinners of yesterday and today who believe He has come. The celebration of Yom Kippur, established by Yahweh on Mount Sinai, was finally eclipsed and made unnecessary by the triumphant and only true Day of Atonement, known to the Christian church as Good Friday.

Every person who has ever lived (Jesus Christ excepted) deserves eternal death, for we have all turned from God, choosing Egypt over Canaan, false gods over Yahweh, self-protection over risk, autonomy over obedience. We are all at the dread mercy of God's grace. But our greatest terror can bend to our most joyous hope, for the good news is that on Calvary's crossed beams God's holy justice and His tender mercy eternally intersect without compromise, winning salvation for all who trust in Christ. This is the gospel, and in the symbolism of tabernacle ritual, this is what Moses saw on the mountain from within the thick darkness of God's glory.

DANGER OF DISBELIEF

They say hindsight is always 20/20, so we may find it easy to fault the Israelites for their soon renunciation of God's promises and commands in the matter of the golden calf. But the truth is, we all suffer a similar ambivalence. It is difficult to maintain faith in God and hope in His deliverance when around and within we find ample reason for impatience and despair—because of our marriages, our health, our children—whatever. Those things we see with our physical eyes so easily blur our spiritual vision. Such was the "seeing is believing" disobedience of the Israelites at the foot of Mount Sinai. Such also was the experience of Peter the fisherman many centuries later.

Peter had been a man of the sea for many years, knowing well its danger. He had always exercised a healthy respect for its unpredictability, but there were other things he feared even more. That is why what happened to him one night on the Sea of Galilee was so astonishing (see Matt. 14:22–32).

Peter and the other disciples had just watched Jesus feed five thousand people with only five loaves of bread and two fish, the first of several extraordinary events. Afterward Jesus had sent them in a boat to the other side of the sea ahead of Him so He could be alone with His Father.

It wasn't long before the disciples began having a hard time of it. Struggling against buffeting waves and a contrary wind, they suddenly saw a form walking toward them on the water. Terrified, they screamed in fear. A storm was one thing; a ghost was quite another. Where was Jesus when they needed Him? Could He banish the apparition as He had calmed the sea?

Then they heard His voice. The "ghost" was saying, "Take courage! It is I. Don't be afraid." And they knew *He* was the apparition, and He *was* there when they needed Him, banishing not the apparition but their fear.

One would think Jesus' walking toward them on the water would be astonishment enough for one night. But what happened next was even more amazing. For Peter, whether from doubt or bravado, impulsively called out, "Lord, if it's you, tell me to come to you on the water." So Jesus invited him, "Come." And he did.

Climbing down out of the boat, Peter began walking on the water toward his Lord. It made no sense. Stepping into a raging sea far from shore was lunacy, even for an experienced seaman. Who had ever heard of such a thing as a man—now *two* men—walking on water? Would Peter trip on the waves?

Suddenly the fisherman realized where he was and what he was doing. Shifting his gaze from Jesus to the waves whipped up by the wind, Peter panicked and began to sink. "Lord, save me!" he screamed, and Jesus quickly reached out His hand. With the storm still raging, He caught Peter, asking, "You of little faith, why did you doubt?"

This was now the second time Jesus had rebuked Peter for his littleness of faith. The Savior had not, however, chided him for his impulsive leap out of the boat. Sometimes He invites us to follow His leading into situations that may appear foolhardy to others. Nevertheless, when we respond to His bidding, we must also believe He will sustain us in our choices. Peter was not wrong to want to walk beside Jesus but he began to sink when what he saw and heard around him caused him to doubt the One he had seen and heard in front of him. How difficult it is to trust our spiritual vision more than our physical sight or intellectual insight. Our disbelief in what is *really* real leads always to disaster.

Yet in spite of Peter's littleness of faith, Jesus saved him from the raging sea, walking with him back to the boat, where one more astonishment awaited them. When they climbed aboard, the wind died down. Is it any wonder that "those who were in the boat worshiped him, saying, 'Truly you are the Son of God'"? Increasingly the disciples were believing in the divine nature of this extraordinary rabbi they called friend.

DEATH AND THE GOSPEL

Peter and the other disciples, however, were not the first to recognize Jesus as Messiah. The Savior had already revealed His messianic identity to a most unlikely candidate: a Samaritan, a woman, a *fallen* woman, an outcast of outcasts (see John 4 again). "You Samaritans worship what you do not know," Jesus had told her, referring to the "mixed religion" of her people. Scripture tells us that the ancestors of the Samaritan woman had "worshiped the LORD, but . . . also served their own gods in accordance with the customs of the nations from which they had been brought" (2 Kings 17:33).

Thus the Samaritans were only part Jewish, both in their racial make-up and in their religion, which accounts for the Jewish custom of treating them as Gentile sinners. In contrast, Jesus had reminded the woman at the well, "we [Jews] worship what we do know, for salvation is from the Jews," referring to the age-old promise of a coming Jewish Messiah who would deliver His people from their sin.

Though neither the woman nor the disciples understood that Messiah's salvation would be from their sin and not from their enemies, Jesus made the connection clear by referring to "salvation" in the context of having just exposed her sinful lifestyle. Surely she did not need convincing of her need for forgiveness; she knew she was caught.

"I know that Messiah . . . is coming," she responded, asserting her own hope for Christ's advent by adding, "When he comes, he will explain everything to us." Her stated hope for Messiah to come and explain things camouflaged her deeper need, which was for Him to come and cleanse her heart from sin. Jesus, however, offered her both when He declared, "I who speak to you am he."

What a time for the disciples to arrive with the food they had bought in town! The woman no doubt had much more she wanted to ask this man who claimed to be Messiah, but not in front of all those men, whose expressions did not put her at rest as Jesus' eyes had done. Leaving her water jug behind, she fled the scene, hurrying back to Sychar, no longer caring that the villagers disdained and avoided her. "Come, see a man who told me everything I ever did," she invited her haughty neighbors, who themselves already knew a good deal about what she had done. "Could this be the Christ?" she excitedly asked. Her news was too good to keep to herself, and because of this sinful woman's testimony about Jesus, the residents of her village "came out of the town and made their way toward him."

The good news is like that—people become gospel-tellers in spite of themselves. This woman who had received Jesus' kindness found herself compelled to tell others about Him, and many would come to faith because of her. It would be her first taste of community in a very long time.

Meanwhile, the disciples tried to ignore Jesus' impropriety in having engaged in conversation with a Samaritan outcast woman. Though they "were surprised to find him talking with a woman, . . . no one asked, 'What do you want?' or 'Why are you talking with her?'" Instead, they skirted the issue, urging Him, "Rabbi, eat something," addressing His fatigue from the journey and His need for refreshment.

But Jesus inexplicably refused their food. "I have food to eat," He said, "that you know nothing about." What did that mean? Who could have brought Him something to eat out here? Hopefully not the woman who had just left! A rabbi eating food made unclean by contact with a Samaritan—why, such a thing was unthinkable!

But Jesus had redemption not reputation (or eating) on His mind, for He already knew His messianic task would lead to a cross. "My food," Jesus explained, "is to do the will of him who sent me and to finish his work." Intimately yoked to His Father, He was nourished by submission, refreshed by knowing and doing whatever His Father asked of Him, though it would mean His crucifixion. Jesus' loud scream, "It is finished," just before His death (John 19:30), would announce the completion of the work His Father had assigned—which was to offer His own blood to atone for the sins of all who put their faith in Him—even the Samaritans hurrying toward Him from the town. Jesus took sustenance from bringing His own will into line with His Father's will, which meant that by His death, God's wayward sons and daughters would be drawn back home to Himself.

How little the disciples understood or embraced Jesus' otherworldly priorities at the well at Sychar! How seldom even we, who have fuller knowledge of God's larger picture, consider trust in our heavenly Father and obedience to His will more nourishing than what this world offers. Submission as refreshment is a foreign concept to us, though it was life-giving to Christ. The disciples did not yet understand it, either.

But the Samaritan outcast seems to have grasped something of the grace of rest, as well as the rest of grace. She caught the connection between forgiveness of sin and the joyous unguardedness of a responsive love. And in that sense, the immoral woman who had run to announce the Messiah's coming was closer to the Kingdom than any of the chosen Twelve standing around Jesus at Jacob's well. Such is the foolishness of the gospel and the abandon of worship.

ONENESS WITHOUT PASSION

Who can comprehend the purposes of God, whose "thoughts are not [our] thoughts, neither are [his] ways" like our own (Isa. 55:8)? Why would Jesus speak the gospel to a misguided pagan who worshiped what she did not even know? Why announce His messianic identity so clearly to a Samaritan and not to the Jewish religious leaders? How inscrutable are God's thoughts, how incomprehensible His ways, how crazy His choices about whom to bless. Why offer grace to the unworthy? Which is to say, why offer grace to anyone?

Surely there were no two people in more dire need of grace than Bill and I were when God finally brought us together in a small Miami church in 1969. Bill had come there to worship what he did not really know, and God opened to him the good news of Christ's atonement for his sins, drawing him back from the edge of disaster. I had come to worship what I did know, but my head knowledge about grace had not yet set my heart at rest in God nor released me to the passion of yielding to His love. As my sister, Peg De Boer, wrote in her spiritual autobiography regarding her childhood, "I knew God loved me, but no one ever told my heart."

Nonetheless, God in His mercy brought Bill and me together, and our marriage in 1970 launched us into a oneness we both believed was intended by Him. We were willing to work hard at our relationship, though we had no idea how pervasively our past relational damage had harmed us both. Part of the reason our marriage seemed so compatible in its early years is that both of us hated conflict and compulsively avoided arguments. Unfortunately neither of us recognized the growing arsenal of anger toward each other we were stockpiling in our hearts. We had become expert at keeping it hidden, even from our own awareness.

Perhaps our biggest error as we entered matrimony was in thinking we could mutually meet each other's deepest needs through our love for one another. It was a most unrealistic expectation, of course, distinctively human but fundamentally wrong. No one's partner can possibly meet the deepest needs of the heart. Loving another person totally unconditionally is too big a responsibility for anyone, no matter how spiritually mature. Only God is up to that big a job.

For God is not like us, though we are made in His image. His passion for oneness flows from His nature of love, both within the Trinity and toward us, His fallen image-bearers. His divine longing for oneness is not a need on God's part to *be loved* but an eagerness to *give love* to those who are willing to receive it. Only God is love, and if we are to love Him or anyone else, it must first come from Him. "This is love," the apostle John declared, "not that we loved God, but that he loved us and sent his Son as an atoning sacrifice for our sins" (1 John 4:10). We cannot give what we have not first received.

Besides, our human longing for oneness is altogether tainted by mankind's fall into sin. We long for oneness because we are created in God's image, but in our sin and self-centeredness we want oneness on our terms, which is to say we are primarily interested in *getting* love, not *giving* it. In fact when we are not loved the way we expect (or demand) to be loved, the real intent of our heart is revealed by our response of anger and revenge. We may leave physically or we may leave emotionally (by absenting ourselves from the hearts of those around us). But whatever shape it takes, the withdrawing of our love and the hiding of our hearts when we have been disappointed shows that our desire for oneness comes not from overflow (as God's does) but from our own deficit.

For the terrible truth is that we cannot love a marriage partner (or anyone else, for that matter) out of our own resources. Our well will dry up sooner than we think when things don't go our way. The calamity of our

65

own and each other's sinfulness will run us to the end of our capacity to love every time. The "living water" Jesus offered the Samaritan woman (and us) comes from the well of His own infinite love for the unlovely, and it is what we desperately need. When we refuse to rest in His sufficiency to sustain our relationships (especially our marriages), it is only a matter of time before our puny attempts to overcome our innate selfishness come up against our innate helplessness to maintain the loyalty and faithfulness we have promised to each other. We may yearn for oneness and give it our very best effort, but unless God brings us to the end of ourselves in trying to make it happen, we will never find it. We will just go on working harder in our own strength until we either give up and settle for aloneness (physical or emotional) or pretend to be something we are not, pretend things are better than they are, pretend our intimacy is deeper than it really is or can be.

That is the way Bill and I lived for over a decade in our marriage. He had embraced God's saving grace, and outwardly his life became far more manageable. He kept his job, settled into faithfully providing for me and our family, attended church regularly, and became the best husband and father he knew how to be, despite having had so few positive role models during his childhood and adolescence.

I too settled fairly comfortably into the routine of matrimony, striving to pattern my external life according to the scriptural mandates regarding sub-missive wives and nurturing mothers. My determination to please God and my family kept my earlier fear of abandonment and loneliness well below the surface of my conscious thought. Though I was a far more controlling wife than I was ready to acknowledge, I sought to love biblically the people in my life at home, work, and church. I was thankful Bill and I were both Christians, committed to making this union last. Our hope for the marriage ran high.

During those early years Bill and I believed in God's saving grace. But in retrospect it's clear we knew very little about appropriating that grace into passionate oneness with God or with one another. Neither of us experienced abiding rest in God as our heavenly Father, for both of us were focused on making up for our earlier losses by trying to control and change each other. Much lay beneath the surface of our life together, fears and feelings we neither wanted nor knew how to face. Superficially we were content with our marriage, unaware that eventually God in His kindness would profoundly disrupt our coping strategies and invite us to struggle to the very end of our attempts to live as though we did not need His grace. Trauma sat poised to pounce. It would not be a pretty sight.

Sin and Terror

"Come to me," Jesus had invited, and we had come, Bill and I, the Samaritan woman, Peter the fisherman, Moses and Aaron, and the Israelites of

66

old. "All you who are weary and burdened" He had named us, inviting us to acknowledge how sick and tired we were of our failure to believe in and act according to our true identity as God's beloved sons and daughters. Our burden of sin was heavy, and we could bear it no longer. We needed Messiah to save us—from slavery and drowning, but mostly from immorality and self-protection and sin of every kind. Desperate for His grace we had come, weary of our battle against sin, burdened by our futile attempts to live life on our own terms, afraid of death and of separation from what was familiar and beloved.

We are all afraid, whether or not we acknowledge or even recognize it. The entrance of sin into our world marked the entrance of terror with its sometimes unconscious stranglehold on our will. We continually face the challenge of doing what is right and not giving way to fear, especially in our most intimate relationships. The Israelites yielded to the uncertainty generated by Moses' prolonged absence, and they fell into idolatry. Peter was terrified of the waves when he stopped trusting Jesus, and he fell into the water. Bill and I were afraid of being hurt again and we fell into patterns by which we hid our true hearts from God and from one another.

The Samaritan woman, on the other hand, feared both exposure and rejection but she gave way to neither her fear nor her shame, choosing instead to do what was right by boldly proclaiming the gospel to her judgmental neighbors. What accounts for the difference between her strong hope and the others' faltering courage?

We cannot read the heart as God can, nor is the mystery of His grace subject to our finite comprehension. But surely our hope does not come until our believing is both accurate and acted on. We must know that Jesus is the Messiah, as the Samaritan woman did, and we must courageously behave according to that truth, as also she did. We must embrace and live out the gospel, believing our sins have been forgiven in Christ and our hearts are cherished by our heavenly Father.

This is the magnificent truth of Messiah's coming and of the efficacy of His blood, shed to pay for our sins. Only faith is stronger than fear; only love overcomes self-protection; only the hope of a future good can move us beyond past disappointment. And it is only the courage flowing from faith, hope, and love that can draw us out of our terror into a growing rest in God.

"I will give you rest," Jesus had promised, repeating the words that centuries earlier Yahweh had spoken to Moses: "My Presence will go with you, and I will give you rest" (Exod. 33:14). Gladly we believed and accepted the gift of His forgiving grace. But even as we put our hope in Him, we did not fully comprehend what His rest would be like or what it would cost us to receive it. Surely rest is God's free gift, but that does not mean it is always easy to receive.

Some there are who hate rest, even physical sleep. The Russian-born novelist and poet Vladimir Nabokov, for example, despised resting. "Sleep is the

67

most moronic fraternity in the world," he wrote in his autobiography. "It is a mental torture I find debasing. . . . I simply cannot get used to the nightly betrayal of reason, humanity, genius. No matter how great my weariness, the wrench of parting with consciousness is unspeakably repulsive to me."[2]

It seems significant that God deliberately built into our very humanity an inescapable need for rest. Try as we might to stay awake, sleep always overtakes us sooner or later. It is as though God imprinted a Sabbath imperative on our genes from conception. Physically we must receive rest, though some may rage against their helplessness to resist the "nightly betrayal of reason." To the dismay of those like Vladimir Nabokov, the inevitability of sleep reinforces God's sovereignty over us.

But hating sleep is not for most of us the problem it was for the renowned novelist. Our reluctance to receive rest is not about physical sleep but about relational connection. The "mental torture" we despise has to do with entrusting our hearts to others, even a kind and loving God. Those conditioned to abuse or slavery, like the Israelites, may find rest foreign, uncomfortable, perhaps even distressing. Others, like the Pharisees of Jesus' day, are accustomed to earning God's favor through strict obedience to His law, and the concept of resting solely in His grace may feel lazy, unsatisfying, not quite enough. Still others, like the Samaritan woman who was convicted by the Holy Spirit for flaunting God's law, may find it hard to believe grace is available to the undeserving. Both the efficacy and the necessity of resting in grace is deeply humbling, for it requires of us all that we admit how hopeless life is without God. We would far rather recite our reasons for refusing to rest in Christ.

But even those of us who have accepted our helplessness and who *want* to enter God's rest encounter obstacles. How is it possible, we sometimes wonder, to enter and abide in the rest Jesus offers? How can we find quietness with God even when all else in our life is chaotic? What choices must we make even in the face of our greatest fear that will profoundly determine whether our hearts remain restless or find safe harbor?

The answers to these questions are not difficult to understand, but neither are they easy to implement. We each must take responsibility for making certain deliberate choices about finding and entering rest. The next chapter will explore how that can be accomplished.

Questions to Consider

1. What kind of "golden calves" do people (including Christians) worship today?

2. How might you, like Moses, intercede for the "undeserving" in some of your close relationships (family, church, work, etc.)?

3. In what ways might your intercession change your attitude in those relationships?

4. How are the following related to each other: Yom Kippur, Good Friday, Eucharist (communion, or the Lord's Supper), and personal salvation?

5. What experiences have you had in which, like Peter, you took a risk in following God and then fell prey to fear?

Regarding the opening story:

Scott simply did not have the resources to fill the gaps in Anne's heart left by her father's rejection and contempt. Anne used Scott's provision to abandon the vows she'd made to him. She feared she might never be happy or well loved and she fell into immorality again and again.

6. What impact did Anne's father have on her adult relationships?

7. If you had had an hour to talk with Anne before she left Scott, what would you have said to her?

CHAPTER FOUR

CHOICE

The Responsibility for Faith

GINNY ROCKED back and forth in her grandmother's old rocker, her movement an apt metaphor for her nervous indecision. "Shall I call or not?" she fretted, knowing the right answer, but loathe to abide by her self-imposed prohibition. She had not spoken to Dawn in four days, and Ginny was feeling engulfed by the familiar panic of disconnection.

The two friends had attempted separating from each other twice before— once a year ago when Dawn's husband had complained that Dawn was paying more attention to Ginny than to him and the children, and again five months ago after Ginny had had to come home from a business trip two days early just to be with Dawn. Both times the women had committed themselves to less intensity in their friendship, but both times they had slipped back into the same emotional enmeshment as before.

This *time, though, Ginny and Dawn knew they had to make the separation stick. Five days ago, after everyone else had left Ginny's twenty-sixth birthday party, Dawn's good-bye hug had lasted too long, and the pull had been unmistakable. Shaken by the experience and its implications, the women had committed themselves to two weeks of not seeing or talking to each other, so they could pray about the future of their friendship. Dawn's marriage was important to both of them, and so was their Christian walk.*

But Ginny was especially lonely and anxious this night, and her hand ached to dial the familiar number that would reconnect her to the woman she felt she could not live without. Would she choose to wait, trusting that God would "never leave [her] nor forsake [her]" as she pulled back from this relationship and established other, more healthy friendships? Or would she go on worshiping at the shrine of her inappropriate attachment to Dawn? Her rocking kept time with her indecision, and she was afraid.

Few things reveal the quality of our trust in God more clearly than having to depend utterly on Him in a difficult or frightening circumstance. Whether our fear concerns our emotional and relationship well-being (as was the case for Ginny and Dawn) or our financial or physical health, what is ultimately at stake is our spiritual rest in God. Is He enough for us? Will we believe what He says? Can we quiet our hearts in His presence and know we are loved? And will we obey Him when everything in us fears the worst?

No believer can escape these questions, nor can any of us escape the consequences of the answers we ultimately choose to act on. We are called to the responsibility of trusting and obeying our heavenly Father. But we, like Ginny, must each make our own choice.

"My Presence will go with you, and I will give you rest," God had promised His people at Mount Sinai (Exod. 33:14). But that was two years and several traumas ago, and there was surely no rest to be found in the Hebrew camp at Kadesh on *this* woeful night. The two years spent fashioning the tabernacle and its furnishings seemed like ancient history now, the miracles of Egypt even farther removed. Tonight the expectation of imminent disaster leaped like fire from tent to tent, the smoke of clamorous lament rising skyward in its wake. Palpable fear had become audible everywhere, wailing and curses piercing the dark desert air. Crouched menacingly in the shadows were anarchy and assassination. The Israelites were at it again.

Poised on the southern border of Canaan, they had been ready to enter the Promised Land. Moses, following God's instructions, had sent twelve men north on a reconnaissance mission, and they had come back with abundant evidence of the richness of Canaan's soil and produce. (These events are recorded in Numbers 13–14.) "We went into the land to which you sent us, and it does flow with milk and honey!" they all exulted (Num. 13:27). Indeed, a single cluster of grapes required two of them to carry it back to the Israelite camp, so rich was the fruitfulness of their appointed place of rest.

However, ten of the spies had returned dispirited at the strength and size of the enemy. "The people who live there are powerful, and the cities are fortified and very large," they cautioned. Caleb and Joshua, the other two spies, had countered this apprehension by declaring, "We should go up and take possession of the land, for we can certainly do it." To which the ten in the majority had replied, "We can't attack those people; they are stronger than we are." Turning to the people for vindication, they cried out, "The land we explored devours those living in it. All the people we saw there are of great size. . . . We seemed like grasshoppers in our own eyes, and we looked the same to them."

So it was that contagious alarm had ignited disbelief and despair among the Israelites throughout the long night. The following morning, no longer believing God would give them rest in this good land of Canaan, they thronged to the open area in front of the Tent of Meeting where Moses and Aaron stood. Then "all the people of the community raised their voices and wept aloud," giving clamorous way to the fear that was sabotaging their hope.

"If only we had died in Egypt! Or in this desert!" they wailed back and forth in dismay. They had forgotten how many of them *had* died in Egypt, and how they had *found* life, not lost it, in this very desert. Envisioning Canaan's armed and dangerous giants, they forgot Yahweh's power and demanded of Moses, "Why is the LORD bringing us to this land only to let us fall by the sword?" Visions of lost battles not yet fought gave rise to another terror: "Our wives and children will be taken as plunder!" As though God had brought them out of abuse only to allow His little ones to be abused again! Their fear grew as they wept the louder, disbelief and perceived helplessness sweeping them toward hysteria.

How could they save themselves from this self-projected looming disaster, this certainty of inevitable defeat? Perhaps they could retreat to the familiar and the predictable! "Wouldn't it be better for us to go back to Egypt?" someone began to yell. Of course! Slavery over risk—the choice seemed obvious. The more they shouted it, the more reasonable it began to sound to all of them.

Faced with the specter of fighting against seemingly insurmountable odds, the Israelites had to choose between fear and faith. Was Yahweh bigger than Canaan's giants? Would He indeed fight on His people's behalf? Or were they fools to trust in someone they could not even see?

In the end, they chose to feed their own and each other's fear, until the prospect of believing Yahweh seemed utter nonsense, even suicidal. They hardened their hearts against the encouraging faith words of Joshua and Caleb, and terror found an open path to their will. Rebellion seemed the only logical choice, and mutiny became the hue and cry.

"We should choose a leader and go back to Egypt," someone screamed above the bedlam, and it began to echo into a unified roar. They would go back to bondage to find safety. But first, their present leaders would have to die.

It mattered not that Moses and Aaron had by this time thrown themselves facedown before Yahweh in the presence of the assembly, realizing that God's wrath had been kindled by the people's rebellion. Nor could Joshua and Caleb dissuade the people, though they tore their garments and pleaded, "Do not rebel against the LORD. And do not be afraid of the people of the land, because we will swallow them up. Their protection is gone, but the LORD is with us. Do not be afraid of them."

It was too late. Words availed nothing. The mob had begun picking up stones—large stones, killing stones—weighing them in their hands, feeling the heft of them. Their minds were made up: They were going back to Egypt, and no one was going to stop them.

BACK TO SAFETY

Going back to bondage for security sounds ridiculous when put that simply. Yet that is what the Israelites' fear had brought them to, and that is what our own fears often bring us to as well. We may recognize the power of our fears; we may even understand how we came to be so fearful of certain things, particularly in the realm of relationships. Yet we find ourselves tempted to go back again and again to our destructive ways of coping with our fears—whether of loneliness or failure or even death itself. Old bondages are just so familiar and the inner pull of them is so strong.

This is the dynamic, for example, behind the power of addictions of any kind. Whatever has worked over the years to keep us from feeling the pain of past or present relationship disappointment is what we turn to when relational "danger" threatens. When we face conflict or stress in our marriages or friendships, with our children or our parents, even in our business or church relationships, the fear of failing or of being harmed looms large, and we must choose our course: to enter the fear believing God will sustain us even in our pain or failure, or to run from the danger into some reliable strategy that has kept us safe in the past. Our bondage to drugs or pornography or alcohol or ministry or perfectionism or friendships or work can become prisons of safety to which we return when the risks of freedom demand more of us than we think we can handle. The giants of rejection and failure and aloneness terrify us, and despite God's promises and power, these threatened "deaths" outweigh our faith, and Egypt looks increasingly good to us.

What was ultimately at stake there in the camp at Kadesh, therefore, was not the physical safety of the people but the strength of their spiritual faith in Yahweh. He had clearly promised, "I will give you rest." But was His word trustworthy? Might He be the kind of God who would have second thoughts and possibly renege on His word? Or was He perhaps unable to deliver on His promises? How many times did God have to fulfill His promises to them before they believed Him enough to actually enter His rest? We all face similar questions.

God offers rest to all who will trust in His goodness and power, but seeds of fear sown in our hearts take deep root in our wills. Thus when our fear causes us to disbelieve God's promises or goodness, our disobedience will not be far behind. In fact Scripture uses disobedience and disbelief almost interchangeably when describing the Israelites' rebellion: "To whom did God swear that they would never enter his rest if not to those who *disobeyed*? So we see that they were not able to enter, because of their *unbelief*" (Heb. 3:18–19, emphasis added). When our fear of being abandoned or betrayed by God is not offset by our greater trust in His power and kindness, the temptation to rebel against Him or to try to save ourselves without Him will overtake us. Thus does fear threaten always to sabotage faith.

Because we have been created in God's very image, we have the freedom to accept or reject the gifts He offers us, and our choices have consequences attached to them. God never stops inviting us to rest in Him, but when we choose fear over trust, He honors that choice. Rest requires faith, and both are gifts from the Father's hands. What happens when we refuse God's gifts?

CHOICE AND CONSEQUENCE

The experience of the Israelites at Kadesh reveals the consequences of refusing the gifts God offers. With stones in their hands and murder in their eyes, the mob began closing in on Moses and Aaron, who lay prostrate before the tabernacle. Suddenly, Yahweh showed up in all His majesty and wrath, and "the glory of the LORD appeared at the Tent of Meeting to all the Israelites" (Num. 14:10). His coming was unmistakable, staggering in its brilliance, terrifying in its reverberations.

"How long will these people treat me with contempt?" God thundered at Moses, as killing rocks dropped harmlessly from trembling hands. The Israelites had intended to stone their leaders, but the real object of their contempt was the God for whom those leaders spoke. "How long will they refuse to believe in me, in spite of all the miraculous signs I have performed among them?" Yahweh demanded. Their disbelief was a chosen thing, a flagrant refusal to believe what had been abundantly substantiated by empirical evidence: God was both good and powerful enough to accomplish what He promised. Their fear had given way to a deliberate rejection of God's offer of rest in the Promised Land.

Now the Israelites would have to live with the consequence of their chosen rebellion and disobedience. "I will strike them down with a plague and destroy them," Yahweh declared to Moses in righteous wrath, "but I will make you into a nation greater and stronger than they" (vv. 11–12).

How tempting this renewed offer of personal peace and personal fame must have sounded to Moses, whose assassination had now been stayed indefinitely by the stunning Presence of the Glory. These people had continued to be a burden to him, and after eight decades of life, he must have been ready for a lot less hassle. Besides, God was justified in His anger, and bringing forth a new family from an old man was something God had already shown Himself capable of doing (see Gen. 21:5). Moses believed God could and would give him rest, but what kind of rest did Moses most desire?

We learn the depth of Moses' passion for God by his persistence in choosing God's honor among the nations over his own dreams or comfort. How little we are like him in that! How often the short-term benefits of personal gain or the peace of "no hassle" keep us from taking into account the larger picture of God's glory shining in our dark world. Moses' intercessory prayer for God's people focused neither on their deserving nor on his own well-being but on Yahweh's reputation. If He were to carry out His threatened reprisal against the Hebrews, "the Egyptians will hear about it!" Moses worried to God, "and they will tell the inhabitants of this land about it. . . . If you put these people to death all at one time, the nations who have heard this report about you will say, 'The LORD was not able to bring these people into the land he promised them on oath; so he slaughtered them in the desert'" (Num. 14:13–16).

Moses then "reminded" God of what He had earlier declared about Himself (see Exod. 34:6–7), that He was "slow to anger, abounding in love and forgiving sin and rebellion." On his face before the Glory, Moses begged God for the second time, "In accordance with your great love, forgive the sin of these people, just as you have pardoned them from the time they left Egypt until now" (Num. 14:18–19).

INVITED TO REPENT

And pardon them God did. But He would chasten them as well, for He had also described Himself as a God who "does not leave the guilty unpunished; he punishes the children and their children for the sin of the fathers to the third and fourth generation" (Exod. 34:7b). Because the Israelites had refused God's gift of rest, they would reap a sorrowful harvest, consigning themselves to a future of wandering and unrest. When we give in to fear and choose disobedience over faith, we miss God's best intentions for us.

Consider the punishment God had Moses announce to the Israelites in the camp on that night of disbelief and disobedience.

> As surely as I live, declares the LORD, I will do to you the very things I heard you say: In this desert your bodies will fall—every one of you twenty years old or more who was counted in the census and who has grumbled against me. Not one of you will enter the land I swore with uplifted hand to make your home, except Caleb son of Jephunneh and Joshua son of Nun. As for your children that you said would be taken as plunder, I will bring them in to enjoy the land you have rejected. But you—your bodies will fall in this desert. Your children will be shepherds here for forty years, suffering for your unfaithfulness, until the last of your bodies lies in the desert. For forty years— one year for each of the forty days you explored the land—you will suffer for your sins and know what it is like to have me against you.
>
> NUMBERS 14:28–34

What a terrible plight the Israelites faced, having to live with almighty God against them! More than that, they had to go back into the wilderness at once, for God had said, "Turn back tomorrow and set out toward the desert along the route to the Red Sea" (v. 25). Their discipline was to begin immediately.

This return to the desert was more than the people could bear and they "mourned bitterly" all that night. Then, when morning came, they made a most foolhardy decision. Refusing to accept Yahweh's discipline, they made preparation to do battle with Canaan anyway. "We have sinned," they said. "We will go up to the place the LORD promised" (v. 40). Surely, they reasoned, Yahweh would honor their resurgent "faith" and give them the land after all, considering their "repentance."

But repentance, if it is genuine, does not rebel against the Lord's discipline. Scripture reminds us that "God disciplines us for our good, that we may share in his holiness. No discipline seems pleasant at the time, but painful. Later on, however, it produces a harvest of righteousness and peace for those who have been trained by it" (Heb. 12:10–11). True repentance always moves us to surrender our wills anew to the God who forgives, even as He imposes on us His correction for our waywardness.

Would the Israelites allow God's discipline to train them into righteous living and inner rest? After all, they had seen the disastrous consequences of Pharaoh's repeated hardness of heart. God's chastisement of His own children, of course, is designed not to cast them out but to draw them back. That is why, when Yahweh consigned the Israelites of that generation to live out their lives as nomads in the wilderness, they should have accepted His reproof, should have suffered their loss of Canaan rest, asking forgiveness of their children for the distress their sin had brought on them. In fact they should have given God glory for the justness of His punishment. These things, unfortunately, they refused to do.

Moses tried to warn the Israelites of the folly of this renewed rebellion. "Why are you disobeying the LORD's command?" he demanded. He knew they could not evade God's punishment by attempting to live as though they had not sinned. There was no turning back the clock on sin; it could not be undone. The consequences had to be paid. The people of Israel needed to learn how to live within the double realities of being both forgiven and disciplined.

Moses knew this better than anyone. More than forty years earlier he himself had had to accept his own forced exodus from Egypt. It had not been easy learning to rest within the parameters God had placed around his life during that time. But those were not wasted years, for God had had much to teach Moses that would someday bring Him great glory, though Moses could not have imagined it during the long days and nights as a wilderness shepherd. God is always up to something far larger than we can imagine, and it is His glory to turn even our sin to redemptive purposes. Who was better prepared to lead God's people through the discipline of forty years of desert wandering than the man who had endured forty years being disciplined by Yahweh in precisely the same way and place? God in His economy wastes nothing.

But the Israelites would not listen to Moses speak from his own experience the words of warning: "This will not succeed! Do not go up, because the LORD . . . will not be with you and you will fall by the sword." Persisting in their disbelief, they marched into Canaan anyway—without God, without Moses, without the protection of the ark of the Lord's covenant. And their enemies "attacked them and beat them down," even as Moses had said.

God is not mocked. What He says is always proved true, and when our disbelief results in disobedience (which it always does sooner or later), there will be disaster if we will not yield to God's discipline. Yahweh's children were still Yahweh's children, and His forgiveness would be reaffirmed every year on Yom Kippur as they saw the high priest emerge from the Holy of Holies and watched the scapegoat being sent into the wilderness bearing their sin. Though their earthly destiny would be constricted, their eternal destiny was assured if they would trust Yahweh again. In fact their desert sojourn would offer them rich opportunity to grow spiritually—to strengthen their own trust in God and to teach their children to trust Him too. But that generation of rebels would not have another opportunity to enter the land of rest they once refused to enter because of their unbelief. Their unwillingness to accept their Father's rod of correction had brought them more suffering than they would otherwise have had to endure. We do indeed reap what we sow.

RECEIVING REBUKE

The discipline God sends into our lives is always custom designed just for us. Seldom does He deal with us exactly as He has dealt with someone else. This is the wonder of worshiping the God who reveals Himself as Father, a person whose very nature is intimately relational. Good parents know which kind of discipline is most appropriate for each child's nature and spiritual sensitivity and they don't buy into the philosophy of "one discipline fits all." Similarly, the stories of God's relationships with His children are not all alike, but are unique to each individual's nature and need.

Moreover, Jesus, who revealed God as Father, treated every person He met according to each one's particular situation, gender, and history. Even within the circle of His closest friends, Jesus knew how best to draw each one into greater understanding and faith in Him.

Consider another story in the life of Simon Peter, the disciple of little but growing faith. (This story is told in Matthew 16:13–17:9.) Not many days after Jesus' walk across the Sea of Galilee, Peter and the other apostles were asked by Jesus, "Who do you say I am?" Their responses would reveal what was in their hearts as well as what was in their minds, for this question was not about their intellect but about their faith. Not surprisingly, it was Peter who spoke for them all, saying, "You are the Christ, the Son of the living God." Boldly, perhaps surprising even himself, the disciple had identified Jesus as Messiah, the One promised centuries earlier to be the deliverer of God's people.

Jesus' words in response to Peter's confession must have thrilled the fisherman's heart: "Blessed are you, Simon son of Jonah, for this was not revealed to you by man, but by my Father in heaven." The long-awaited Messiah had finally appeared in their midst as an itinerant rabbi, and the Father in heaven had Himself revealed it to an impulsive, little-faithed fisherman.

Jesus went on to say to Simon, "And I tell you that you are Peter, and on this rock I will build my church, and the gates of Hades will not overcome it." Jesus offered Peter heady words, and he must surely have envisioned a place of prominence for himself in Messiah's coming kingdom. This was the fisherman's red-letter day.

Immediately afterwards, however, Jesus began to explain what kind of messianic kingdom His followers could expect. He began teaching his disciples "that he must go to Jerusalem and suffer many things at the hands of the elders, chief priests and teachers of the law, and that he must be killed and on the third day be raised to life." This they could not believe. A dying Messiah was altogether incongruent with their expectations. The salvation God's people were expecting was not from their sins but from their enemies, the Romans.

Refusing to bend his own messianic preconceptions to Jesus' announcement about His coming death, Peter instead tried to force Jesus into *his* mold, drawing Him aside from the other disciples and rebuking Him. "Never, Lord!" he declared. "This shall never happen to you!" Messiah would reign, not die. Christ would be a king, not a corpse. Peter could not imagine that Jesus would in fact be both, though not in that order. The disciple was determined to alleviate Messiah's morbid apprehension regarding the Jewish leaders. The Rock would teach the Creator what the future held.

What happened next may surprise us, for the image we often hold of Jesus is that of a mild-mannered Clark Kent who sometimes changed into powerful, helpful, polite Superman. But when Peter refused to believe Jesus' own words—that He *must* die and then return to life—the words the fisherman spoke came not from the "Father in heaven" but from God's archenemy, the devil, who was trying to thwart God's redemptive purposes by tempting Christ to resist His crucifixion. This level of disbelief called not for gentle correction but for strong and immediate discipline.

Drawing Peter back to the circle of disciples, Jesus reprimanded him sharply, warning him, "Get behind me, Satan! You are a stumbling block to me; you do not have in mind the things of God, but the things of men."

Peter and the others must have been aghast. The newly named Rock of Christ's church had been publicly rebuked as Satan's spokesman for refusing to accept Jesus' revelation of Himself and His destiny. When we fail to believe the word of Christ, when our own expectations or circumstances take priority over the Father's revelation, God minces no words. This disbelief comes from the pit of hell and smells like smoke (as my former pastor, Steve Brown, used to say). Forget about "polite"; the truth will surely set us free but it will likely shock us first.

RESTING IN DISCIPLINE

God in His disciplining of us is not out to coddle us but to offer us an unequivocal opportunity to change, to either harden or soften our hearts, to either reinforce our strategies for making life work or to rest in His sovereignty. Whether His exposure of our sin is gentle or mind-boggling, He is relentless in inviting us back to His embrace by shining the light of His gaze into the darkness of our hearts. The Israelites had been invited to repent of their rebellion by accepting Yahweh's just discipline but they showed their true hearts when they chose to rebel again. And within a week of Peter's flip-flop from God-inspired testimony to Satan-seduced denunciation of Jesus' coming crucifixion, God gave this man another chance to show what was most deeply in his heart.

The setting this time was a mountain in Galilee, where Jesus had retreated to pray with Peter, James, and John. (This story is found in Luke 9:28–36.) How comforting—and important—for us to know that Peter's earlier failures of faith had not excommunicated him from the circle of Christ's intimate friends! Peter and the other disciples had evidently fallen asleep sometime during their mountaintop prayer vigil but when they awoke, it was to find themselves surrounded by the brilliance of a different revelation of Jesus than they had ever seen before. His face shone like the sun and His clothes were bright as lightning. He was talking with Moses and Elijah, who had appeared "in glorious splendor" with Him. Appropriately enough, considering Peter's recent rebuke, the three shining men were discussing Jesus' approaching crucifixion.

Overcome and terrified by the glory around them, Peter nonetheless became spokesman again. Without even knowing what he was saying, he opened his mouth and words came out. "Master, it is good for us to be here," he blithered. "Let us put up three shelters—one for you, one for Moses and one for Elijah." His unrestrained instinct was not to worship in silent awe but to define, contain, and sustain the mystery of the moment by reducing it to the mundane and manageable.

All at once a voice interrupted Peter, speaking from an enveloping cloud: "This is my Son, whom I have chosen; listen to him." Like the Glory suddenly appearing at Kadesh, the Voice provoked instant reverence and demanded obedience. "Listen to My Son," the Father commanded, and we can be sure Peter's mouth was stopped and his ears opened. Silence was a good choice.

Unlike the Israelites who had persisted in their rebellion, Peter displayed a willingness to repent of his presumption and disbelief. He had not bailed out when Jesus had said he had little faith, nor had he left Jesus in indignation when the Messiah called him Satan's messenger boy. Nor did he now keep talking on the mount of Jesus' transfiguration. And when the Father had stopped speaking and Jesus finally stood alone again with His visible glory fading, Peter continued to keep his mouth shut, obeying Jesus' instructions that they were to tell no one about the experience until after Jesus' resurrection. What a secret for an incautious man to have to keep!

Of course Peter would not appreciate the full meaning of Jesus' revealed glory or His true messianic mission until many weeks later, after Jesus' crucifixion and resurrection, after even His ascension into heaven and the sending of His Holy Spirit. But throughout Christ's earthly ministry the fisherman of growing faith was willing to respond to discipline, and he kept following hard after Jesus. It was not easy for this headstrong disciple to rest in his Lord, for there was much he did not understand yet he was quick to do something anyway. But his love for Jesus was genuine, and he would one day enter a new level of rest in Christ, for he did not refuse to repent.

CHOOSING BUSYNESS

There are times when disbelief wears a more subtle mask, a more benign appearance. Such was the experience of another of Jesus' close friends, whose busyness on His behalf kept her from resting in His presence. Martha was her name, and her story is told in Luke 10:38–42.

Scripture actually tells us very little about Martha, but some things are clear. She loved Jesus, she had a generous spirit, she was preoccupied with doing things right, and she was not a woman at rest.

Martha loved Jesus. We don't know when or how they met; He grew up in Galilee, many miles north of Bethany, her village near Jerusalem. But she and her family had become Jesus' close personal friends, for we read that "Jesus loved Martha and her sister and Lazarus" (John 11:5). We sometimes forget that Jesus had a social life, visiting His loved ones as He traveled throughout Palestine. He had no home of His own, but many did what Martha had done: she "opened her home to him."

This meant, of course, that in her generosity to Him she opened her home to Jesus' disciples as well, and that made quite a crowd. Anyone who has ever given a dinner party without catering knows the amount of work involved in preparing even a simple meal for that many people. We don't know what kind of kitchen help Martha had but we know her preparations for Jesus' dinner party were a labor of love on His behalf. She longed to bless Him with a lovely home-cooked meal. This she could do well; she knew how to serve.

Nonetheless, Martha became irritated when her sister, Mary, neglected to help her and instead "sat at the Lord's feet listening to what he said." Serving was one thing; having to do all the work alone was another. It seemed grossly unfair to Martha.

Meal preparation can be hectic, and Martha "was distracted by all the preparations that had to be made." Distracted from what? Perhaps from enjoying Jesus' presence in her home even in the midst of her party planning. "All the preparations that had to be made"—maybe they didn't all *have* to be made. When we are doing God's will, He does not overburden us. Jesus Himself said His yoke is easy and His burden light (see Matt. 11:30). Faithful work is a good thing, but a harried and distracted spirit is not God's intention for us in our serving.

What sentences might Martha have been saying to herself as she bustled about her chores without Mary's help? Did she call out to Mary and get no response? Was Mary sitting in the middle of Jesus' disciples so Martha dared not interrupt? When the busy hostess finally could take it no more, why did she lash out at Jesus instead of Mary? And did she disparage Jesus in front of everyone or did she draw Him aside?

Martha was not wrong in wanting her sister's help. Nor was her busyness in and of itself a bad thing. "As we have opportunity, let us do good to all people, especially to those who belong to the family of believers," the apostle Paul teaches (Gal. 6:10). Even Martha's motive—her desire to bless her good Friend—was praiseworthy. What, then, was *not* praiseworthy about her behavior that evening?

ISSUES OF UNBELIEF

Though not readily apparent, even to herself, Martha's underlying problem was disbelief. Her first angry words to Jesus honored His position but questioned both His goodness and His love for her. "Lord, don't you care," she accused, "that my sister has left me to do the work by myself?" This was not an attack against Jesus' omniscience (surely He knew that her frustration had been building), but a doubting of what His heart was toward her. Jesus' failure to chastise her sister for her "laziness" was to Martha a vote *against* her and *for* Mary—how could He be so insensitive when she was doing all she could for Him?

"Don't you care?" These were the same words the disciples had thrown at Jesus when they thought they were about to drown (Mark 4:38) and similar also to the implication behind the Israelites' shouts flung abroad in the bedlam: "Our wives and children will be taken as plunder" (Num. 14:3). It is, moreover, the question *we* ask when our own health or safety or job or preciousness is in question—"Lord, don't you care?" This doubt, springing so naturally to our minds and mouths when our personal world is amiss, is at its root a failure to believe in God's goodness and in His love for us, and it always undermines our rest in Him. If He is not good, if He does not care, how can we relax in trusting Him? This was the deeper question in Martha's heart, and it resides within us all as well. No wonder we so seldom go off duty. Disbelief in God's goodness always sabotages our rest in Him. It may evidence itself in blatant rebellion or more subtle accusations of uncaring. But however God's sovereignty or character is maligned, the offense is capital, deserving death.

Nonetheless, I have often empathized with Martha, because I too have worked hard for the Lord and have at times felt unappreciated and abandoned by Him. And I too have moved from the disbelief of self-pity to the arrogance of demandingness. "Lord, do things *my* way for a change!" I insist (usually to myself, lest I appear unspiritual). Martha said it aloud to Jesus:

"Tell [Mary] to help me!" Surely, she reasoned, He owed her this much for all her trouble.

Teaching God how to run any aspect of His universe has to be the height of presumption. But telling Him to force someone else's volition violates not only His sovereignty but the other person's freedom of choice as well. Mary had chosen to honor Jesus by sitting at His feet, just as Martha had decided to love Him by setting a fine table before Him. Who was right? Both of them. Who was the more beloved? He loved them equally. Yet because Jesus loved them both, He admonished Martha for her disbelief (which was separating her heart from His) and affirmed Mary for her worship (which was strengthening the connection between Him and her).

It is worth noting that Jesus did not run from the chaos in Martha's heart nor did He try to fix what was wrong with her—strategies men often employ to deal with the feminine disruption that seems so inscrutable to the masculine mind. Faced with emotions in a woman, which are neither fixable nor fathomable, many husbands (or fathers or boyfriends or bosses) throw up their hands and retreat from the chaos. Jesus, however, had the courage to *enter* Martha's disruption and speak words of truth and kindness without trying to correct what was "wrong" with her or to change her into someone more "manageable."

"Martha, Martha," the Lord gently chided, speaking her name twice to indicate their intimate and loving relationship. "You are worried and upset about many things, but only one thing is needed." Was He addressing her busyness or her unrest, the "many things" or the "worried and upset"? Probably both, because for Martha the busyness was camouflaging the fear (that Jesus didn't care about her) and the anger (that He had not come to her aid), which were keeping her from resting in Him.

Jesus' chastening words, however, were intended not to humiliate Martha but to invite her back to faith in His love for her. It was grace, not shame, by which He meant to call her to rest in Him. The "one thing" needed was that Martha remember and receive again the love Jesus had for her—not necessarily in the contemplative way Mary had chosen but within the context of her own servant ministry. If the intimacy of our relationship with Christ and our worship of His goodness are not the source of our serving, then our activity will exhaust and exasperate us, as it did Martha.

"Mary has chosen what is better," Jesus went on to say, "and it will not be taken away from her." In following her heart and her passion to know Jesus more, Mary's teachableness and worship pleased the Lord, even as Martha's desire to serve Him (which ran deeper than either her fear or her anger) gladdened Him and His disciples. We each must learn to recognize and exercise our unique giftedness for God's glory. But we must also beware of two dangers: judging others because their gifts differ from ours and allowing *anything* to ruin our own intimate rest in God's unfailing love for us.

Martha, Mary, Peter, the Israelites—*all* of us—must heed Scripture's advice: "Let us . . . make every effort to enter [God's] rest" (Heb. 4:11). It is our only hope.

AN UNFIRM FOUNDATION

Sometimes we live our whole lives without truly resting in God. Our busyness, our careers, our families, even our church involvement may so preoccupy our energy that we don't recognize how low our spiritual fuel is running. We go through the motions of worship, both personal and corporate, but we're not quite at home with God, not really at ease in His presence.

For the first fifteen years of our marriage, Bill and I were largely unaware of any major spiritual struggles, for we were slow to recognize how little we rested in Christ. We tried hard to maintain our lives and our marriage, and it took well over a decade for us to run to the end of our attempts to love each other in our own strength.

This did not feel like a deliberate refusal to enter God's rest. Bill and I simply did not know there was a better, more passionate way to live. Our unexamined strategies for dealing with our unacknowledged fears had kept us from recognizing the gaps in our souls, and we had learned to live without hope for a richer walk with God or one another. Occasionally, however, I suspected a deeper taste of oneness ought to be possible, at least with God.

One Sunday, for instance, I heard a pastor read these words, referring to Christ: "Whom having not seen, ye love; in whom, though now ye see him not, yet believing, ye rejoice with joy unspeakable and full of glory" (1 Peter 1:8 KJV). I remember the stab in my spirit at the phrase, "joy unspeakable and full of glory," an inner mix of sadness and longing. I had professed Christ in my teens and had always wanted to love and serve God. Yet nothing in my walk with Christ had brought me that kind of joy, though I was profoundly drawn to it that morning. What was wrong with me, I wondered, that my relationship with Jesus so little resembled what Peter was describing?

I didn't know it then, but the reason I couldn't experience unspeakable joy was that I had shut down many of my emotions, joy among them. My childhood had taught me that feelings were dangerous, so I had gradually deadened my soul so I could avoid pain and keep my life manageable. Like the ancient Israelites, my passionless and often trustless response to others was the bitter fruit of my refusal to open my heart to anyone who might do me harm, including Bill, including even God Himself.

My lack of trust in Bill, in fact, was one of the fatal flaws in the very foundation of our marriage. For despite my father's alcoholism, I continued to seek his paternal guidance more than my husband's for many years after Bill and I were married. A good friend even told me one day as we discussed a particular problem in my marriage, "You trust your father more than you trust Bill." She was right, and I knew it; I just didn't know how to change that part of my heart. Bill knew it in his spirit too, though he could not have verbalized it, and the rift it caused in our oneness would not be mended until I was prepared to trust and "submit to [him] as to the Lord" (see Eph. 5:22). It would be many years in coming.

For the truth is, I was able to suppress my distrust of Bill for more than fifteen years into our marriage. We thought we were the perfect Christian couple, committed to each other and our family, worshiping regularly, and trying to live up to the expectations of our families and of our church community. Not until our life together began to crumble did we think to take an inside look and examine both our hearts and our marriage for possible problems.

Unfortunately it's possible to construct a relationship on a faulty foundation and keep it intact for some time. Bill was a good worker, a faithful husband, an involved (though often angry) father, and a regular churchgoer. He seldom discussed the disappointments of his past, but within six months of our marriage he did resume his pattern of numbing with alcohol the pain of those unresolved losses. This pattern terrified me more than I would admit until years later.

My own youthful traumas and strategies had also caused deep fissures in the foundation of our marriage. For instance, my way of dealing with Bill's increasing alcoholism (I couldn't call it that at the time) was similar to what I'd seen my mother do: I redoubled my efforts to control it—that is to say, I tried harder to control *him*. I loved Bill and I had a wonderful plan for his life. I knew who he could and should be and I took it on myself (though of course I always asked God for His help) to change Bill into the image of him I held in my heart. It seemed right to me, but it would in the end lead to death—i.e., the destroying of our marital oneness. Lack of trust is a pernicious enemy of intimacy.

What was happening to Bill and me during those years can best be compared to building a lovely home in a sandy field. Our marriage looked pretty good from the outside, but inside the floors were beginning to sink, the walls were cracking, and the ceiling had an ominous sag to it. Bill's anger was becoming more unmanageable all the time, erupting more and more often into fits of disproportionate rage. I would respond to his raging not by expressing my terror or seeking help to deal appropriately with the situation but by trying to calm Bill down and then walking on eggshells to keep him from exploding again. Between my attempts to control his drinking and his rage, I almost never felt truly at rest in my own home, not with Bill, not even with God.

In fact neither Bill nor God had my wholehearted devotion. Bryan Chapell in his book, *Each for the Other*, could have been describing my life when he wrote, "A wife who marries with the intention of reforming her husband rarely loves him deeply. Instead, she delays giving her whole heart to him until after he reflects the perfection of her makeover. Thus she is forever deprived of oneness with her spouse as he is in the present."[1]

I thought I was loving Bill, but I was really in love with an illusion. The real Bill had far less of my heart than either of us knew. The marital oneness Bill and I had tried to build was soon to disintegrate, constructed as it had been on the unstable foundation of our mutual fear. And our individual oneness with our heavenly Father was in jeopardy as well. It would not be long before He would show us how very little either of us knew about receiving and entering God's rest.

FEARSOME ONENESS

Christ's invitation had been there all along: "Come to me, all you who are weary and burdened, and I will give you rest" (Matt. 11:28). We long for the joy of rest—not just Bill and I but all of us—for it is our nature to desire the peace of restored oneness with God. We were from the beginning created for intimacy with Him, and though our yearning for His presence has been damaged by sin and its consequent fear of His holiness, we long for restoration nonetheless. Yahweh's promise to the Israelites of finding rest in the Promised Land would be a physical manifestation of the deeper spiritual reality Christ pledges to all believers—rest in His forgiveness and presence now, and eternal rest someday in the promised "land" of heaven.

Yahweh's invitation to enter the rest of Canaan and Christ's later invitation to come to Him for rest are the same, for Yahweh and Jesus are One. Even more than that, when we respond to God's invitation and receive His promises, He becomes one with *us* in love and purpose. How magnificent this yoking of the Three-in-One God with His beloved!

But this too is needed: "Take my yoke upon you and learn from me," Jesus said, "for I am gentle and humble in heart" (v. 29). He obeyed His Father in all things—are we willing to take that risk? He was gentle and humble in heart—will we agree to let that spirit rule our lives? He counted even death a price worth paying to win our hearts to Himself—do we love even our spouse this much? The cost of oneness is exorbitant, even dangerous, and many will refuse the rest Christ offers because they fear what their oneness with Him will require of them.

The Israelites refused God's yoke of obedience and in choosing to rebel, they chose against rest. Similarly, Bill and I yielded to our fear, yoking ourselves not to rest in Christ's plan for our lives but to a vicious cycle of alcoholism and co-alcoholism. Every husband and wife long for the kind of intimate marital relationship that lets them rest their hearts in each other. But it is more difficult to submit our lives to God as Christ yoked His will to

His Father. And it is this submission to God's love and leading that alone can empower us for the risks of faith necessary to bind our hearts to the one we have covenanted to love until death.

The tragedy of the Israelites at Kadesh is that they refused Yahweh's promised rest by not believing they could overcome the giants in the land with God's help. We too fear the giants in our land, particularly the ones that inhabit our own homes, our own hearts, and our most intimate relationships. The mystery of marriage confounds us, for that level of intimacy feels alien to us, and we know not how to safely navigate our way. Danger to our hearts looms large, and we cry out, "Remove the giants! We feel like grasshoppers!"

But God knows best and sometimes He leaves the giants there and reminds us that, yoked to Him in intimacy and love, our faith in His strength can defeat any giant we may have to face. For we are not grasshoppers but beloved sons and daughters of the great King. Someone has said that to thrive we all need one person who is simply crazy about us, and many people live their entire lives never tasting the joy of knowing they're loved for being precious, not for being good. It is this we crave, this the rest we long to enter—that our heavenly Father (if not our earthly father or mother) knows us intimately and delights in us.

Often it is hard to remember that we are God's delightful children, created in His image and redeemed by His blood. Christ Himself indwells us by His Spirit, and His righteousness has become ours. But this too is an area of choice for us. Do we believe He loves us? Will we move into our fear with the confidence of being His children? Our willingness to believe our true identity is crucial to finding the joy of resting in Him.

Any movement into rest has its peril. It always requires something of us to not demand escape from life's troubling circumstances but instead to bless others from an inner, God-given tranquillity in the midst of those circumstances. How can we experience the quiet of Christ even in the context of a driven, apprehensive, sometimes hopeless world? What, after all, is the purpose of our oneness with Christ as He summons us to rest in Him?

The next section will explore these and other questions regarding Jesus' invitation to rest in His grace. Surely it must begin with our willingness to humble ourselves in receiving from our heavenly Father what we cannot procure for ourselves, which is the topic of chapter 5.

 ## QUESTIONS TO CONSIDER

1. When, if ever, has fear been the deciding factor in causing you to make a sinful choice?

2. What bondages or "prisons of safety" have kept you from living in relational freedom?

3. How has God's discipline been a kindness to you?

4. What experiences of anger, anxiety, or busyness hinder your present rest in Christ (as they did for Martha)?

5. What choices might you make this week that would allow you to rest more fully in God?

Regarding the opening story:

The unhealthy emotional dependence between Ginny and Dawn was damaging not only Dawn's marriage but also each woman's intimacy with God.

6. What biblical principles should guide Ginny and Dawn in deciding the future of their relationship?

7. Would the dilemma faced by Ginny and Dawn be less likely to pose a problem for men? Why or why not?

Part 2

REST

AND ITS

COSTLY

ENTICEMENT

CHAPTER FIVE

HUMILITY

The Cost of Receiving

"I HATE BEING NEEDY!" *Luanne exclaimed to the other members of her support group. "I do just fine depending on myself. But when I have to ask Mike for help, I feel vulnerable—not just vulnerable but ugly. I don't want to admit I long for his kindness, because that would give him more power than I want him to have."*

"I agree," Angela responded. "If anything happens and I lose Joe, I want to be able to just go on with my life without missing him too much."

"When my husband died a year ago," added Michelle, "it wasn't just the abandonment and loneliness that got to me. It was the helplessness of needing something I couldn't provide for myself. I still struggle with that frustration."

"I think I understand what you mean," interjected Patty, the group leader. "But have you considered the impact your feelings have on your relationship with God? Do you think He wants His children to need Him? Perhaps we should define what we mean by 'needy,' because some kinds of dependencies might be spiritually appropriate, even necessary."

The group was silent for a time, made thoughtful by Patty's comments. Somehow the awareness was growing that there was more to their aversion to "being needy" than they had considered before. Maybe needing love was not all bad, though it certainly had brought them pain. Perhaps God wanted to teach them something they had not yet learned.

Acknowledging dependence on God is often difficult for men and women accustomed to living self-sufficiently. Resting under the sovereign rule of a Being infinitely holy and altogether powerful demands of us both faith and humility, for admitting we desperately need God will deal a deathblow to our pride.

It is a delicate balance to achieve. On the one hand, every person must accept responsibility for his or her own choices and must be willing to pay the consequences when those choices are wrong. But when it comes to the eternal consequences of our sin against a holy God, there is nothing we can do to save ourselves. Oswald Chambers accurately observed, "we cannot earn or win anything from God; we must either receive it as a gift or do without it."[1] The humility of receiving from God what we cannot do for ourselves is the cost of our salvation.

In a similar way, there are things we must ask for and be willing to receive from other people, especially those to whom we are most intimately connected. We must accept our innate neediness—not the unhealthy neediness of a clinging vine dependent on another person for identity or worth but the legitimate need we all have for human connectedness and love. It is the humility of needing others that opens us to a deeper level of human intimacy. And it is the humility of needing God that opens us to repentance and grace, restoring us to fellowship with Him.

Yet the willingness to need requires much of us, for we are more accustomed to earning and accomplishing than to desiring and asking. This chapter concerns the humility we must exercise if we are to receive from God and from others what we legitimately need.

The day had begun, no doubt, like any other day. Of course there was the usual apprehension of war readiness, but a business-as-usual mood prevailed in the city. Danger threatened but was not imminent. Protected by strong walls and a rain-swollen river, the city's inhabitants managed their fear by working hard. The innkeeper was no exception. (This story is recounted in Joshua 2.)

Her work had started early and would end late. Traders, adventurers, rogues, sorcerers, soldiers—over the years she had entertained them all. Her stock-in-trade included meals, conversation, a bed, and sometimes herself. She would tend her customers' animals, keep their sordid secrets, collect her hard-earned money, and send them on their way. More often than not, a piece of herself went with them. It was not a good life but it paid the bills. Her own sorrows and dreams she kept to herself. Rahab was her name.

Perhaps it was late afternoon that day when they came, two nondescript travelers looking for a place to rest from their journey. What was it her practiced shrewdness recognized in them? Did they seem to lack the hardness and world-weariness of her usual jaded clientele? Did their eyes betray the absence of cruelty in their hearts? Why did she trust them as soon as she saw them? And why did she feel compelled to hide them before the king's messengers came banging on her door?

"Bring out the men who came to you and entered your house," the king's men demanded, "because they have come to spy out the whole land."

"Yes, the men came to me," she admitted, "but I did not know where they had come from. At dusk, when it was time to close the city gate, the men left. I don't know which way they went. Go after them quickly. You may catch up with them."

Now the day had become decidedly *unlike* any ordinary day. Concealing the spies beneath the flax on her roof was treason, a capital offense. Moreover, she could not know for sure what the enemy hidden above might do to her, even though she had just saved their lives. Her bargaining chips with them were few but powerful. She would appeal to their God, about whom she had heard so much.

SURPRISED BY FAITH

The city was Jericho, and the two men hidden on Rahab's roof had been sent by Joshua, commander in chief of the Israelite army, to spy out the land west of the raging Jordan River. Forty years had passed since Moses had led God's people out of Egypt and across the Red Sea on dry ground. During those four decades, all Israelite men of military age who had escaped Pharaoh's bondage had been buried in the desert where they had wandered because of their unbelief.

But the stories about Yahweh and what He had done to the Egyptians had not died, nor had they been forgotten. In fact those stories had been resurrected and retold in light of more recent events occurring just east of the Jordan River, across from Jericho. There, shortly before the death of Moses, the army of second-generation Israelites had fought against Sihon and Og, two Amorite kings who had attacked them and whose armies they had utterly defeated. No Amorites had survived, and thousands of Israelite families had settled into the vacated homes of their enemies.

95

The king of Jericho and the other Canaanite kings west of the Jordan River now feared that they and their people would suffer a similar fate. This threat of military disaster should have moved them to repent of their idolatry and wickedness, considering the obvious power of the Israelites' God. But like the Egyptians forty years earlier, the Canaanites' terror had moved them instead to hardness and to preparation for war. They would consult their mediums for advice; they would sacrifice their children to appease their bloodthirsty idols; they would fight desperately to preserve their lives and their depraved culture. But they would not acknowledge Yahweh as God nor bend the knee to Him.

All, that is, except Rahab. Her words to the spies after she had sent the king's men away revealed not rebellion against Yahweh but faith in Him. "I know that the LORD has given this land to you," she testified, "and that a great fear of you has fallen on us, so that all who live in this country are melting in fear because of you. We have heard how the LORD dried up the water of the Red Sea for you when you came out of Egypt, and what you did to Sihon and Og, the two kings of the Amorites east of the Jordan, whom you completely destroyed. When we heard of it, our hearts melted and everyone's courage failed because of you," she declared. How these words must have thrilled the hearts of the spies as they listened to what Rahab said.

But then the unexpected happened. This woman whom the spies had just met—a prostitute whose religious experience had been limited to the worship of rapacious gods and demonic powers—this woman declared her belief in the God of her enemy, saying, "The LORD your God is God in heaven above and on the earth below." What incredible words of faith from a pagan woman who knew next to nothing about the ways of Yahweh! It was one thing for her to have heard stories about Him and to describe for the spies the Canaanites' fear of their God. It was another to declare personal faith in Yahweh's almighty power over all other gods.

And it was even more amazing that Rahab would seek and expect to find salvation from this God about whom she had heard and in whom she had come to believe. "Please swear to me by the LORD," she entreated the spies, "that you will show kindness to my family, because I have shown kindness to you. Give me a sure sign that you will spare the lives of my father and mother, my brothers and sisters, and all who belong to them, and that you will save us from death." Surely she had learned to barter favor for favor in her dreary occupation. But this time she was prepared to offer the spies a present help in exchange for a future deliverance, with only a "sure sign" as guarantee that they would reward her for her protection.

"Our lives for your lives!" the two spies agreed. "If you don't tell what we are doing, we will treat you kindly and faithfully when the LORD gives us the land." Kindness and faithfulness—what had Rahab known of these in the degradation of her daily work? How could she even conceive of an all-powerful God who was also loving and gracious, when all her gods were lascivious and cruel? How had her own terror of Israel's God given way to faith instead of to rage or to revenge against His representatives?

Believing Is Receiving

The answer, of course, is that Rahab's faith was a gift from God, just as faith is God's gift to anyone who believes in Him (see Eph. 2:8–9). A Canaanite by birth, Rahab would become an Israelite by rebirth, an alien no longer but embraced by the covenant through the faith gift she had received from Yahweh. Rahab's choice to cast her lot with Yahweh's people instead of her own meant she was the first to "enter God's rest" in the Promised Land of Canaan— not just because her home was already there but because along with her gift of faith she had received also His gift of rest, bringing herself and her family under the covering of Yahweh and His people. God's light to the Gentiles (those born outside the bloodline of Abraham's descendants) had come to shine on this Canaanite family in Jericho.

God, of course, seldom works His purposes on only one level. His gift of grace to Rahab was also His gift of encouragement to the Israelites, those born into His covenant family and named by Him as His "firstborn son" (Exod. 4:22). Rahab's words to the spies would strengthen the hearts of all God's people, who would be told that their enemies were "melting in fear" for dread of them. The prostitute's confidence in God's yet-to-come victory would especially shore up the courage of the soldiers who would soon cross the turbulent Jordan River and fight their first battle in Canaan.

But as Rahab awaited the battle that would seal her new identity as Yahweh's daughter, she could not have envisioned the long-range role she was playing in God's larger story, a role far beyond the courageous stand she had taken to protect the spies who had come to her. For Rahab would not merely be rescued from the death that would soon befall her countrymen. She would also be embraced by the family of God and would one day marry Salmon, one of the princes of Judah. This prostitute would become a princess, her identity transformed not by her own determined efforts to change herself or her lifestyle but by placing herself under the care of Yahweh and His people. More than that, many centuries later there would come from the descendants of Rahab and Salmon a special Child, even the promised Messiah, who would save His people from their sins (see Matt. 1:5).

This would be the most outrageous of makeovers, one that would confound God's enemy and turn to God's praise. For the shame Satan had hoped to bring on Rahab through her sexual abuse and prostitution and childlessness would be swallowed up in her eternal joy at becoming a wife and mother and ultimately an ancestress of God's own Son. Her shame would change to glory. This is the wonder of God's great grace, for only He can transform terrible evil into marvelous good.

All this Rahab could not have foreseen, however, when she sent the spies on their way. All she had to depend on as she waited in her inn at Jericho was the word of the two men whose lives she had saved, along with the "sure sign" they had given her. For as she waited, sustained only by her faith in Yahweh, she was to demonstrate her faith by hanging a scarlet cord from the window of her house (which was built into Jericho's outer wall) so Yahweh's soldiers could see where she lived when they surrounded the city. She also was told to bring all her family inside her house so they too could survive the coming Israelite attack.

Surely God, who wastes nothing, intended by this sign in Rahab's window not only to remind her of her promise to the spies but also to remind the Israelites of their own deliverance from Egypt. For the red rope dangling from the brothel of Jericho would be reminiscent of the blood of the sacrificed Passover lamb, which had been smeared across the tops and sides of the door frames of their houses, saving all those sheltered inside from the angel of death. This scarlet symbol of Rahab's faith would identify which house was hers but it would also symbolize for the Israelite men who would attack Jericho that their own faith in God had saved them too from death. Thus above the bloody carnage of Jericho would hang the red cord signaling the blood of the covenant, even the blood of the Christ who would be the long-awaited fruit of the redeemed woman waiting inside the city wall.

THE SUBMISSION OF WAITING

Meanwhile, on the east bank of the Jordan River, hundreds of thousands of Israelites also waited. For forty years they had been doing that very thing—waiting for God to tell them when and where to move. When the pillar of cloud representing His presence had lifted from the tabernacle and had begun moving, the people had broken camp and followed wherever it went. When it had stopped, they had stopped, and there they had stayed until God's cloud started them on their way to yet another camping place. Their entire lives had been spent learning submission in God's waiting room, and now they were waiting once again.

This submission of waiting had been a hard-won discipline, learned over the course of four decades of following God's pillar of fire and cloud when it moved—and *only* when it moved. Their parents' generation, accustomed to the slave mentality of forced obedience to raw power, had over the years given way to a generation of adult children, disciplined to *choose* obedience to a stern but compassionate Father. Many of the soldiers waiting on Jordan's tumultuous shore had seen with their own eyes the consequences of disbelief—community leaders swallowed by the earth, neighbors consumed by fire from the Lord, aunts and uncles bitten by snakes, parents dying of a virulent plague—they had seen and they had learned (see Numbers 16–25).

Perhaps no other generation of people on earth has ever discovered more experientially than they did how closely sin is related to punishment. If they had felt the inclination to rebel against God (and which of them had not?), their motivation to instead discipline themselves to obedience was vastly strengthened by seeing firsthand the cost of *not* submitting to Him. They had learned the hard way to wait patiently on God's leading, for even Moses, the man whom they had seen enter Sinai's glory, had been disciplined for distrusting and dishonoring this holy One who dwelt in pillar and tabernacle.

Their waiting on Jordan's shore, however, was different. For they were finally on the verge of actually entering the Promised Land of Canaan, and their learned submission to God would soon be tested. Their battle skills had been honed in the wars against Sihon and Og, but the conflict ahead in Canaan would test far more than their war readiness. What was most in question was their willingness to trust Yahweh's battling on their behalf. God's promise to deliver their enemies into their hands was not mere rhetoric to them—their very lives depended on it.

Moreover, the Israelite army would enter Canaan without Moses' familiar leadership. God had forbidden him and Aaron to inherit the Promised Land because they had failed to honor Him as holy in an incident involving the Israelites' complaint about no water fit to drink. When the two leaders went to God facedown, perhaps expecting to have to intercede again because of the people's rebellion, God had offered grace not vengeance, telling Moses to speak to a particular rock formation and water would come out for the people to drink.

But instead, Moses had said to the people, "Listen, you rebels, must we bring you water out of this rock?" Then he had struck the rock twice with his staff, and water had come gushing out (see Num. 20:10–11).

God had intended to be kind to His people, but Moses had been angry with them. God had wished to bless the people, but Moses had wanted them to pay for their grumbling. God had said to speak to the rock, but Moses had spoken to the people and had struck the rock—two times. God had said the rock would (miraculously) bring forth water, but Moses had used his shepherd's rod and had said, "Must *we* bring you water?" [emphasis added].

Had Moses thought that God *should* be angry with the Israelites? Maybe he had wanted another opportunity to feel noble by interceding, and God was being kind without his intervention. Or maybe Moses was simply tired of the whole thing—the recurring complaints, the weight of responsibility for these rebels, the bruising of having played middleman between Yahweh and His children. Whatever Moses' reason for disobeying God, the root of his disobedience was a lack of trust in God's decision to be kind, and the result was insisting on his own way of handling these rebels. If he had to show them God's kindness, he'd at least make them pay first.

Before we cast stones at Moses, however, we would do well to look at our own hearts. How do we respond when the unrighteous flourish? When injustice prevails? When the one who has harmed us is blessed by God? When our own cause is not vindicated? When we have done things right and God does not avenge the wrong against us but instead shows His mercy toward the undeserving? Do we not become angry and sometimes take vengeance into our own hands—if only with unkindness or gossip or a fit of pique or self-pity?

How unfair of God to have judged Moses and Aaron so harshly, we think. Besides, the people got their water anyway, so what difference did it make? Why did Moses and Aaron lose their opportunity to enter the Promised Land just because of this one sin? After all they had been through in bringing the Israelites through forty years of desert wandering, why would God punish them now?

But God was more interested in His glory than in indulging Moses' emotional outburst. Much is required of those who represent God, for they must be as ready to offer grace as to speak judgment, even though it is easier to intercede for the unrighteous than to watch God choose not to reproach the wicked. None of Moses' sins was minor, for he spoke on God's behalf and represented His attitude toward the people. However understandable Moses' anger may have been, God was passionate for His own honor, and both Moses and Aaron were punished for their sin of dishonoring Him: They would not be allowed to enter the Promised Land with the Israelites. Moses, unlike Aaron, would at least see Canaan from a mountaintop, but neither would go in (see Deut. 32:48–52; 34:1–8).

Consequently, Israel's army would have to follow someone else into Canaan, and that someone was the man who had led them to military victory east of the Jordan River—Joshua, son of Nun, a man chosen by God as "a man in whom is the Spirit" (NASB). Before Moses had died, he "took Joshua and had him stand before Eleazar the priest and the whole assembly. Then he laid his hands on him and commissioned him," after which Moses was taken to heaven from Mount Pisgah at one hundred twenty years of age (Num. 27:17–18, 22–23). The mantle of leadership had been transferred to Joshua, and "the Israelites listened to him" (Deut. 34:9).

As the Israelite nation waited in their camp near the flooding Jordan River, many no doubt recalled a similar impossible crossing forty years earlier at the edge of the Red Sea. Except for Joshua and Caleb, however, all adults who had seen God part that sea lay buried in the desert, and now this second generation of Israelites (many of whom had crossed the Red Sea as children) faced their own crisis of faith. Would they follow Joshua, or would they too give way to fear and try to choose a new leader to take them back the way they had come, back to slavery? Could Joshua's authority withstand the test as Moses' leadership had?

To undergird Joshua's position, God spoke to him as He had forty years earlier spoken to Moses in the burning bush. "Moses my servant is dead," God said to His new commander in chief. "Now then, you and all these people, get ready to cross the Jordan River into the land I am about to give to them—to the Israelites. I will give you every place where you set your foot, as I promised Moses. . . . No one will be able to stand up against you all the days of your life. As I was with Moses, so I will be with you; I will never leave you nor forsake you" (see Josh. 1:1–18).

But God's gracious promise of His abiding presence was accompanied by words of warning: "Be careful to obey all the law my servant Moses gave you," He admonished Joshua. "Do not turn from it to the right or to the left, that you may be successful wherever you go. . . . Be strong and courageous. Do not be terrified; do not be discouraged, for the LORD your God will be with you wherever you go" (vv. 7, 9).

Three times Joshua was reminded to be strong and courageous—i.e., to hold firm to his faith in Yahweh and not to give way to fear. The earlier generation of Israelites had failed in both categories and had not entered the rest of the Promised Land. Now God was reminding this generation that faith (His gift) and obedience (their response to that gift) were to go hand in hand as they entered the battle. Joshua's challenge as their leader was to believe God's promise (that He would give them every place where they set their feet) and to follow His commands (to carefully obey the law) in submission and gratitude. Would Joshua receive God's offer and enter His rest or would his faith fail?

It appears Joshua lost no time deciding. When God gave the order to move, "Joshua ordered the officers of the people: 'Go through the camp and tell the people, "Get your supplies ready. Three days from now you will cross the Jordan here to go in and take possession of the land the LORD your God is giving you for your own."'" For years God's people had followed Him in the pillar of cloud and fire when it had moved and now they recognized God would lead them through the word of Joshua. "Whatever you have commanded us we will do," they said to Joshua, "and wherever you send us we will go. Just as we fully obeyed Moses, so we will obey you. Only may the LORD your God be with you as he was with Moses" (vv. 16–17). Soon God would prove that He was indeed with Joshua as He had been with Moses, able to lead His people into the rest He had promised them.

THE UNDESERVING

Joshua's readiness to cross the raging Jordan at God's command required not merely courage but also humility in accepting Yahweh's provision of faith. For faith must be received from God; it cannot be self-generated. The apostle Paul reminded the Ephesian Christians, "It is by grace you have been saved, through faith—and this not from yourselves, it is the gift of God—not by works, so that no one can boast" (Eph. 2:8–9). Faith is always the Father's unmerited gift.

Rahab, too, would receive an inheritance among the Israelites, but not because she deserved it or had somehow earned it. Surely God did not approve of what she had done when she gave her body to the many men who frequented her inn. For in breaking Yahweh's Sinai covenant (which she had not yet heard), she had grieved the heart of her heavenly Father (whom she did not yet know as Father). Nevertheless, she was elevated to equal status with God's chosen people. Was this not a gift of God's grace, His favor undeserved and unearned?

The amazing thing about grace is that no one deserves it, neither alien nor covenant child, neither Canaanite prostitute nor Israelite commander in chief. How very different the lives of these two believers had been! Joshua had spent untold hours as Moses' right-hand man, going to Sinai with him and remaining in the holy Tent of Meeting for long periods of time (see Exod. 24:13–14; 33:7–11). Rahab meanwhile was making a living trading sexual favors for profit from the roughest among an utterly depraved people. Joshua thus knew more about Yahweh and enjoyed a richer relationship with Him as His covenant child than Rahab could even have imagined in her wall-built inn. But neither deserved to receive the grace God offered.

Unbelievable as it seems—in fact unfair as it may seem—God did not love Joshua more than He loved Rahab, not even during those years when Joshua was faithful and Rahab faithless. God's love is like a laser beam in its constancy, equally unwavering and penetrating to all toward whom He directs it. Joshua and Rahab were equally God's chosen ones, beloved by Him, recipients of His gift of faith, and responsive to His call on their lives because of that faith. In fact, there is nothing they could have done or not done that would have motivated God to love either one of them any more or any less.

This is the wonder and bewilderment of the gospel. Both Israelite leader and Canaanite prostitute received grace without having earned it. And both rested in God's Word as they awaited with eagerness the fall of Jericho—he in the camp of God's army, she in the stronghold of God's enemy. Who but God could have contrived so elaborate a scheme for accomplishing His purposes while at the same time thwarting His enemy's wicked design? Satan had maliciously anticipated that Rahab and Joshua would get what they both deserved—eternal death for their sin. But his evil intent would be turned to God's glory, the glory of His love and mercy toward sinners. It is no wonder the ancient serpent despises grace.

HUMILITY AND GRACE

But Satan is not alone in hating grace. In our fallenness we all abhor being dependent on God, reduced to asking and receiving, humbled into needing what we are unable to provide for ourselves. We resist being dependent on the love of others, even God. Deep in our hearts runs the rebellion God's enemy urged on our first parents in the Garden of Eden and on Jesus in the Garden of Gethsemane—the spirit of choosing our own way over God's. We by nature strive to run our own lives, to earn our own way, and to need no one but ourselves as we seek to find rest in a restless world. Even when our hearts are connected to God and to His Christ, we think we can bless Him more with our doing than with our receiving. Needing His grace runs counter to our determination to earn His favor by our own best efforts.

The words of the apostle Peter are again typical of our own response to Jesus as He proffers grace and invites us to receive instead of earn. The scene this time is an upstairs room in Jerusalem at the time of the annual celebration of Passover, which commemorated the night when the angel of death passed over the Israelite homes in Egypt because of the lamb's blood smeared on their doorposts. Passover was traditionally a family feast, and Jesus' celebration with His disciples signified the new "family" He was instituting—the family of faith, which would soon be referred to as the church. During this supper, Jesus would identify Himself as the Passover Lamb, declaring His broken body and shed blood to be the basis of the new covenant they would observe instead of Passover from then on, in memory of the deliverance from sin His approaching crucifixion and resurrection would accomplish. But before beginning the feast for which He had eagerly awaited, Jesus offered His disciples an object lesson on receiving grace. (This story is found in John 13:1–17.)

The disciples had just been arguing about who would be the greatest in Christ's coming kingdom, and in sharp contrast to their perception of greatness, Jesus took on Himself the task of the lowliest servant, which was to wash the feet of the Passover guests. This He did, not out of self-contempt nor a forced humility but out of a quiet assurance of His true identity as the powerful Son of God. The apostle John tells us: "Jesus knew that the Father had put all things under his power, and that he had come from God and was returning to God; so he got up from the meal, took off his outer clothing, and wrapped a towel around his waist" in preparation for washing His disciples' feet. Jesus knew who He was, and even doing the most menial of jobs (or suffering the most shameful of deaths) could not diminish His intrinsic dignity nor sway Him from His purpose of showing those He loved "the full extent of his love." We too if we will embrace our identity as God's beloved, can enter the "rest" of living unselfishly and unself-consciously.

103

When the Savior came to Peter, however, the outspoken fisherman refused to allow Jesus to be servant to him. "You shall never wash my feet," he declared, for he could not allow his King to carry out so lowly a function. No doubt Peter meant to honor Jesus, but the Master defined honoring Him in altogether different terms. "Unless I wash you," Jesus said, "you have no part with me." That is to say, unless Peter (and all of us) will allow Jesus to be our servant, unless we permit Him to give us what we do not deserve and cannot earn, unless we are willing to receive His cleansing, we cannot be connected to Him. The humility of Christ's foot washing demanded the reciprocal humility of Peter's willingness to receive. And though Peter did not understand fully what Jesus was doing, his passionate desire to be part of his Lord moved him to the opposite extreme. "Then, Lord," Simon Peter exclaimed, "not just my feet but my hands and my head as well!" If receiving cleansing was prerequisite to connection with Jesus, Peter wanted to receive all the cleansing he could.

Would that our own desire for greater intimacy with Christ matched Peter's! What this disciple lacked in understanding he made up for in passion, longing to bring all of himself under the new covenant he did not yet comprehend. Very soon he would desert and betray the One he loved, and the memory of having received Christ's foot washing would be instructive of how very much more he would yet need to receive from Jesus in the way of forgiveness, restoration, and cleansing. We too must do as Peter did, yielding ourselves more and more to Christ's gracious stooping to serve and to save us.

A New Identity

Jesus had said, "Come to me," and they had come—Peter and the eleven and many others besides, for they were weary of the struggle to perform and burdened by their recurring sin. "I will give you rest," the rabbi had promised, and it sounded good to them. The leaders of the Pharisees would have said, "Come to us, and we will give you thirty-nine categories of work you are not allowed to do on the Sabbath, along with a list of spices you are required to tithe, and guidelines for avoiding contact with a dead body, and our interpretation of every commandment, and . . ."—the requirements would have gone on and on. Part of the weariness Jesus mentioned had come from the meticulous "doing" demanded by the Pharisees. No doubt Jesus' promise of rest from these burdens came to His listeners like a breath of fresh air. Someone once penned these words to describe our invitation to Christ's rest:

> Lay your deadly doing down, down at Jesus' feet.
> Stand in Him, in Him alone—gloriously complete!
>
> AUTHOR UNKNOWN

The rest Jesus offers is not the rest of inactivity or laziness. The gift He offers has its own "requirements." For one thing, as we have just seen, those who desire Jesus' rest must receive it and not try to earn it. Yielding our autonomy and acknowledging our need for His grace is a recurring struggle for us all.

But along with the requirement to receive and not strive to earn Christ's rest, there is also the invitation to identify ourselves with Him as we rest in Him. "Take my yoke upon you," Jesus said, presenting an image that conjures up close connection, even oneness. For when two or more draft animals are yoked together, they pull as one—no longer plural but a single team. Jesus' invitation to be yoked to Him is an invitation to oneness with Him in identity and purpose.

When we consider the nature of Jesus—that He is true God as well as true man—our being one with Him seems almost ludicrous, like yoking an elephant to a gnat. What humility that God chose to reveal Himself in human form, the eternal Word made flesh, embracing us in His stooping so that by His death we could be one with Him. This is what Christ prayed for us as He faced the crucifixion that would win our salvation—that because of His faithfulness we would know for ourselves something of the oneness with the Father He Himself had enjoyed from before the foundation of the earth (see John 17:20–23).

Like Rahab, who yoked herself to Yahweh and His people in rejection of her Canaanite identity, we are invited to rest in being known as Christ's beloved people, no longer belonging to Satan or feeling at home in our alien culture. If we choose to receive His rest, we must likewise receive His yoke—a sort of engagement ring as the Bride of Christ, showing that our oneness with Him here on earth takes precedence over all other claims on our affection, for we are pledged to oneness with Him through all eternity.

As a further picture of the intimacy of the yoking to which Jesus invites us, God gives us (through the words of the apostle Paul in Ephesians 5) the image of marriage: Christ as the wooing Bridegroom and we believers as the responsive Bride. It is a fitting image, for within the yoke of marriage husband and wife are in some mysterious way no longer two but one—one in heart and in spirit and in body—yet still two persons. Similarly, we who are the Bride of Christ retain our individual identity, but we are one with our Lord through His Spirit. Moreover, our "marriage" to Him means we have taken His name and are identified with Him, so that those who interact with us can see Christ in us and can know we are intimately bound to Him.

When Jesus invited His followers, "Take my yoke upon you," He was offering a sort of "marriage proposal" to any whose hearts were drawn to intimacy with God. Those individuals (both then and now) who accept the "ring" of His yoke are thereby betrothed to Christ, a covenant as binding as marriage in first-century Judaic society. Perhaps that is why Jesus never married while living on earth as a man—He was already "engaged" to His church. The apostle Paul in Ephesians 5 compares the intimacy between a redeemed husband and his wife to the oneness between Christ and His betrothed Bride-to-be. This can be taken to mean that a husband is to behave like Christ toward his wife, and she must show to her husband the church's response to her Bridegroom. This is mystery indeed, as Paul has said.

MYSTERY OF ONENESS

How can a saved man, for example, be both bride to Christ and husband to a wife? How can he live out the paradigm Paul presents when he says, "Now I want you to realize that the head of every man is Christ, and the head of the woman is man, and the head of Christ is God" (1 Cor. 11:3)? For a husband to live as Christ's Bride, he must submit himself to Christ as head (emulating Jesus' submission to His Father's headship) and simultaneously be Christ-like head to his wife in servant leadership, according to Jesus' own model of John 13 foot washing and John 19 life-sacrificing.

In other words, because of and in the strength of a husband's own submission to the headship of Christ, he must pursue a gentle but persistent movement toward his wife for her protection and cherishing, teaching her of the nature and goodness of Christ Himself through his own sacrificial love for her. In initiating and sustaining a strong, compassionate involvement with her at every level, he will reflect Jesus' own wooing of her heart. In this way she, as God's beloved daughter, in imitation of the church's responsiveness to Christ, can experience the freedom and encouragement she needs to gladly use her Spirit-generated gifts for the advancement of God's kingdom. Under her husband's cherishing, a wife will flourish and grow.

No husband can accomplish so sacred and costly a responsibility in his own strength, of course, for no one can muster sacrificial love. For a man to fulfill the scriptural mandate that husbands love their wives "just as Christ loved the church" (Eph. 5:25), he must persist in bending his own neck to Christ's yoke, providing the Holy Spirit ample room in his heart to live out Jesus' life in and through him. Only thus will he be fit for the hard work of spiritual leadership through intimately knowing, gladly serving, and humbly asking forgiveness of the wife God has entrusted to him.

And how, on the other hand, can a woman be bride to both Christ and to her husband, submissive to Jesus as her Lord and to her husband as her head? In other words, what would it look like for her to "submit to [her husband] as to the Lord" (Eph. 5:22)? If he is a redeemed man (and the apostle Paul was addressing his words to Christian husbands and wives), he will be indwelt by the Holy Spirit, and she must seek to offer him the genuine respect and glad responsiveness to his love that she shows to Christ because of His sacrifice for her. As believers we are called to submit our lives to His sacrificial leadership; as wives, we are to nurture a similar willingness to submit to our husband's Christ-like leadership.

Neither submission to God nor submission to a husband comes to any wife without struggle. This struggle will be at its core an internal battle, not an external striving against our husbands when they fail us (though that is where it is often focused). Submission is always a heart issue, a question of whom we trust enough to yield our hearts to his leadership. Yoked to the perfect Christ, we struggle to follow Him with a glad heart. Yoked to an imperfect man, we think we will lose ourselves altogether if we offer our hearts to him. It is one thing to receive his kindness as we receive Christ's kindness; it is another to live without protecting ourselves from his unkindness. It is when our husbands fail us that we consider ourselves fools for trusting their leadership. And fail us they will at some time or another.

It is then that Paul's instructions to submit to our husbands *as to the Lord* must become the focal point of our energy. For whatever keeps us from trusting our husbands (what they do to disappoint or harm us) is what we fear in our relationship with Christ as well (that He will not come through for us in the ways we want or expect). If we cannot rest in His love, we will not be able to rest in our husbands, either. Moreover, if we *do* learn to face our fears and come to rest our hearts in Christ, we will grow in our courage to risk trusting our husbands as well. Chapter 8 of this book will explore this complex process in greater detail.[2]

Like Jesus, who loved His heavenly Father and submitted all things to His headship, a wife is called to honor and follow her husband in those things that do not violate the redeemed image of God in her or in him. If at any time he is not modeling Christ's love toward her, she must not stop longing to rest in him, even though embracing her longing will likely cause her much sadness. She must pray that God's presence in her husband will increase. She must also remain willing to trust her heavenly Father's power to direct and to protect her life even through her husband's imperfect leadership.

Meanwhile, she must also take the risk of telling her husband honestly what is in her heart, as Jesus did with His Father. For Scripture tells us that "during the days of Jesus' life on earth, he offered up prayers and petitions with loud cries and tears to the one who could save him from death, and he was heard because of his reverent submission" (Heb. 5:7). As a wife opens her heart to her husband with candor and a longing to rest in him, there will be something in her desire for him and in her longing to respond to his love that will show him how to long for and gladly submit to the loving headship of Christ.

A godly wife cannot respond to her imperfect husband in a Christ-like way without remaining intimately connected to God through His Spirit. If she tries to create a loving relationship with him in her own strength, redoubling her efforts to earn his love whenever he fails to model Christ to her (or making him pay for not loving her well), she runs the risk of becoming bitterly disappointed or even hateful toward him. Only God can love her fallen husband with the persistent strength and forgiving love he needs. Only God through His Spirit's presence in her heart can enable her to submit to her husband with Christ-like humility and the expectation of good from him.

In short, both husband and wife, yoked to Christ, are called to live out toward one another the passionate oneness between Christ and His Bride, the church. This they cannot do unless the Holy Spirit rules in their hearts, producing in each of them the one life of Christ. Their mutual submission to Jesus and to each other can then teach the world that Christ sacrificed His life for His own and that redeemed sinners are passionate to follow Him in devotion and service.

It is mystery indeed, but glorious mystery, this oneing, this yoking. Even our fear of intimacy—with God and with one another—is part of the awe-struck worship to which we are drawn as we respond to the One who designed us for Himself and for each other. For when we consider our incalculable power to bless or harm the Savior we love and the spouse to whom we are yoked (to say nothing of their power to bless or harm us), we do well to be afraid. The mystery of oneness is dread mystery. How can we mutually submit ourselves to the one who may not reciprocate our love? How can we find the courage to say that even our fear of rejection cannot stop us from loving well? How do we stay yoked to Jesus and to the one with whom we have repeated covenant vows, so that our identity as Christians and as husbands and wives will be true? Will not our frailty and terror overwhelm us?

A STRUGGLE TO RECEIVE

This is the dilemma we face, especially those of us willing to acknowledge the dark recesses of our own hearts. We recognize that our desire for intimacy is often blindsided by the dual realities of our own sin and of the relational disappointments we have known. We've experienced how the oneness we desire can melt down in the heat of fear and anger when we have been or are being unloved. Rest for our souls is elusive, because we continually strain against the yoke of being identified with an imperfect person, unwilling to live in the tension of longing for more than we are receiving. So much in ourselves and in the other blocks our marital intimacy.

More than that, it seems inevitable that one spouse will pursue oneness more fervently or at an earlier point in time than the other. It was so with Bill and me in our journey toward oneness. The struggles we began experiencing in the sixteenth year of our marriage arose from my desire for more depth in our relationship than Bill thought he was able or willing to pursue. This distancing between us drove us farther and farther apart, almost to the point of divorce.

The external focus of our conflict was Bill's drinking, which I was determined to control because I believed (rightly so) that it was thwarting the oneness of heart God intended us to enjoy. My own attempts to control his drinking, of course, were also thwarting our oneness, but that I could not yet perceive. In fact the reason I finally began to affiliate with a support group for family members of substance abusers was all wrong. I wanted to "fix" Bill once and for all by learning how to more effectively control his dependence on alcohol (his way of diminishing his pain). Then, I thought, he would stop drinking and all our problems would be over.

What I actually learned in those meetings, however, was that I could control no one's decisions but my own, no one's spiritual growth but my own, no one's passion for oneness but my own. In other words, I had to give up my long-standing attempts to force Bill into the mold I had mentally fashioned for him, and learn instead how to love him as God loved him— just as he was—without letting his moods or choices dictate my own.

These things I had to learn in the context of the worst marital battle I could have imagined. Bill was furious that I was attending "those stupid meetings," and I vacillated back and forth in my willingness to keep going to them anyway. The following years were not an easy passage for Bill and me. Our anger regarding our many past and present losses, long submerged in denial, continually erupted in bitter outbursts and unbridled recriminations. Over time we ran out of all our reasons for loving each other and for staying together—except one: We had spoken covenant vows in front of God and a whole bunch of people and we were reluctant to break those promises. So we stayed together and fought things out for six long years, both our lives hanging by the thin, precarious thread of commitment.

In many ways our journey resembled the journey of the Israelites out of Egypt toward the Promised Land of Canaan. Both Bill and I had lived in the bondage of fear and self-contempt for years before we met each other, and though God had redeemed us before we married, neither of us knew much about living free. Bill's alcoholism and my obsession with control were the golden calves we most frequently worshiped during those years, though there were other idolatries claiming our allegiance as well. The "slave mentality" with which we had entered our marriage had kept us from understanding our new identity in Christ, and we experienced very little of what it meant to be at rest with God. We were just too busy trying to stay in charge of each other and of our own lives.

Bill and I had no major Kadesh experience in our marriage, no event where we rebelled big-time against God and were disciplined with years of wilderness exile. But our lives often felt desert-dry, our hearts more bent on striving to manipulate each other than on resting in what God wanted us to receive from Him. Internally we wandered for years with little sense of place or peace, for we were appalled at the prospect of living at the mercy of grace. Bill and I loved each other as best we knew how, and both of us wanted our marriage to work. But our love eventually began running dry. We had few tastes of deep joy during our years of destructive conflict over Bill's drinking, because we found it so difficult to accept God's discipline and to submit our lives utterly to Him. Neither of us could see a way out of the wilderness we were in, and rest seemed to be just a mirage destined to evaporate time and again—probably (we thought) for the rest of our lives.

DESPERATE FOR GRACE

I remember vividly the moment when I recognized how deeply angry I was at Bill for what he was putting me through with his unwillingness to repent. As I was watching him lift weights one day, I said to myself, *I simply do not love this man anymore!*

At that moment, God's voice in my heart asked, *Do you think I love this man?*

Stunned and angry, I paused briefly, then responded, *I don't see how You can! And I really don't think You should—haven't You been paying attention to what's been going on here?*

To which He replied, *Do you really think it is any harder for Me to love this man than to love his wife?* And I had nothing more to say. My voice was stopped.

We all represent God if His Holy Spirit is living in us. I was being honest when I admitted I no longer loved my husband, but God would not let me stop there. He wanted to draw out what was most deeply in my heart, which was His presence in me. When I found my voice again, my spirit had been humbled into confession and entreaty: *Lord, I do not love this man, but I know You do. If You want me to love him again, You must change my heart and give me Your love for him. My own resources are not enough.*

It was the prayer He had been waiting for, the prayer He had spent many years bringing me to pray. As long as I could cling to my own resources, I would not need Him. But when I knew myself devoid of love and desperate for His Spirit to flow into and through me, He could fill my empty heart with His love and my empty mouth with words of forgiveness and my empty hands with acts of kindness. Then and only then can any of us represent Him well.

Many have asked Bill and me, "How did you do it? How could you have lived without giving and receiving what you were designed for as husband and wife? Where did you find the strength to go on?" To which we now reply in retrospect, "By God's grace we lived one day at a time." I had never had to live that way before, had never had to cling to God so desperately, crying out to Him, "If You do not come I am undone!" I had always managed my world fairly well. But during those years, my life had become altogether beyond my control, and I could no longer live without God meeting me time and again to reassure me He was still there. It was a terrifying passage. It was also glorious.

No one creates the strength to persevere; it is a gift of grace. No one can self-generate love when it has died; it must come from God. No one finds lasting hope unless it is in abandoning oneself to God and His purposes. Without grace, without the humility of receiving rest from God and of being yoked to Him, there is no hope for restoring genuine oneness.

Nor is there any guarantee that if one or the other spouse responds to God's grace that the marriage relationship will necessarily be restored. The only certain fruit of any person's brokenness before God is the realization that He cannot fill any but empty hands and the reassurance that He will be present in the middle of sorrow and longing. It may not sound like much and it seldom feels like enough this side of heaven. But the tastes of grace Bill and I received from the Father in the midst of our pain were all that sustained us as we experienced the dying of the marriage relationship we had constructed.

As we look back, we can see that much of what died during those years *had* to die—Bill's dependence on alcohol to numb his pain, my trust in control to numb my own; his rage, my appeasing; his demand to always be right, my insistence that I never be hurt; his emotional withdrawal from me, my worship of his emotional presence with me. There were many destructive and self-centered habits we had brought into our marriage and had reinforced during our first fifteen years together, habits we had to recognize, confess, and revoke. Like Rahab, our time of crisis exposed what was really in our hearts, and we were backed into choosing whether or not to repent of our sin and stand firm in being yoked to God and to each other. We struggled to know whether we really wanted to go on receiving His rest and the yoke of identity and submission that went with it. There remained important decisions for us both.

GIVING GIFTS

Ultimately, of course, if both partners in a marriage are one with Christ, it eventually changes their hearts, for His Holy Spirit is the agent of powerful inner transformation. People drawn to Christ's love, who have received His grace and have yielded to His yoking, find their hearts softened and their capacity for loving others enlarged. This heart change also increases their desire to bless their Savior with a responsive love and heartfelt worship. For the humility of receiving God's kindness prepares us as nothing else can to praise and adore Him. Those who know themselves well loved must find expression for their gratitude.

Such was the experience of Jesus' good friend Mary, the sister of Martha and Lazarus, who humbled herself to receive what Jesus had to offer and found it was far more than she had expected. While Martha opened her home and offered her hands to Jesus, Mary opened her heart and offered her worship to Him. She listened to what He taught and she believed Him when He explained that He must soon die. And unlike Peter, she did not deny the reality nor try to deter Him from His death-bound path. Though her heart was filled with sorrow, she was moved to consider what she might do to honor Him before He would no longer be a visitor in their home. Her sister had given Him a lovely meal. What could she give her Lord to express her love for Him and her grief over His approaching death?

How wonderful that when Jesus captures our hearts, when we are humble recipients of His truth and His grace, He is also ready to receive what we long to offer back to Him. Jesus, like an enamored fiancé, does not come to us empty-handed, but brings gifts custom-designed to delight and enhance each member of His Body, the church. He also rejoices to accept from us the responsive outpouring of our hearts. He ate Martha's good food and was grateful. He would receive another kind of blessing from her sister. (This story is told in Matthew 26:6–13 and John 12:1–8.)

They were gathered at a meal again, and Martha was serving, this time without complaint. Mary had evidently been pondering Jesus' words concerning His coming betrayal and death. His disciples had heard His teaching too but they were having trouble accepting it. A dying Messiah was not congruent with their expectation of a reigning Messiah, and Jesus' triumphal entry into Jerusalem had confused them even more. But Mary believed Jesus' teaching about His death, and though it grieved her, the gift she chose for Him reflected the faith she had placed in the truth of His words.

While the guests chatted around Martha's table, Mary approached Jesus with a pint of very expensive perfume, pure nard, produced in the Himalayas from the spikenard plant. She poured it out on Jesus, and "the house was filled with the fragrance of the perfume." What an extravagance of both faith and worship! When some at the dinner party criticized Mary for this "waste" of money, Jesus rebuked them, extolling both her action and the believing heart that had motivated it. "She has done a beautiful thing to me," He said, validating that once again she had chosen well. "When she poured this perfume on my body," He went on to explain, "she did it to prepare me for burial."

Nard was a spice often used to anoint the body of a deceased loved one, both as a final act of honor and to camouflage the odor of death. In anointing Jesus, Mary was declaring both her honor for Him as worthy of this expensive and lavish gift and her belief that His words about His coming death were true. This double blessing of love and faith was a response to Jesus' gift of grace to her, the reciprocal offering of her own gift back to Him. Jesus affirmed her heart and received her adoration with glad thankfulness. Then He added another strand to the circle of love between them by offering her yet another gift, the promise of perpetual recognition for her adoring generosity. "Whenever this gospel is preached throughout the world," Jesus told the guests around the table, "what she has done will also be told, in memory of her." And so it has been, and I have told it yet once more.

And in the repetition of the story of Mary's love outpoured on her soon-to-die Savior, we are reminded that we too can be changed as we respond with a reckless abandon of love to the One who first loved us. The echoes of Christ's patient invitation to rest in Him sound daily in our own hearts and daily we can come again to Him and bend our necks anew to His kind yoke. Jesus' "Come unto me" is for everyone and is never retracted. Those who do not come have chosen *not* to come; they have not been turned away.

How is it with our own hearts today? The Holy Spirit enjoins us, "See to it, brothers, that none of you has a sinful, unbelieving heart that turns away from the living God. But encourage one another daily, as long as it is called Today, so that none of you may be hardened by sin's deceitfulness" (Heb. 3:12–13). Sin would seduce us away from receiving God's gifts with a humble heart, but "today" Jesus calls us to come.

Fear and disbelief can easily sidetrack us from steadfastly remaining yoked to Christ in identity and purpose. Tests of our faith come time and again, and though Satan intends them to derail our faith walk, the Holy Spirit longs to turn them to our benefit by strengthening both our submission to God and our dependence on His gifts for our very lives. The next chapter will examine in greater depth the continual testing of our determination to find our rest in God alone.

 ## Questions to Consider

1. What disturbances might Satan have stirred up in Rahab's heart after she helped the two spies escape?

2. How has God humbled you in order to give you a blessing?

3. What in your experience helps you identify with the following: (a) Rahab asking the spies for protection; (b) Peter's response to Jesus' washing his feet; (c) Mary's worship of Jesus with expensive ointment?

4. How has your yoking to Christ in identity and direction been difficult for you?

5. What marital benefits might proceed from a husband being yoked to Christ in sacrificial service to his wife, or a wife being yoked to Christ in submission to the care and protection of her husband?

6. How might your own intimate relationships change if you were yoked more intimately to Christ?

Regarding the opening story:

Despite what she says, Luanne *does* want to receive Mike's kindness—God made her that way. Angela's fear of genuine involvement with Joe is keeping her from entering the mutual trust and interdependence her heavenly Father intended her to enjoy. And Michelle's frustration in longing for the oneness she misses as a widow is an integral aspect of the cost of giving and receiving love. Patty was right to suggest that neediness isn't all bad and that God wants us to need Him.

7. How would you respond to Luanne's declaration that she hates being needy?

CHAPTER SIX

OBEDIENCE

The Allure of Reckless Faith

THE APARTMENT WAS SMALL, *compared to the spaciousness of the home Brian could no longer visit. He had agreed to the separation, had admitted the debilitating effects of his pornography addiction on Sue Ellen and the children, had spent the past nine months in counseling, and had committed to meeting biweekly with an accountability group of men from his church. He had to admit the apartment was lonely, except for the times when his children called and wanted to see him. Those were his good days and they kept him encouraged in his waiting.*

To say Sue Ellen was skeptical about Brian's changed heart would be an understatement. He knew how different he was, how sorrowful for having hurt those he most loved, how excited about his new relationship with God, how willing to do whatever it took to win back his wife's trust. But he also knew he could not convince Sue Ellen of those inner changes. God would have to move in her heart, and most of the time Brian was content to wait on God's timing.

But the last week had been difficult for Brian—lonely and sexually frustrating. His friends had been supportive—even when he'd called one of them late at night just to talk. Yet thoughts of divorce had begun slipping sideways into

115

his thinking, breaking through even his joy in the Lord with unnerving stabs of discontent and a longing for greater intimacy than he was experiencing.

Then it happened—not just once but three times. As thoughts about divorce entered his mind, he heard a firm and unequivocal "No!" echo in the back of his mind. Brian knew the voice. He also knew he would obey what God had said. His frustration remained undiminished, his longing for intimacy unsatisfied, his apartment still small and lonely. But the voice reminded him that he had yielded himself to God and had determined with God's help to woo the woman he loved until she made a decision about her own heart toward God and toward him.

Though pursuing Sue Ellen seemed futile, Brian would obey God and persevere, depending on his heavenly Father's presence one day at a time. Eventually Sue Ellen would reveal what she most deeply wanted, and then Brian would know what to do. Until then he would listen and obey, no matter what.

There are times in the lives of all believers when doing what God tells us to do feels not just difficult but nonsensical, maybe even dangerous. When our urgent prayers are met with God's silence, or when His direction for our lives contradicts reason and seems to jeopardize our physical, emotional, or relational safety, then our faith is tested in ways that will cause us either to bolt back to the familiarity of self-determination or to cling desperately to God and find joy in His provision. When we become willing to trust God in the silence of postponed or disappointing answers to our prayers, we will more deeply and joyously come to know His heart.

Down the scarlet rope and into the dark the two men descended, rappelling from Rahab's window and dropping to the ground outside Jericho's walls. Swiftly and silently they made their way into the western hills. There they remained in hiding for three days before fording the Jordan River and heading back to the safety of the Israelite camp. The next time they crossed the Jordan it would be on dry ground. And the next time they saw Jericho the red rope hanging from a window in its wall would mark both their escape and Rahab's.

The spies had completed their mission, reporting excitedly to Joshua, "The LORD has surely given the whole land into our hands; all the people are melting in fear because of us" (Josh. 2:24). What déjà vu this must have been for Joshua, the former spy, now commander in chief. Forty years earlier he had said to his countrymen regarding this same enemy, "Do not be afraid of the people of this land, because we will swallow them up. Their protection is gone, but the LORD is with us" (Num. 14:9).

Unfortunately that entire generation—including the parents of the spies now standing before Joshua—had disbelieved his long-ago report and had been shut out of God's rest because of their disobedience. Now this second generation of Israelites would have opportunity to make a better choice. Would their faith pass the test of obedience this time? Would they believe the spies' words of encouragement and hope? Would they follow Joshua into danger, not just struggling to enter the rest in the Promised Land but resting in the promises of Yahweh at every step along the way? This would be the test of their rest.

A UNIQUE TEST

A good test in academic circles is one that challenges but does not overwhelm the test taker. That is to say, a test or exam must cover the subject taught, yet be doable by any student who has prepared adequately for it.

God's test of rest, however, was decidedly different. At Yahweh's direction Joshua had brought the people of Israel to a new campsite on the eastern banks of the flooded Jordan River, which the two spies had twice managed to ford. But there was no way hundreds of thousands of soldiers with their armament, their wives and children, their livestock, and their household goods could safely transverse this raging water. Why did God choose harvesttime (when the river always flooded) for this crossing, instead of waiting for a more navigable season?

Superficially it may have been because once the Jordan was breached, the Israelites would need the harvest of Canaanite crops for food (see Josh. 5:12). But God also had a larger purpose in bringing His people to a test that was not just difficult but impossible to pass in their own strength. He intended to show His strength through their weakness. What they could not do, He would do for them. A rain-swollen river lay between them and the land God had promised to Abraham almost five hundred years earlier, and the only way they could enter it was to rest in God's power on their behalf. This was to be a test not of *their* competence but of His.

Ancient peoples often believed their battles were ultimately won or lost not by armies but by the gods of those armies. Victory affirmed not just military or strategic predominance but the superiority of the winning nation's deities. There was more at stake on the eastern shore of the Jordan than merely the Israelites' survival. If the Israelites could be brought across the flooded Jordan River, it would prove that Yahweh was more powerful than Baal, the Canaanite god "who was believed to reign as king among the gods because he had triumphed over the sea-god."[1] Thus it would establish Yahweh rather than Baal as legitimate claimant to the land into which He was sending His army. Joshua explained that God intended to miraculously bring the Israelites into Canaan "so that all the peoples of the earth might know that the hand of the LORD is powerful and so that [the Israelites] might always fear the LORD [their] God" (Josh. 4:24).

Therefore, it was for God's glory as well as for His people's good that the Israelites gathered to breach the dangerous waters of the Jordan River, their first step into the land of God's promised rest. (This story is told in Josh. 3:1–5:12.) Going on ahead of them would be the ark of the covenant, carried by the priests. The people were to follow the ark because, as Joshua said, "Then you will know which way to go, since you have never been this way before." The ark, where Yahweh dwelt in His dread glory, would lead them as they had been led in the wilderness by pillar of cloud and fire—God showing them the way and they walking wherever He led. What an abandon of trust and obedience Yahweh was asking of them! Keeping a respectful distance from the holy ark, the people were to obey God by following their spiritual leaders into grave danger, believing that Yahweh's rest awaited them beyond the river.

Yet, paradoxically, the Israelites had to enter God's rest *before* they obeyed God by crossing the Jordan into Canaan. Thirty-eight years earlier at Kadesh their parents had refused to rest in God and had fallen into disobedience. In contrast, Scripture warns us to "make every effort to *enter* [God's] rest, *so that* no one will fall by following their example of disobedience" (Heb. 4:11, emphasis added). In other words, entering rest (i.e., entrusting our lives to God) *precedes* obedience. We must keep on believing in His love for us and keep on resting in His grace *so that* we can obey. What is our heart attitude toward God? Will our hearts be hard or submissive, stubborn or gentle, self-determined or humble? If we are not letting Jesus' own gentleness and humility rule in our hearts, our obedience will falter every time the risk becomes too great. This is the test of rest.

THE OBEDIENCE OF REST

From the eastern shore of the Jordan River the first to walk the faith-test into danger were to be the ark-bearing priests. The weight of gold in the ark they carried would surely drown them if God's word failed. Sometimes when we move into rest, we must take a step of "unreasonable" faith. Would we dare trust God with our very lives as those priests did? Would we tell our feet to step into the fast-flowing current of the river, not knowing for sure whether or how God would provide safe passage? Which of us would not demand more surety than simply Joshua's word that God had said, "Go"?

Yet follow God into danger they did, foolish as their trust and obedience may have seemed. What could have motivated them to such recklessness of faith? Why would they abandon the safety of Jordan's shore for the peril of possible death? What sort of vision could sustain that kind of risk?

We are not told what the ark-bearing priests were thinking or feeling. We know only what they did. But one thing is sure: They valued God's purposes above all else, trusted His word enough to stake their lives on it, desired His glory more than their own futures. When God woos our hearts and we respond to His love, we are enthralled at His presence and long to be with Him wherever He leads, even if it means enduring loneliness—or carrying a load of gold into a raging river. God's wish becomes our command, whatever it may be. We sometimes do crazy things when we're in love, but we're not sorry to be doing them.

And miraculously, "as soon as the priests who carried the ark reached the Jordan and their feet touched the water's edge, the water from upstream stopped flowing. It piled up in a heap a great distance away, . . . while the water flowing down to . . . (the Salt Sea) was completely cut off. So the people crossed over opposite Jericho" on land that was wide and dry (Josh. 3:15–16). The priests had risked their lives to walk the Israelites into rest, halting halfway across the Jordan to stand still, holding the ark of God's presence, which protected the people as they hurried past them into Canaan.

When all had crossed and twelve men had carried ashore huge memorial stones from where the ark stood in the middle of the Jordan, the priests brought their holy burden out of the riverbed, and immediately the Jordan resumed its flooding. The "test" was over. The Israelites' trust in Yahweh had issued forth in obedience, and their obedience had brought them into the land of rest. The stone monument built in the new camp at Gilgal declared God's power, memorializing the people's "reckless" faith and reinforcing the future faith of coming generations of Israelites.

How like God to make obedience not only the fruit of rest but also and simultaneously the path into rest. If we put our trust in Him, resting in His promise, we will obey whatever He tells us to do. And when we obey, He brings us into the "land of rest" where even our work transcends drudgery to become fruitful and satisfying. Scripture tells us that the earlier generation of Israelites—the ones He led out of Egypt—"did not go in [to God's rest], because of their disobedience" (Heb. 4:6). The message of God's promised blessing "was of no value to them, because those who heard did not combine it with faith" (v. 2). If those just-freed Israelites had rested in God's promise to give them Canaan despite the giants and fortifications there, they would have listened to Joshua and Caleb, obeyed God's marching orders, and saved themselves thirty-eight years of nonproductive desert wandering—as well as their own untimely deaths.

Faith in God's words and obedience to His leading must always go hand in hand. Scripture says that Rahab was "considered righteous for what she did when she gave lodging to the spies and sent them off in a different

119

direction" (James 2:25). In receiving Yahweh's gift of faith she imperiled her own life to save the spies. Joshua also gave evidence of his faith when he risked leading Israel against impossible odds in the taking of Canaan. If faith is to prevail it must be "activated" as it is received. We all face crises of faith whenever we hear the gospel preached. Will we merely receive the good news in our hearts or will we also translate our faith into action? Will we be ruled by our own passion for personal safety or will we yield ourselves to God's plan to use us for His glory and for our good? Is our deepest desire focused on achieving our own brand of success, or will we seek passionately to do His will above our own? How large is our perception of God and of His purposes through us? How often do we "combine [God's message] with faith" by resting our hearts in Him and obeying Him no matter what the risk?

If our hearts were so totally sold out to Christ that we would follow Him into any danger, what inner tranquillity would characterize our lives! Like the battle-ready Israelites crossing the Jordan, we could be confident our work would fit into God's larger story, and we could rest secure in the knowledge that our lives had meaning beyond our own fleeting happiness. Even if we were to lose our lives following Him, our faith and obedience would make us everlastingly fruitful for the Kingdom of God in ways we might never imagine, and our joy in Him would be eternal. This is the allure of knowing God intimately and submitting to Him in reckless faith.

SACRAMENT AND CELEBRATION

Following priests into a held-back river along with hundreds of thousands of other hurrying people required a different kind of risk than would be asked of God's soldiers next. Even building the stone memorial in the new camp was a corporate celebration of faith distinct from the individual acts of faith that were to come.

God had called a people to Himself, the descendants of one man, Abraham. These descendants had now become a huge nation comprised of twelve tribes, hundreds of clans, and thousands of particular families, along with many non-Hebraic servants and other Gentiles attached to the Israelite community. But God was also interested in forming and perpetuating an intimate relationship with each individual, promising to be God to him and to his family, and requiring of him obedience to His laws and purposes. The sign of this intimacy, the covenant token God gave to Abraham that was to be bestowed on all his dependents and descendants for all generations to come, was circumcision.

Circumcision refers to the surgical procedure of cutting away the foreskin from a male's reproductive organ. Performed on all Hebrew boys when they were eight days old, this rite symbolized the purification from sin required by a holy God as He drew into relationship with Himself an unholy people. The physical removal of "unclean" flesh stood for the inner purging of a person's heart, which had been made unclean by sin. Moses referred to this symbolism when he instructed the people, "Circumcise your hearts, therefore, and do not be stiff-necked any longer" (Deut. 10:16). Touching the very core of masculine identity and procreativity, circumcision reminded the boy (as he grew to manhood) and all those who had witnessed his circumcising that everyone's sin requires the shedding of blood if it is to be washed away. Prefiguring the blood shed by Christ to take away sin, circumcision acknowledged each person's dependence on and submission to Yahweh to cleanse his heart and to sustain the covenant connection.

This heart-cleansing symbolized by circumcision was required of all who wished to be intimately yoked with a sinless God. It's interesting that the covenant sign of oneness with Yahweh was applied not only to Abraham's personal offspring but to all of his household. "Whether born in your household or bought with your money, [every male who is eight days old] must be circumcised," God instructed Abraham (Gen. 17:13). In other words, Gentiles were included in the covenant from the beginning, their relationship to Yahweh being established by their connection with Abraham's family and their trust in the God who had chosen this family as His people (see Gen. 12:3). The covenant was not merely racial (connected genetically to Abraham) but relational (connected to Yahweh by faith in His promises). Yahweh would be God to all who believed in Him, all who were willing to seal their faith by receiving the covenant sign of circumcision.

Thus God's consecrating of a people to Himself was individual as well as corporate; every child born to or bought by or attached by choice to a descendant of Abraham belonged within God's covenant family and was to be marked with circumcision. Though only the boy-child received the physical token, the girl-child was included in the covenant by virtue of her father's circumcision. When these covenant children reached adulthood, they would give evidence of personally accepting their covenant identity and obligations by observing the covenant commandments, receiving forgiveness through the sacrifices offered for sin, and marking their own sons with the bloody sign of circumcision.

Unfortunately God's covenant of circumcision, intended as a perpetual requirement for all of Abraham's seed, had for some reason been neglected during the Israelites' forty years of wandering in the desert. Thus no one (except perhaps Joshua and Caleb) had crossed the flooded Jordan River ceremonially identified as God's man. But as soon as the nation had settled into Gilgal, their new campsite west of the Jordan, God told Joshua to circumcise every soldier before proceeding into battle against the Canaanites. The renewal of this sacrament would represent the people's cleansing in preparation for receiving from Yahweh the land of Canaan that He had promised Abraham (see Gen. 12:7). In contrast to the terrible wickedness of the Canaanite culture, which they would soon destroy, Yahweh's soldiers would inherit the land as cleansed men, having received the covenant sign, embracing even its pain, to declare themselves yoked to God and consecrated to His purposes for them.

Nonetheless, from the standpoint of military strategy, disabling an entire army by circumcising them just before going into battle must have seemed like lunacy, especially considering the overwhelming military odds the Israelites faced as they camped in enemy territory. Even though "they remained where they were in camp until they were healed," it surely meant each man had to believe against all reason that Yahweh's timing regarding this holy but excruciating sacrament was no mistake (Josh. 5:8).

The Israelites' cost of declaring their faith in God was considerable, but after the men had been circumcised, God declared, "Today I have rolled away the reproach of Egypt from you." The disgrace associated with the Israelites' former identity as slaves was dismantled forever by their receiving in their bodies the sign of Yahweh's cleansing of their hearts. Moreover, the event would be memorialized for centuries to come by the naming of their camp "Gilgal," which "sounds like the Hebrew for *roll*."[2] Dwelling in Gilgal would for many years signify resting in grace.

But there was another purpose God had in telling Joshua to make flint knives and circumcise the Israelites. Circumcision was a God-ordained prerequisite for the celebration of the Passover, which God intended His people to observe before embarking on the conquest of Canaan. Evidently the Israelites had not observed Passover either since their sojourn at Sinai, and God wanted to remind them not only that they were yoked exclusively to Him (in circumcision), but also that He would exercise the same power to deliver Canaan into their hands as He had exercised in freeing them from their Egyptian abusers (which Passover commemorated).

Therefore, on the first day in Canaan, even before the men were circumcised, every Israelite family chose a baby lamb or kid from their flocks and brought it into their home to live for four days, making it a family pet for a time. On the evening of the fourth day (the designated time for Passover), while the men were still in postoperative pain from circumcision, each family sorrowfully killed the baby animal that had been living with them, and marked their tents with its blood. This ceremony, fraught with the ambivalence of sadness and rejoicing, reminded the Israelites of their deliverance from their death-bound slavery in Egypt. It also prefigured the eventual death of the future "Joshua"—Jesus, "the Lamb of God, who takes away the sin of the world" (see John 1:29). This death would also be marked with ambivalence, for God's unspeakable sorrow in sacrificing His Son would mingle with His joy at receiving back to His embrace His rebellious children, bought from the bondage of sin by the blood of His Son.

Finally, "the day after the Passover, that very day, [the Israelites] ate some of the produce of the land: unleavened bread and roasted grain. The manna stopped the day after they ate this food from the land; there was no longer any manna for the Israelites, but that year they ate of the produce of Canaan" (Josh. 5:11–12). The Israelites' new life in the new land had begun.

And if God's people could have seen it from their tents' blood-spattered doorways in Gilgal, they might have caught the symbolism of Rahab's blood-red cord suspended from her Jericho window as she awaited her own deliverance from death. God had extended His love to this undeserving woman for His own purposes, just as He had extended His love to Abraham's undeserving progeny for His own purposes. How inscrutable are God's thoughts and His ways past comprehension! Yet now His glory—which is the truest reality of all—was about to shine in a new way in a world of desperate darkness. The second generation of Israelites had passed the test of faith and obedience, which their parents had failed many years earlier. And now the two sacraments, circumcision and Passover, had prepared God's people outside Jericho's walls for their role in displaying that glory.

GLORY IN DEATH

The events that display God's glory often occur in the most unlikely ways and places, and He uniquely draws each of us to abandon our lives to Him according to His own larger method and timetable. Usually in fact we are unable to either predict or understand how God will be glorified by particular circumstances or losses in our world or in our own lives. Such was the experience of both Martha and her sister Mary when their brother, Lazarus, died after a brief illness. (This story is recorded in John 11:1–44.)

The sisters had sent for Jesus, the Healer, when Lazarus took sick, of course. More than once they had seen His power over disease and they knew their brother would be healed if Jesus could get to his bedside in time. But Jesus, on receiving the message that His beloved friend was sick, had said to His disciples, "This sickness will not end in death. No, it is for God's glory so that God's Son may be glorified through it." That is why, although "Jesus loved Martha and her sister and Lazarus," He nonetheless "stayed where he was two more days" before heading for their home in Bethany. In the meantime Lazarus died and was placed in a cave, sealed inside by a huge stone, bound by death and by layers of linen strips wound around his body.

If Martha and Mary had known Jesus was purposely delaying His return, would they not have doubted that He truly loved them and Lazarus? From their perspective, Jesus' healing of Lazarus was the best possible event that

123

could have occurred. Even God's glory may not have seemed to them a better purpose than restoring their brother to health. They might have argued that the healing of Lazarus would in itself reveal the glory of God and of His Son Jesus.

The question is age-old and will not go away: How can something bad or painful have a positive purpose in God's overall plan? How could the physical pain of circumcision or the emotional pain of a loved one's death turn to God's glory? What kind of a God is He after all? For that is always the deeper question—Is God good or not?

When Jesus finally arrived at the funeral wake of His dear friend, both Martha and Mary affirmed His power, each declaring to Him individually, "Lord, if you had been here, my brother would not have died." Even some of the professional Jewish mourners, seeing Jesus' tears at Lazarus's grave, said, "Could not he who opened the eyes of the blind man have kept this man from dying?" Many believed in Christ's power to heal. But did they trust in His goodness?

The faith of Lazarus's sisters and of their friends regarding what Jesus could have done stopped short of expecting He could or would do anything more now that Lazarus was in the grave. How natural that they did not expect Lazarus's immediate resurrection. We too would doubt in similar circumstances. After all, the percentage of dead persons who have come back to life again is exceedingly small.

But what we all forget is that God's plans are far larger than our own, and He will do for His own glory and for our good such things as we cannot imagine, for they are beyond the explanation of natural cause or common sense. God makes a dry path through sea and raging river, walks on waves, and calms storms. Forces far greater than wind and water are subject to His word. Shattered families are restored. Fiercely destructive habits are broken. Terrible crimes are forgiven by the victims of those crimes. Hard hearts are softened, and love overcomes hate. Prostitutes become women of purity, and murderers become zealous to protect instead of to destroy life. The same power that heartened Israelites and amazed disciples has not diminished in the least.

Nor has the purpose of that power changed over the centuries. "Fear the LORD your God," Moses instructed the Israelites (Deut. 6:13). This fear, which Scripture commands us to have toward God, however, is not the terror of judgment or annihilation but a holy awe and wholehearted obedience, offered to our heavenly Father in response to His love for us. Jesus then and now, even Yahweh of old, is bent on displaying who He is so that His people's faith will grow, their love will be enlarged, their obedience will become more ready, and His own glory will shine in His world. Thus the final end of our righteous fear will be to show forth God's glory.

124

In every situation, therefore, Christ Jesus, for the revelation of His Father's glory, invites us—woos us, really—to rest our faith in Him, not in ourselves nor in someone or something else. This He did at Lazarus's grave site, instructing those present to remove the stone from in front of the cave's entrance. Martha objected, however, accurately reminding Jesus that "by this time there is a bad odor, for he [Lazarus] has been there four days." From Martha's perspective, not only did the situation seem impossible, but Jesus' request seemed unpleasant, repugnant, even pointless. Why add insult to injury, disgust to sorrow? Why not simply accept the loss and get on with life?

But Jesus had another agenda, and He would not be deterred. "Did I not tell you," He asked Martha, "that if you believed, you would see the glory of God?" That is to say, if Martha would allow Jesus to disturb her brother's dead body, He would allow her to see God's goodness, the glory of His grace. *Which is greater,* God is always asking His children, *your comfort or the greater purposes of My plan?* Will we do what He asks with reckless indifference to its seeming foolishness or will we insist on playing it "safe and sane"? Responding in faith to Jesus' love and tears, Martha instructed that the stone be rolled back, reopening the tomb of her dead brother. Everyone waited expectantly, wondering what Jesus would do next.

Looking up, Jesus first thanked His Father for answering His prayer, so that the faith of those around Him would be strengthened. Then He shouted, "Lazarus, come out!" The people must have thought He was crazy—they had seen with their own eyes a dead body carried into that tomb.

But out Lazarus did come, somehow finding his way to daylight, "his hands and feet wrapped with strips of linen, and a cloth around his face"— looking just the way he had when they had buried him four days earlier, except now he was moving on his own. Clumsily he emerged, the onlookers no doubt instinctively backing away, for who had ever seen such a thing before? Besides, Lazarus *did* smell bad. More than that, who wanted to become ceremonially unclean by coming in contact with a dead body—if it *was* a dead body—who could tell? How could the Jews unravel *this* theological dilemma? No one had categories for comprehending so remarkable a revelation of the glory of God.

Nevertheless, Jesus offered those present yet another invitation to faith. Calling the dispersing crowd to come back closer to Lazarus, despite the risk of contamination and the odor of death, Jesus presented him to the people and said, "Take off the grave clothes and let him go." Lazarus could not unbind himself, and though only God could release a man from the bondage of death, He would allow His people to help unbind the released prisoner from the shackles he still wore.

We all bear the consequences of our early losses and disappointments, and it is in the context of the love and encouragement of community that we find the healing and hope only God can give. God's larger purposes involve revealing His glory by allowing His people to cooperate in the completion of His work of deliverance in the lives of others, as well as through miraculous intervention that reveals His goodness. Joshua would complete God's salvation begun by Moses. The Israelite community would embrace Rahab, the former prostitute. Lazarus's sisters and their friends would complete the task begun by Jesus' work of resurrection. And God would be glorified through it all, because it is the work of His own Holy Spirit in us that enables us to cooperate with His work in others.

SAFETY OVER REST

For this too is the allure of reckless faith—the adventure of partnering with God for His glory. What humility God exercises in allowing us to show forth His glory when we submit ourselves to His plan and play whatever role He asks us to play, no matter how mundane or unpleasant that role may seem to us. When we humble ourselves to receive His grace and then offer it to others, we too participate in showing forth the glory of His love. Would that we more regularly believed God can bring good out of evil and can use us in the process, even when we are unable to see that process clearly.

All too often, however, we forget that God is up to something far bigger than we can imagine. We are so tightly bound not merely by our human frailty but by our smallness of vision. The here and now of our lives and our preoccupation with personal comfort and hassle-free relationships keep us from perceiving—let alone embracing—God's larger picture. Even though our underside view of God's purposes prevents us from fully comprehending the majesty of God's tapestry, our greater failure is that we forget there is a tapestry, and we can't imagine that our particular thread is important to the beauty of the whole. Then, when we forget, we fail to rest in God, choosing instead to trust our own devices.

This is what happened to Peter in the hours after he and the other disciples had celebrated their last Passover with Jesus in the upper room. Christ had just spoken to them again about His approaching betrayal and death, but somehow it was not taking hold of their perception of reality. They did not want Jesus to die, could not conceive of His death, would not believe that He *had* to die. Christ's earthly kingdom and their place in it were far more real to them than the truth spoken to them by the rabbi from Nazareth.

Thus, even when they left Jerusalem and made their way to the familiar olive grove opposite the city, the disciples' hearts were focused more on Jesus' earthly kingdom than on the danger about which He had so recently spoken. True, Peter loved Jesus passionately and had sworn to defend Him with his life, showing his Lord the sword he carried for just that purpose. And Peter, James, and John had agreed to pray with and for Jesus when they arrived at Gethsemane, for their hearts had become intimately knit with His over the three years of His public ministry. But their Master's struggle was one these men could not have fully discerned.

How could they have known what His death would cost Him, even beyond the physical agony of crucifixion? Who saw the sweat fall like drops of blood on the ground as He prayed while they slept? Who heard His pleas that another cup of sorrow replace the one He had agreed to drink immeasurable eons ago? Who saw or could have understood the angel's ministry to Him in His extremity? Even if Jesus' special friends had not given in to the utter fatigue of their uncertainty and grief, could they possibly have understood the dreadful drama about to unfold amidst the ancient olive trees?

Was this a test of their trust in Jesus? Without a doubt. Judas had failed the test, choosing to betray his Lord with a kiss. But could not Peter have chosen to rest in Jesus' words instead of resorting to slicing off Malchus's ear with a sword when the soldiers came to arrest Jesus? Of course. Could the others have stayed in Gethsemane to encourage their Lord when He was seized, instead of running to save their own skins? Certainly.

But this test of faith was one that God Himself would pass if they failed—which they did and which all of us do in one way or another. Jesus would remain true to God's call on His life, His faith in His Father's goodness the most passionately reckless of all. Though all His disciples forsook Him, Jesus allowed Himself to be taken into a custody He would not physically survive. Allured by the joy of reuniting us to God, Christ yielded to His ardent desire to obey His Father, enduring the cross, unabashed by its shame (see Ps. 40:8; Heb. 10:5–7; 12:2). God's anointed Son would rest in His Father's plan, though it meant He would die, and in this dying be separated from the Father He loves with an eternal, incomprehensible abandon.

Jesus would not fail the test of rest, and the wonder of the gospel is that His "passing grade" becomes ours as well. The disciples' failure would cause them (and their Lord) much grief, but it would not cost them their salvation, for that salvation was won by the very death from which they fled in the Garden of Gethsemane. When we forget who we are and fail to rest in the One who loves us, we do harm to our souls but, because of the cross, we are not destroyed.

No one is exempt from having to take the test of rest—not Joshua nor Rahab nor the Israelite soldiers nor Mary nor Martha nor Peter nor the disciples nor you nor I. We all will be asked to trust God and obey what He says. Our exemption is not from the taking of the test, nor is it from the failing of the test, for all have sinned and come short of trusting and glorifying God in all we do. But there is one kind of exemption for all who believe, if we will receive it from God's hands. It is the gracious exemption from the eternal consequences of our failure, for our faith is the channel by which the Father views us as righteous because the Son is righteous and stands in our place.

Jesus had said to the grieving Martha outside her home, "I am the resurrection and the life. He who believes in me will live, even though he dies; and whoever lives and believes in me will never die" (John 11:25–26). This "never die" refers not to our physical life but to our hope for eternal life, secured by Jesus' willing sacrifice of Himself in our place to restore us to His Father. From before the foundation of the earth the Triune God had intended not to terrorize us with His holiness but to love us back into relationship with Himself through the gospel of salvation through Christ's atonement. Our faith in Jesus' death on our behalf is able to banish our greatest terror, so that even our own physical death can be welcomed as a doorway into an eternal life of intimacy with God. Acknowledging our unrighteousness and receiving the grace of God's forgiveness in Christ is our only hope.

FAITH TO WAIT

Yet how hard it is to live at the mercy of grace. We'd rather be strong than helpless, offerers not askers, forgivers rather than suppliants. As much as we are drawn to abandon our hearts to God in response to His love, somehow it goes against our grain to need instead of earn. It feels more comfortable to be one up in our relationships, not indebted to someone else. Grace, though we know we can't live without it, is often hard to receive.

It is, no doubt, a control issue with us. Few things frighten or dismay us like sensing that our lives are out of our control. Bill and I discovered at different times and in different ways in the midst of our marital turmoil that giving up control and receiving grace—from God or from each other—was one of the most difficult things we had to do. We had become experts at managing our lives and defending our own behavior, and it felt altogether foreign to rest in God instead of in our own resources. God had to substantially disrupt our marriage before we became ready to leave our wilderness of self-sufficiency behind.

We did not cross the Jordan together, Bill and I. When I was forced to come out of denial regarding Bill's alcoholism, I was plunged into recognizing how helpless I really was. I could not change Bill's heart; only God could. I could not even change my own heart; only God could. And in my struggle to let Him be in charge of both of us, I began to have brief periods when I rested in Him and not in myself nor in Bill. Once in a while I'd catch a vision of myself as the Father's beloved daughter or as the Bridegroom's beautiful betrothed. The cherishing I had demanded from Bill I continued to desire from him but I came to depend increasingly on God's cherishing when Bill was not able to give it to me. These glimpses of rest were preparation for my Jordan crossing, for they encouraged me to behave like a spiritual daughter of Sarah, who put her hope in God and did not give way to fear (see 1 Peter 3:5–6).

The test of rest came for me at one of the lowest points in my life with Bill. I stood on the banks of the raging river of his refusal to face his alcoholism and I wanted to give up and go back to being in charge again—at least of my own life. Desperate for relief from my pain and waiting, I left home for a weekend by myself and dreamed of separating from Bill and starting over.

But God had other plans. He wanted me to walk into the seemingly impossible, to commit my life anew to this man, realizing I was likely to live the rest of my life covenantally bound to a man who would not meet my God-given longing for protection and cherishing and sacrificial love. I did not think I would survive such an existence, but God made it clear to me that this was the Jordan River He wanted me to set my foot into, with no guarantee of the outcome other than His presence with me no matter what happened. He wanted me to focus on His plan for me, not on what He might or might not do in Bill.

I could feel the menacing waves lap at my feet as my Father invited me to trust in His goodness and not in my own strength or survival mechanisms. Would I be daughter or rebel? In anguish I cried out the words of Moses, "If your Presence does not go with [me], do not send [me] up from here" (Exod. 33:15)! And when He assured me again of His commitment to my good, I walked into the flood, not without fear but willing to trust Him to sustain my life in the midst of my fear, knowing I would not be destroyed.

The next day I returned to my marriage, achingly lonely but knowing I was not alone. I had set foot in a small corner of the promised land of God's rest.

Bill, however, did not inhabit the same land yet, nor was there assurance that he ever would. He was still angry, still rebelling against what I was inviting him to do, still refusing to believe God wanted his hard heart so He could change it to a son's soft heart. So I lived alone in the land, struggling to rest more and more not in Bill but in God. True to His Word, the Father was with me, but I missed Bill terribly. There are few experiences more exquisitely painful than spouses sharing a house without sharing their hearts. It is not God's way, and I was unspeakably lonely.

Bill's Jordan test came months later, when something I did infuriated him and he headed purposefully down the hallway of our home to our bedroom, intending to pack his bags and leave. Neither of us can say what happened in his heart while I sat crying, waiting to hear the door slam behind his leave-taking. But when he walked back down the hallway, he came to me on the patio instead of going to the front door, and something was profoundly different in him. His anger had melted, replaced by sorrow over having hurt me. He admitted he was mystified by and helpless before his own rage and he wanted help in sorting out his life. I had to tell Bill I could not help him, and he acknowledged that this Jordan crossing had to be his own step of faith in God and he would not demand that I help him in it.

129

Bill had decided, as I had earlier decided, to stay in the marriage and strug-gle to heal our brokenness. This was God's work in him—Christ's presence in him revealing itself to me. And though I was hesitant to trust overmuch in Bill's change of heart, I knew to thank God for my husband's words, which affirmed his hatred of the sin he saw in himself. For this hatred of sin could not have come from himself. It was the Holy Spirit's work I was seeing in him, and my glimpse of God's glory in this once-raging man caused me to stand in awe of the Father's work.

And so it was that Bill joined me in God's land of rest, becoming cir-cumcised of heart and recommitting himself to God and to me. Together we observed a most tentative Passover, afraid to hope for too much, yet both willing to need the grace we had tasted. It was good to have him with me.

Nonetheless, we were painfully aware there were still giants in the land—most notably his addiction to alcohol and mine to self-sufficiency. Our sep-arate Jordan crossings had been only the first steps on a long and perilous journey. We were different people at eighteen years of marriage than we had been when our journey into change had begun three and a half years earlier. To be sure, our identity in Christ was more clear to us both. But how we were to live that out was far from clear to either of us.

A Chosen Yoking

Entering rest is not just a onetime event but a continuing *walk* of faith. It is a process begun when we open our hearts to God's forgiveness in Christ, but it is also an ongoing journey built on the confidence "that he who began a good work in [us] will carry it on to completion until the day of Christ Jesus" (Phil. 1:6). Our walk of faith in this life will not be one of perfect obedience, because the enemy of our souls retains strongholds in our hearts that must be torn down gradually over time. There are walled cities yet to be taken by our ongoing dependence on God's power in us, and in all too many circumstances we refuse to rest in God, relying instead on ourselves or someone else. Consequently our passion to respond to Jesus' invitation of rest must be reaffirmed time and again.

The rest Jesus offered His followers made use of a familiar agricultural image (Matt. 11:28–30). He said, "Come to me, all you who are weary and burdened, and I will give you rest." If He had stopped there, we might have assumed He would take away all our troubles and we would live the remain-der of our lives with no fatigue, no burdens, nothing to bother us ever again.

But this is not what Jesus meant by rest. When the Israelites crossed the Jordan, they were consecrated by circumcision and Passover not to a life of ease but to a life of struggle and warfare. Martha and her sister faced sor-row and death, though they were deeply connected to Jesus. Peter experi-enced the misguidedness and the failure of his faith when he ran from the

Garden of Gethsemane. Bill and I had much work to do when we recommitted our hearts to God and to one another. What, then, did Jesus mean when He promised us rest?

The imagery in Jesus' next words is most instructive. "Take my yoke upon you," Jesus said, "and learn from me." A yoke is an implement for farm animals, a piece of wood shaped to fit their necks or shoulders, linking them together for plowing or pulling loads. Usually a yoke was forced on the draft animals by their owner, but Jesus makes it clear that His yoke, a figurative image of our being bonded to Him, is to be a received yoke, a chosen yielding, a willing submission to Him. Those who are drawn into the joy of trinitarian love will be yielding to the allure of *taking* Jesus' yoke, receiving the "rest" of going wherever He directs, and learning from Him how He wore His own chosen submission to His Father's leading. God will not force either our obedience or our love, for neither is genuine unless it is gladly given.

This is the incredible humility of our God—that He woos but does not force. God surely has the power to coerce our obedience. But because He is a person who loves, not a tyrant who compels or a puppeteer who controls, He invites us to choose His yoke as an act of responsiveness to His initiating love. Our willingness to rest in Him and to yield to the yoke of His passion for us must flow from our desire to please the One whom we love because He first loved us. In this way, we make complete the circle of trust and obedience and reciprocal love flowing within and from our incredible God.

However, because of our losses and habits of self-protection, we often find ourselves terrified of being at the mercy of God, even though we have had rich tastes of His forgiveness and grace. And if we are going to accept Christ's yoke, we will have to make a conscious, faith-filled choice to move into our terror and stretch our necks to receive His yoke of oneness time and again, in spite of our fear. We can't stop being afraid, but we can admit our fear to Him and still choose to follow Him wherever He leads us.

This the Israelites did when they crossed the Jordan into the "rest" of fighting for Canaan—the warfare to which God had called them. This was the connection of love to which Jesus' disciples, male and female, submitted when they aligned themselves with Him. And this is what Bill and I did as we made our individual Jordan crossings and entered a new kind of fray in which we would be allies instead of antagonists.

Being linked in relationship with God to accomplish His purposes is seldom restful in the usual sense of the word. Rather, it represents a willingness to follow Jesus' example by abiding in God's love and submitting our own agenda to our Father's eternal plans, exchanging our own ideas of fulfillment for His redemptive purposes, and sacrificing our own personal comfort to the greater good of His glory. Our rest will not be in our achieving, our circumstances, or our good intentions, nor can it be in ourselves or in someone or something else. Rather, we must come to rest more and more

131

in the goodness and forgiveness of the God who loves us. Being yoked to Him will not allow for passivity, but will harness us to Christ as we joyfully labor together for His kingdom in whatever direction He chooses.

We are daily invited to enter our terror and find rest—not in ourselves but only in our oneness with Jesus Christ, who lives within us by faith. If we are yoked to Him for better or worse, reckless in our abandon to His love, our greatest desire will be to glorify Him and to revel in His presence. Surely this will require that we grapple unceasingly with choosing faith over fear, rest over striving, and submission to Christ over self-determination. However, we will also become more and more willing to pay that price.

Receiving Jesus' yoke is always a risky affair, equally so for men and for women, though differently for each one. The next two chapters will explore the perils of living at rest in Christ, first for men (in chapter 7), and then for women (in chapter 8). Willing submission to the yoke of the Savior is not easy for any of us, as we shall see.

QUESTIONS TO CONSIDER

1. What biblical characters "passed God's test of rest" by obeying Him in spite of difficult or dangerous circumstances?

2. Describe a time when you obeyed God and someone else's life was blessed because of your obedience.

3. What in your experience corresponds to Martha's reluctance to open the tomb of her brother, Lazarus, as Jesus asked her to do?

4. How would you answer someone who believes God is not good because so many bad things happen in our world?

5. What help might your church give to those who are "bound in the grave clothes" of past sin or trauma or addiction?

6. How have you reacted when, like Peter, you have deserted Christ out of fear for your own well-being?

Regarding the opening story:

Brian is not finding his waiting and wooing to be without suffering. He must wonder often how the pain of his loneliness will fit into God's larger story.

7. In what way could Brian be said to be yielding to "the allure of reckless faith" regarding his marriage? Would you encourage or discourage his choice?

Chapter Seven

Movement

The Peril in Godly Manhood

Nikki tapped the ash from her cigarette into the elegant milkglass bowl gracing her mother's coffee table, relishing the thought of her parents' helpless irritation when they returned from vacation and discovered her violation of their no-smoking rule. She would be long gone by then, of course. Eddie was due any minute, and the two of them would be halfway to Colorado before her parents would discover she had left. Nikki's satisfaction at deceiving them brought a wry smile to her face. "I'll run my own life, whether they want me to or not," she congratulated herself.

Then the memory intruded itself again, as it had several times in the days since she'd decided to run away. In her mind's eye she saw her father straining toward her, relief flooding his face and overflowing his eyes. "Oh, Nikki, honey," he was saying as he scooped her sobbing seven-year-old frame into his strong arms. "I'm so glad we found you!" Then, hugging her close, he was repeating over and over into her tangled hair, "I'll never let you get lost ever again, sweetheart. Daddy will always protect you, always protect you, always protect you."

133

The memory gradually faded like exhaled smoke, and Nikki's mind went to other more recent and less comforting scenarios—her anger at her father's endless business travel and sports preoccupation, the spiteful arguments with her mother, the hours spent in her bedroom alternately seething and crying. Nikki's resentment built again as she crushed out her cigarette with unnecessary force and walked to the front window. Eddie was no prize but he was her ticket out of town. She could ignore his drinking and occasional violence if he would just take her away.

Why, then, this ambivalence? Staring unseeingly at the front yard, Nikki thought of the cartoon she once saw of a young child standing on his mother's dresser, ready to jump down into a blanket held on four corners by his little friends, one of whom was saying, "Someone ought to stop us before we hurt ourselves."

That's how Nikki felt, suddenly wishing her father would surprise her by coming home early to protect her from her own foolishness. "Daddy, where are you?" The sound of her own voice startled her, and she felt tears welling up in her eyes.

Just then, Nikki's musing was interrupted by three insistent honks coming from the driveway. Eddie had arrived, and her father had not come home. She grabbed her purse and headed for the door.

Children never outgrow their longing to be protected by the strength of their fathers. For girls, especially, knowing there is a good man guarding them from damage—physical, emotional, or sexual—establishes a security essential to the confidence necessary for them to face the world's evil and unpredictability. Eventually a girl's desire for protection is transferred from her father to her husband or to other good men in her life, but until then, her father is her main man.

God's own commitment to protect His people from evil and to establish righteousness and justice in His world is intended to be emulated by His image-bearers—men in particular. When they make every effort to provide safe places for their families, churches, and the broader community of human culture, God's own nature shines through them, and genuine rest becomes possible. And when they fail to make this effort, there are always some who suffer.

The two preceding chapters (chapters 5 and 6) dealt with two requirements for entering the rest God promises to those who come to Him in faith: humility to receive from Him what we cannot procure for ourselves and an abandon to His leading that will demand our faith in both His power and His goodness. This chapter focuses on the risks required of men when they rest in God, and the next chapter will examine the distinctive risks asked of women when they move into God's rest.

✎

Joshua was on his face, nose to dust, not in subjugation but in obeisance. Before him stood the tall figure of an armed man, sword at the ready. Behind the figure rose the city walls of Jericho, gates closed tightly against any who might go in or out, its inhabitants and king drained of courage in the face of the Israelites' miraculous crossing of the Jordan River. Joshua's prebattle reconnaissance of the Canaanite stronghold had been interrupted by the sudden appearance of this formidable warrior. (This encounter is described in Joshua 5:13–15.)

It was not that Joshua had given way to fear of someone larger or more adequately armed than he. Israel's commander in chief was no coward. He had followed protocol, approaching the figure with the appropriate question for establishing identity: "Are you for us or for our enemies?" he had asked. He'd been ready to face either Israelite or Canaanite but he was not prepared for the answer he had received.

"Neither," the man had retorted sharply, "but as commander of the army of the LORD I have now come." That is when Joshua had dropped to the ground. He had heard Yahweh's voice before, but this was the first time he had seen His appearing. Israel's military leader knew the commander of God's celestial hosts outranked him hands down, and he was, after all, a very good soldier. He would do what he was told.

"What message does my Lord have for his servant?" asked Joshua, speaking facedown. Yoked to God and to His purposes, Joshua would go in whatever direction God might point through the armed warrior at whose feet he bowed. And God's commander replied with the same words once spoken to Moses, "Take off your sandals, for the place where you are standing is holy." Worship of Yahweh was the first order of the day, and Joshua shed his battle shoes in reverence and awe. Like Moses before him, he would do what God wanted him to do, despite the risk. Unlike Moses, however, he didn't first argue with God. Joshua's mentor had taught him well.

And so on holy ground Joshua received his instructions for taking the city of Jericho. The stage was set for the war to begin, the war that would not only afford the multitude of God's people a place of rest from their enemies but would also reveal the omnipotent glory of Yahweh Himself. Jericho's residents were right to be terrified. The God of the universe was about to do battle with them!

HOLY ZEAL

What might have gone through Joshua's mind when the Lord's commander said he was neither for Israel nor for Israel's enemies? Why hadn't the commander of God's army declared himself *for* Israel and *against* Canaan?

Certainly God's invisible angelic force was an entity distinct from Israel's army camped at Gilgal, and God's cosmic warfare far exceeds the scope or even the grasp of the best military strategist. His celestial army has purposes—then and now—which no mortal man can comprehend. In terms of identity, the commander of the Lord's army was neither Israelite nor Canaanite.

But was Yahweh's supernatural army neutral in this war about to be fought? Surely the presence of this heavenly commander reminded Joshua that God Himself had promised His people: "I will send my terror ahead of you and throw into confusion every nation you encounter. I will make all your enemies turn their backs and run" (Exod. 23:27). God was *not* neutral about the events soon to take place in Canaan, since He was going to defeat Israel's enemies for them. What, then, did God want Joshua to understand before outlining His battle plan against Jericho?

In order to comprehend God's "position" regarding the Israelites' war against Canaan, we must understand His purpose for ordaining that war. Undergirding the divine purpose, of course, is the divine character, so we must first consider just what kind of God Yahweh is. Of particular importance are His attributes of holiness and justice.

The holiness of God is impossible for us to fully understand, compromised as we are by the inescapable presence of moral corruption. As Bible scholar A. W. Tozer has written, "only the Spirit of the Holy One can impart to the human spirit the knowledge of the holy."[1] And when God's Spirit *does* impart to us intimations of His holiness, the experience inevitably undoes us. "Woe to me!" cried the prophet Isaiah when he saw the vision of the Holy One. "I am ruined! For I am a man of unclean lips, and I live among a people of unclean lips, and my eyes have seen the King, the LORD Almighty" (Isa. 6:5). The brilliance of Yahweh's holiness blinds us, for He is "the absolute quintessence of moral excellence, infinitely perfect in righteousness, purity, rectitude, and incomprehensible holiness."[2] No wonder Isaiah was undone. And no wonder Joshua was on his face before the holy commander of Yahweh's army.

Moreover, because God is holy, the universe He created in perfection has a moral dimension "built into" it from the beginning of time. Even when evil entered our world through Adam and Eve's fall into sin, morality was not destroyed, though a moral "disease" infected our entire world, posing a deadly threat to our survival. And because God is both holy (by nature incapable of evil) and loving (caring for His fallen image-bearers), He wages unrelenting war against this wickedness wherever it exists in His universe. It is a warfare we usually cannot observe but it rages invisible and unheard at every moment.

A. W. Tozer uses the metaphor of terminal illness to describe God's hatred toward the moral disease of sin.

Since God's first concern for His universe is its moral health, that is, its holiness, whatever is contrary to this is necessarily under His eternal displeasure. To preserve His creation God must destroy whatever would destroy it. . . . He hates iniquity as a mother hates the polio that would take the life of her child. . . . Every wrathful judgment in the history of the world has been a holy act of preservation.[3]

In other words, when God moves in holy zeal against the evil in our world, He is acting in our best interest and in the best interest of His entire creation. He is also acting in perfect consistency with another of His attributes: His inescapable justice. Justice has to do with moral equity or rightness, and as God's image-bearers, we too are designed to long for justice to triumph over injustice. Even our children complain, "That's not fair!" and demand that wrong be set right. This call for justice is the heart's cry that the moral order God built into the universe would prevail.

And because God gets to be God, and because He is zealous for righteousness to reign in His world, His justice *will* ultimately prevail. All unrighteousness will be called to account when Christ returns in His glory, overthrowing evil and ushering in God's eternal Kingdom. But even before Christ's eventual second coming, God sometimes intervenes in human history to right certain wrongs that would otherwise destroy our world. This He did, for example, with the universal flood in Noah's day, and with the destruction of the wicked cities of Sodom and Gomorrah in Abraham's day. This He also planned to do with the decadent people of the land of Canaan.

God is decidedly not neutral about sin. When the figure before Joshua announced himself as commander of the Lord's army, he was declaring that the approaching war against Canaan was not a national conflict nor even a territorial dispute. This war would carry out God's divine justice against moral depravity gone utterly amok. The Israelite army, in destroying the Canaanites and their corrupt culture, would be God's vehicle for bringing His justice to bear against a desperately evil and unrepentant segment of human society.

Deserving Judgment

What had the Canaanites done that was so bad? Sometimes we recoil from the notion that God commissioned the Israelites to devote to the Lord all living beings in Canaan, referring to "the irrevocable giving over of things or persons to the LORD, often by totally destroying them."[4] How could God order His chosen people to carry out His divine death sentence against the people of Canaan in hand-to-hand combat? Our Western perception of justice, which is man-centered and preoccupied with individual rights, can easily obscure the larger question of good and evil, right and wrong.

137

God's river of justice cannot be contained in the tiny vessels of our finite perception of what is "fair." Without seeing the Israelites' war in Canaan from God's perspective, we would be tempted to call Him cruel for ordaining it. We would reproach Him for the death of children instead of blaming their deaths on the desperate wickedness in the land, which had reached its fullness and had become so degrading that the culture itself was self-destructing. When we question God's kindness, we not only lie about the nature of God, but we also fail to comprehend the depth of the wrong in Canaan that cried out for the justice that would make things right.

Actually the Canaanites' degeneracy had been intensifying for centuries. Some four hundred years earlier God had spoken with Abraham about the sin of the Canaanites (or Amorites, as they were then called). "In the fourth generation your descendants will come back here [to Canaan]," God had told Abraham, *"for the sin of the Amorites has not yet reached its full measure"* (Gen. 15:16, emphasis added). In other words, the Amorites/Canaanites would have four generations in which to repent before God would intervene. If they refused to repent, God would drive them out of the land, not only to make way for Abraham's descendants but also to finally punish them for having utterly abandoned themselves to wickedness and decadence.

This four-hundred-year period of grace ended when God yoked Moses to Himself for the purpose of delivering His people from Egypt. Now, forty years after their deliverance, the Israelites themselves were being yoked to God for the purpose of carrying out His judgment against the rampant evil in the land of Canaan.

Considering the severity of God's judgment on the Canaanites, their wickedness in their culture must have been very great. What exactly was the nature and extent of that wickedness?

Sexual Perversity

For one thing, the moral decline of the Canaanites had mired them in the abasement of sexual perversion and unbridled promiscuity, resulting in the predictable moral and physical diseases accompanying that kind of lifestyle. Don Hudson, in the book *The Silence of Adam*, describes how the Canaanite version of the creation story was fashioned according to what Near Eastern men knew about their own hearts. He writes:

> In the ancient Near East, men feared chaos above everything. Men of old lived in perpetual terror of being thrown into chaos at any moment. They lived in fear of famine. They lived in fear of infertility. They lived in fear of marauding enemies. So what did they do with their chaos? They made gods in their image—gods of violence and sexual perversion. And they worshiped

their gods with violence and sexual perversion to appease them, to persuade them to banish the chaos of their world.[5]

Scholars tell us that archeologists "have recovered texts from the ancient Canaanite city-state of Ugarit . . . [which] fully support the Bible's portrait of these tribes."[6] Both Scripture and archeology confirm that the:

gods of the Canaanites were brutal and highly sexed. One myth actually portrays Baal having intercourse with a young cow. Religious rites employed sex between persons not married to each other in order to stimulate the gods and goddesses to grant fertility to the land and to their livestock. . . . The Canaanites even designated homosexual priests and priestesses as their "holy ones." These were employed as cult prostitutes.[7]

These practices, commonplace throughout the land of Canaan, had enmeshed religion with sexual perversion and license—something emphatically forbidden by God. He had said through Moses, "You must not do as they do in Egypt, where you used to live, and you must not do as they do in the land of Canaan, where I am bringing you. Do not follow their practices" (Lev. 18:3).

Yahweh went on to be very specific about the sexual behavior His people were to avoid: "No one is to approach any close relative to have sexual relations," He commanded, naming all the family relationships that must not be sexualized by a man: mother or stepmother, sister or stepsister, granddaughter, aunt, daughter-in-law, sister-in-law, daughter or stepdaughter (Lev. 18:7–17). Then He continued:

Do not have sexual relations with your neighbor's wife and defile yourself with her. . . .

Do not lie with a man as one lies with a woman; that is detestable.

Do not have sexual relations with an animal and defile yourself with it. A woman must not present herself to an animal to have sexual relations with it; that is a perversion.

Do not defile yourselves in any of these ways, because this is how the nations that I am going to drive out before you became defiled.

LEVITICUS 18:20–24

What an indictment! God declared that "all these things" were done by the people living in the land. This was a condition no longer responsive to minor course adjustments in Canaanite culture. This depravity must be purged from the land for, as God rather graphically declared, "Even the land was defiled; so I punished it for its sin, and the land vomited out its inhabitants" (Lev. 18:25).

Satanic Worship

But sexual immorality, vile and violent as it had become in the religious practices of the Canaanites, was coupled with other more decadent and conscience-less sin. Violating the natural bond between parent and child, the Canaanites' religious practices included sacrificing their children to the red-hot arms of their god Molech to appease the idol's wrath and secure its favor. Again, God was adamant to protect His own little ones, commanding the Israelites through Moses, "When you enter the land the LORD your God is giving you, do not learn to imitate the detestable ways of the nations there. Let no one be found among you who sacrifices his son or daughter in the fire" (Deut. 18:9–10). Yahweh demands no such sacrifice from His people, for His own Son is the One who would pass through death for us, that we and our children might live.

No, it was Satan who provoked the Canaanites' debauchery and wickedness, for they had given him entrance to their souls by worshiping demonic powers. "Let no one be found among you," God further warned His people, "who practices divination or sorcery, interprets omens, engages in witchcraft, or casts spells, or who is a medium or spiritist or who consults the dead. . . . The nations you will dispossess listen to those who practice sorcery or divination. But as for you, the LORD your God has not permitted you to do so" (Deut. 18:10–11, 14).

The Canaanites had given themselves over to sexual defilement and the atrocities of demon worship, debasing themselves and dooming their children to physical and moral death. This is the reason God's judgment would fall on them at the hands of the Israelites. "The contrast between the moral and religious vision of the Canaanites and that of the Scripture could hardly be more pronounced," writes one scholar. "The issue at the time of the conquest . . . was whose view of morality, and whose concept of God, would survive. Seen in this perspective, the command to exterminate the Canaanites was not only justified, but necessary for the good of all humanity in the coming ages."[8]

GOD'S CHOOSING

God had consecrated the Israelites through circumcision as a people yoked to Himself and set aside for holiness. In contrast, the Canaanites were a people who, because of their chosen yoking to God's enemy, Satan, had been set apart and devoted to destruction. God intended to demolish all remnants of their evil worship practices, telling His people, "Do not bow down before their gods or worship them or follow their practices" (Exod. 23:24). More than that, Yahweh instructed them to "break down their

140

altars, smash their sacred stones, cut down their Asherah poles and burn their idols in the fire. For you are a people holy to the LORD your God" (Deut. 7:5–6a).

It is not that the Israelites were "a people holy to the LORD" because they were better than the Canaanites, for all mankind is lost in sin and subject to a pell-mell slide into moral decline apart from God's grace. Rather, God had yoked Himself to them in order to draw them to Himself, demonstrating through them His holiness and His righteous justice against evil. Moses had warned the people:

> Do not say to yourself, "The LORD has brought me here to take possession of this land because of my righteousness." No, it is on account of the wickedness of these nations that the LORD is going to drive them out before you. It is not because of your righteousness or your integrity that you are going in to take possession of their land; but on account of the wickedness of these nations, the LORD your God will drive them out before you, to accomplish what he swore to your fathers, to Abraham, Isaac and Jacob.
>
> DEUTERONOMY 9:4–5

The Israelites would destroy the Canaanite culture because of its irredeemable moral decay, not because of their own innate moral superiority. What set the Israelites apart was not their goodness but their chosenness. "The LORD your God has chosen you out of all the peoples on the face of the earth to be his people, his treasured possession," Moses had told them (7:6b). They were descendants of God's chosen servant, Abraham, and God fully intended to keep His covenant promise to Abraham's offspring.

Thus two purposes are clear regarding God's destruction of the Canaanites, and both reveal the very nature of God. First, God in His holiness and justice would use this war to cleanse the land of Canaan from the wickedness of this utterly corrupt culture. Simultaneously He would reveal the glory of His goodness and grace in using this destruction to fulfill His covenant vow of giving Abraham's descendants the newly cleansed land. In this, God brings together both His righteous judgment and His faithful love to establish justice on earth and to reveal His grace to those whom He loves and who love Him in return.

The psalmist acknowledges God's dual purposes with these words celebrating the Israelites' conquest of Canaan:

> We have heard with our ears, O God;
>   our fathers have told us
> what you did in their days,
>   in days long ago.
> With your hand you drove out the nations
>   and planted our fathers;

you crushed the peoples
    and made our fathers flourish.
It was not by their sword that they won the land,
    nor did their arm bring them victory;
it was your right hand, your arm,
    and the light of your face, for you loved them.

Psalm 44:1–3

Not only God's powerful arm but the light of His face was revealed in the destruction of Canaan, for He loved the people He had chosen. They had received the mark of circumcision and had celebrated Passover not as mere rituals but as the joyous coming of Yahweh in His love. This presence of the Holy One had invested symbol and sacrament with meaning and power, and God's people had been changed. Though still ordinary men and women, they were marked as belonging to and empowered by an extraordinary God.

God's destruction of Canaan is a word of warning for us all. Left to ourselves apart from grace, we are as wicked as the Canaanites and deserving of the destruction they experienced. Only God's kindness in wooing us to salvation can redeem us from death and enable us to desire obedience over wickedness. This is the gospel, embraced by the second generation of Israelites out of Egypt, but rejected by the Canaanites, including the inhabitants of Jericho. All, that is, except Rahab and her family, who waited and watched as the Israelites initiated their battle plan to take the city.

Walls Come Down

And a strange battle plan it was. The soldiers of Jericho had the advantage of entrenchment as a hill city with virtually impregnable walls— probably fifteen feet thick and twenty-five feet high, the average size of city walls in that era.[9] What military strategist would have proposed a seven-day plan involving no attempt to storm or breach the walls, and calling for only one day of actual combat?

Yet that is what the commander of the Lord's army instructed Joshua to do. For the first six days the armed men of Israel, in obedience to the divine directive, marched around Jericho once each day, saying nothing and then returning to camp for the night. No weapons were used against the enemy until the seventh day, on which they marched in silence around the city walls seven times instead of once.

These daily marches were not totally silent, however, nor were the soldiers the only ones marching. Central to the battle strategy was the presence of priests carrying the golden ark of the covenant and circling the city of Jericho in the middle of the fighting men. The holy ark was the physical representation of the very presence of Yahweh Himself, signifying the supernatural and sacred nature of this battle. Seven priests heralded the ark's presence by blowing loudly on their trumpets, and the eerie echo bouncing back from Jericho's towering walls was the only sound heard besides the clanking of thousands of weapons as the priests and soldiers circled the city each day.

Finally, on the seventh day, after the army's seventh circuit around the city, Joshua gave a signal, and the silence was shattered by a terrifying blast of the priests' instruments, followed immediately by the battle cries of hundreds of thousands of Israelite men. Suddenly the walls protecting the people of Jericho began to crumble, then collapsed so completely that Yahweh's soldiers could charge straight up the hill and attack the exposed city from every side.

Then, in accordance with God's instructions, the warriors "devoted the city to the LORD and destroyed with the sword every living thing in it—men and women, young and old, cattle, sheep and donkeys" (Josh. 6:21). Only Rahab and her family were spared, delivered to safety by the spies she had rescued, and taken to a place outside Israel's camp. There they would wait and be taught the ways of Yahweh so they could be assimilated into the Israelite culture.

Before the day was out, Jericho was burned. Only the articles of silver, gold, bronze, and iron were saved, brought out and carried into the treasury of the Lord's house. The biblical account of Jericho's destruction concludes with these words, "So the LORD was with Joshua, and his fame spread throughout the land" (v. 27). The war to take Canaan was off to a victorious start, and God's holy judgment against the evil in the land had begun, accomplished by armies angelic and human.

PERSONAL PASSION

The presence of "the army of the LORD" in the taking of Jericho, however, must not keep us from appreciating the risks the Israelites took in fulfilling God's command to totally destroy the evil in the land. Though very few Israelites died during the entire campaign against Canaan, we are not to suppose that God's promise of supernatural help protected His people from the work of fighting this war on His behalf. The Israelites' victory over Jericho had not occurred without each soldier facing the realities of danger, fear, fatigue, injury, and hard work in the winning of it. This was hand-to-hand combat and it required of each man courage, energy, discernment, strength, commitment, and deep faith in Yahweh.

Every moral battle—then and now—involves risk, even though its participants are yoked to God to accomplish His purposes. The fight to destroy evil and make way for holiness is seldom neat or leisurely, whether fought physically in the dusty ruins of an ancient city, or spiritually and morally in the homes and marketplaces of present-day civilization. There is constant cosmic warfare against holiness and grace, and though God's enemy is doomed, his power and influence can yet be felt everywhere. Ever since Adam was placed in the Garden of Eden to "take care of it" (Gen. 2:15)—i.e., to protect it—God's men have been called to wage war against spiritual danger and unrighteousness wherever they find it. Good men long to protect those they love from harm and damage. Often this masculine battle against evil is fierce, and always it is relentless. At stake for these men is the sanctity of their homes, the physical and spiritual well-being of their wives and children, and the establishment and maintenance of a just and righteous society in which the worship of Yahweh can flourish. It is a war rife with danger, and not everyone is willing to risk fighting it.

But the Israelites under Joshua did risk waging the war in Canaan, beginning with the battle for Jericho. Moses had said, "The LORD your God . . . will subdue [the Canaanites] before you. And *you* will drive them out" (Deut. 9:3, emphasis added). It was God's battle, but they had to physically fight it. While their wives and children waited and prayed in the camp at Gilgal, they moved forward to drive out evil from the land. No doubt the swords and spears of their enemies seemed far more real to them than the invisible armament of God's celestial warriors. As mortal men, they took the blows and chased the enemy and defended their comrades and wiped the blood and sweat from their faces and ached from the swinging and plunging of their weapons and nursed their wounds, bruises, and broken bones.

Warfare in ancient times was confusing and noisy and bloody, filled with the horrifying sights and sounds of pain and dying. This was no bomb dropped anonymously out of an airplane. The Israelite soldiers would see their enemies die inches away at the point of their weapons. It was a violent and shockingly in-your-face reality no one can understand who has not seen war up close and personal. Assaulting wickedness with brute force was not easy, was not pretty, was not Sunday-school sanitized. Not only at Jericho but at every battle that would follow in the taking of the land, the Israelite soldiers had to risk moving out of the comfort and safety of camp and into an arena of mortal danger. God's men, when they rested in Him, battled to destroy evil (in themselves and in the world) to bring God glory and to establish His rule in the land He would give them. Not only their life's work (in the fields they would inherit from the Canaanites, for example) but also the well-being of their wives and families would be at stake.

A MAN'S DILEMMA

The risks a man is called to take as he comes to rest his soul in God are far different from the risks most men expect when they consider what it

144

means to live out their masculine identity in today's western culture. A manly man by society's standards is mostly silent, rather aloof, physically and/or socially powerful, and emotionally unflappable. Most men feel they don't really qualify—except for the silent part—but neither are they sure what an alternative model for masculinity might be. Don Hudson, who with his colleague, Al Andrews, conducts seminars on biblical manhood, writes, "We are a generation of men who do not know who we are, why we are here, or where we are going. All of us are on this journey called manhood, but few of us, if we are honest, feel at ease with the path we tread."[10]

In the face of such uncertainty, who is there who can teach a man how to be a man? In today's culture, where fathers are conspicuously absent from so many homes either physically or emotionally, who will model manhood for the sons (and daughters) growing up there? Who will teach our young people what a good man acts like? Even of the fathers who *are* present in their homes, how many are teaching their sons how to be not merely men but godly men? More even than that, who is to say what a godly man is? Except for the record of Christ's life, Scripture is full of stories about men who failed (sometimes in major ways) to maintain their courage or their purity or even at times their faith in God. Is a godly man one who experiences moral victory *most* of the time or in *most* areas of his life? Why was God so willing—even eager—to show us the failures of every man portrayed in the Bible, except for Jesus Christ? What does it mean when we affirm (as Christian psychologist Larry Crabb accurately declares), *"The only way to be manly is first to be godly"*?[11] What does it mean to be a godly man? And how do men get there?

There are no easy answers, no formulas, no package deals for accomplishing the task. For one thing, no two men are the same—not in genetic patterning nor in childhood experiences nor in adult choices. Even those who have taken Jesus' yoke and are indwelt by His Spirit are not alike, though they are one in Him. The Holy Spirit is in the process of conforming each to the image of Christ, but even when they get Home each will reflect Jesus' likeness differently, uniquely.

What is true for all men, however, is that, because they are God's image-bearers, they are designed to make a positive impact in their world, especially in their relationships. As God brought order out of chaos in creating the world, and as He created and entered relationship with beings who would image Him, so men are called to bring order out of chaos in the world and in their relationships, particularly within the intimacy of marriage and in their interactions with their children. Larry Crabb summarized the essence of masculinity as *movement*—or more explicitly, "Spiritual manhood involves the courage to keep on moving—in the middle of overwhelming confusion—toward relationships."[12]

145

The Movement of Men

All men are designed for movement—especially toward relationships—but only God's grace enables a man to make consistently *good* movement into his world. For because of the fallenness of mankind, men often choose bad movement instead of good, and the result is always harmful—damaging to others and destructive of their own souls as well. Who can number the ways a man can move badly? And who would want to name them? Too many of us have experienced them firsthand, and our hearts have not forgotten, though by grace we may have forgiven and been forgiven.

There are many hindrances to a man's good movement, but one of the greatest is fear—fear of failure, fear of being exposed as inadequate, fear of the chaos that looms large without and within. And nowhere is a man's terror of chaos more easily aroused and revealed than in the context of personal relationships.

Men fear and hate chaos because they fear and hate whatever makes them feel out of control. That is why they so often focus their lives primarily on things they *can* control—whatever falls within the realm of their greatest area of competence. They will struggle to become really good at something (or several things), and anything that falls outside that arena of expertise and felt adequacy they try to avoid. My husband, Bill, uses a military analogy, saying, "Once a man has captured the high ground (a hill, for example), he doesn't want to go into the valley to fight at a disadvantage. He will wait for the fight to come to him on his terms." If a thing can't be managed, it will often not be attempted. If a man can't be assured of at least a measure of success, he won't want to step into the ring. He will either turn the other way or convince himself it isn't important or worthy of his effort.

A variation of this theme is to be found in the man who will try anything just to prove he *is* adequate. But even in this case, his attempts are often centered in areas in which he believes himself physically, mentally, or vocationally equipped to make a good showing. His successes bolster what is often a below-the-surface need to prove himself adequate, rather than a confident movement into a challenge to bless others and glorify God. Such men will tackle a task to bring order out of chaos, but it will be a chaos they are pretty sure they can amend.

Unfortunately there are few arenas in life more unmanageably chaotic than relationships. God has created us in His image, free to choose for or against relationship with Him and free to enter or avoid relationship with anyone else. Even within those relationships we choose to forge, we are free to make choices about what to do and who to be. This freedom is very important to us.

What we often forget, however, is that freedom of relational choice is also important to every other person. For this reason, we must not approach any relationship with a management mentality if we want it to thrive. We cannot control spouse or boss or parent or sibling, nor even employee or partner or child or friend. Certainly we cannot control God, either, though that doesn't keep us from sometimes trying.

In many relationships, of course, we can bring to bear consequences for what the other person chooses to be or do. A woman's boss, for example, can try to force her to do something by threatening to fire her—though she can choose to leave the job and trust God for her future if she believes God is leading her to that. Parents can and should bring consequences to bear if their children disobey, but they cannot change the child's heart nor control the child's spirit. A spouse may succeed in pushing his or her partner to begin or stop a certain behavior, but the partner's inner attitude cannot be managed. No one can control another person's will. God has designed each person to carry that responsibility alone.

That is why relationships are so chaotic. They may be entered but they cannot be managed. They may be perpetuated but not predicted. They are responsive to our concern but not to our competence. A person described as "good" at relationships may just be good at appeasing others (or possibly good at manipulating them), rather than being good at nourishing them. This chaos of unmanageability in relationships is frightening, especially when it concerns those we love most. As Larry Crabb says about men:

> We're . . . afraid to face what might happen if a wife, a son or daughter, or a friend slipped out from under our control and stepped forward in his or her unpredictable individuality. . . . We're not sure if we want people to make their own choices as they relate to us. Can we handle what might happen if people close to us actually were freed?[13]

This reality presents a serious problem to someone whose self-image is tied up in a quest for competence and a fear of inadequacy—precisely the predicament in which many men, especially married men, find themselves. Don Hudson confesses about himself, "All my life, I desired—I *begged*—God to remove the chaos of my world so I could become a man. I wanted him to flip a switch in my soul so I could change. I would not move forward in my world until I felt adequate."[14] Don's colleague, Al Andrews, adds:

> When I moved beyond the predictable and into something more chaotic, there was a greater chance that my incompetence would be exposed. I would be more likely to make a fool of myself; there would be a greater possibility of failure. Like most men, I do not enjoy such exposure. It is better to . . . play by the rules, and get through unscathed. Avoid risk. Stay away from chaos.[15]

What a dilemma! The close personal connection that a man naturally desires as God's image-bearer, drawing him to the intimacy of marriage, is the

147

very thing that is least subject to his attempts to prove himself competent. For not only is the relationship itself chaotic in its unpredictability, but the woman in his life is herself more subject to the chaos of emotions and hormones and relational disruption than he is as a man. Unrecognized by both husband and wife, these dynamics often conspire to keep her feeling unloved and him feeling inadequate. What can be done about this catch-22?

ENTERING CHAOS

Perhaps there is some help to be found through greater understanding of our differences as men and women. Certainly we could all benefit from increasing our communication skills and learning the "love language" our particular spouse best understands. But these are often merely cosmetic solutions or, at best, helpful tools for addressing the deeper heart issues involved in moving toward genuine oneness in our marriages. Men may be metaphorically from Mars and women from Venus, but does knowing that help us deal with our terror of intimacy and our intractable self-centeredness as husbands and wives?

Surely from God's perspective most marriages need more than superficial course adjustments if they are to richly reflect Christ's relationship with His church, as the apostle Paul admonished the Ephesian Christians (see Eph. 5:25–30). It seems almost an insult to Jesus' enormous cost in dying for His Bride if we simply settle for fewer hassles in our marriages instead of pursuing a terrifying and joyous passion for each other that somehow mirrors Christ's own passion for us.

The truth is, as God entered chaos to create His world and as Christ entered the chaos of our sinful world (and the chaos of engaging intimately with His fallen people) to win His Bride through suffering and sacrifice, so each man is called to enter the chaos of his wife's "world," willing to suffer and sacrifice himself on her behalf. "Husbands, love your wives, just as Christ loved the church" is no simple command (see v. 25). It touches at the deep terror in every man's soul—the terror of chaos and the threat of exposed incompetence. Most men don't bargain on this when they marry.

But the man who longs not only to stay committed to his marriage but to richly impact for good the woman he has covenanted to love—this man will have to face the darkness of his terror and enter it with the intent to bless his wife, though he won't have a clue how to do it. The same is true of any good man seeking to enrich the lives of the women he knows, as Jesus always did. Such a good man will have to speak when he doesn't know what to say. He will have to act without any formula or rules, for there is no formula except to pay attention to a woman's heart and know what harms and blesses her, and no rule except the command to love as Jesus loves the church (see Eph. 5:28–29 and 1 Peter 3:7).

Sometimes a man will demand a formula, even from his wife or another woman in his life: "What do I have to do to make you happy?" Not only does the question fail to set her heart at rest, it is not her job to answer it. It is God's job, and God doesn't often speak to a man in specifics, not even in his extremity. What God *does* do is promise His presence, saying, "Never will I leave you; never will I forsake you" (Heb. 13:5). And in the strength of believing that promise a man can plunge into the darkness of chaos to speak words and perform acts of love reflecting God's character, desiring but not demanding appreciation or response.

For this too is true: No man can love anyone, not even his wife, as Jesus loves His church. Only Christ has that depth of submission to His Father that enables Him to obey perfectly the command of love. And if a man has not the presence of Christ in him, he cannot enter chaos with the courage required to love others unto death—even the death of his own pride and self-centeredness—especially the particular imperfect feminine member of the Bride of Christ to whom he is married. His terror is not subject to his own control, nor will it recede for very long because of a spiritual pep talk or a spurt of renewed interest in God. Only the ongoing presence of Christ Himself within him can urge a man to step into a darkness God alone can lead him through, with only a foot-lamp to light his way—and sometimes not even that, but only God's whisper of encouragement. To enter the terrifying chaos of relationship will require utter dependence on the God who alone knows beginning from end, and who has told us only that in the end He wins.

Something much larger even than the survival and deepening of one's marriage is at stake, though that is no insignificant accomplishment, especially in today's culture. The rest of the story concerns God's larger battle against evil, which He invites us to wage alongside His heavenly warriors. The battle of Jericho was big—a miraculous victory against enormous odds because Yahweh was helping His people. But it was just a minor skirmish, not only in the conquest of Canaan but in the ongoing spiritual warfare that continues even to this very day. When men do battle for God's Kingdom by taking up their spiritual weapons against evil to protect their wives, children, churches, and culture, they are part of a much larger story than they might realize. In fact they may never recognize until they get Home the vital role they played in defeating God's enemy, even the enemy of our own souls.

No battle in any war is insignificant, of course, but only the five-star general may understand its place in the whole. In the unseen war between God and His enemy, cosmic forces contend daily, hourly, for the eternal souls of men, women, and children throughout our world. Each evidence of masculine kindness, each marriage saved, each husband and wife spared the trauma of brokenness, each child protected from the ravages of divorce, each church strengthened by the spiritual revival of even one of its members—these are the not-so-small victories that move the Bride of Christ toward her wedding day when she will see her Beloved face-to-face. And it is the courageous movement of God's men into chaos that wields enormous power to accomplish these things in God's strength. And of special importance is a man's battle to preserve his marriage by doing the hard work of wooing his wife with Christ's own passionate love back to his heart. Much, much is at stake.

AVOIDING DANGER

The sad reality of men's nature, however, is that they (like women) are imperfect beings who struggle against their own fallen nature and sometimes lose. Many start out with great intentions but they wander from the path somewhere along the way. Even in their relationship with God—perhaps especially in their relationship with God—men are sometimes unwilling to enter the chaos of intimacy with Him. In fact, sometimes it seems safer to not be in relationship with Him at all.

No one—man or woman—is willing to risk being identified with Christ all the time. Our courage fails, our fears overwhelm us, and instead of risking, we run. Instead of remaining yoked, we try to slip out from the wooden crossbars and go off in our own direction, not God's. This Peter did on the night Jesus was betrayed. It was the worst night of his life. (This drama unfolds in Matt. 26:17–56.)

The evening had begun with Jesus washing the disciples' feet. Then, during the Passover meal, He had declared that He would be betrayed by one of them and be led off to His death. Yet Peter and the others still clung to the hope that it would not happen.

Later had come the Gethsemane debacle—Peter, James, and John falling asleep while Jesus prayed, the line of torches coming their way, Judas kissing Jesus' hand to betray Him, the soldiers with their swords and clubs roughing Him up, Peter's swordplay and Jesus' restoration of the ear Peter had lopped off, the disciples' flight from the garden as Jesus was led away—the night had become a nightmare of confusion and noise and cowardice and desertion.

When the dust had finally settled and the reality of Jesus' arrest had begun to sink in, the AWOL Peter found himself compelled to seek out the place where his beloved Lord had been taken. Remembering his outspoken avowal to Jesus, "Even if all fall away on account of you, I never will," Peter was determined to not desert Jesus a second time. He would find Jesus, stay to see what happened, and hopefully accompany Jesus home when He was released.

What Peter had evidently forgotten, however, was Jesus' prediction to him, "I tell you the truth, . . . this very night, before the rooster crows, you will disown me three times" (v. 34). Peter hadn't believed it, for he was sure of his own love for his Lord. He had fallen into the pitfall of self-deception that ambushes anyone who thinks a particular sin is beyond his or her capacity to commit. "I could never do such a thing!" we declare with perfect sincerity. But the truth is, we are all capable of committing any debasement if our situation becomes desperate enough. Naïveté about our inclination toward evil leaves us frighteningly vulnerable to Satan's seduction.

But Peter wasn't thinking about Jesus' warning as he stood warming his hands at the fire in Caiaphas's courtyard outside the place where Jesus was being interrogated. Long months ago Peter had accepted Jesus' invitation, "Take my yoke upon you and learn from me, for I am gentle and humble in heart, and you will find rest for your souls" (11:29). He had taken Jesus' yoke, telling Him, "Even if I have to die with you, I will never disown you" (26:35). This was a man who had committed himself to identifying with the One to whom he was self-yoked for life.

Yet shivering in Caiaphas's courtyard, Peter was finding no rest for his soul. He was troubled and afraid, his loyalty toward his Lord at war with his fear for his own survival. He loved Jesus but did he really want to identify with Him just now? Yes. And no. Raging within this very human disciple was huge ambivalence at being one with a man likely to soon be tortured and put to death.

Peter hadn't really bargained on how hard this would be. In the warmth of the upper room he had sworn his allegiance, but in the chill of this dangerous courtyard he swore something else. He swore that he was *not* connected to Jesus, swore to those around that he was *not* His disciple, swore loudly to all who might listen that he had never even *met* the Man. Then a nearby rooster crowed the end of this terrible night, and One who *had* listened to the fisherman's denial looked Peter's way while being led bound through the courtyard. And in the eyes of Jesus, Peter saw a depth of love and sorrow he knew he would never be able to forget. That is when he finally remembered—too late—the words of Jesus' warning and he went out into the frigid dawn and cried and cried and cried.

RISKS OF INTIMACY

Anyone who has received Jesus' rest and is yoked in oneness to Him has walked in Peter's sandals. Drawn into the circle of Jesus' love and identified as a son or daughter of the God of the universe, our desire to obey and honor our King nevertheless ebbs and flows. We are ambivalent, wanting to walk His way but drawn time and again into fear and self-protection. We

151

agree to keep watch with Him and then fall asleep. We declare at church that we are His children, but at work or at home we behave like orphans or runaways. Sometimes we're like Rahab hidden in Jericho's wall, willing to risk our future in order to be connected to God and His people. At other times we're like the disciple in Caiaphas's courtyard, afraid to risk admitting we even know Jesus.

Bill and I experienced firsthand the struggle between fear and faith after our individual decisions to stay together and seek healing for our marriage. Our marital discord had shaken us badly, and though Bill began seeing a Christian counselor, he wasn't ready to admit his drinking was addictive—he believed he had it under control. The conflict in my soul between faith in God and fear regarding my future will be recounted in the next chapter. But Bill's inner struggle to rest in God required different risks from mine. What was true for us both, however, was that the enemy of our souls and of our oneness was not about to roll over and give up. Jericho lay dead ahead, and though the battle was the Lord's, we would have to fight it.

The war Bill and I had been waging had focused on his alcoholism, but, though the drinking had driven a deep wedge between us, it was not the battleground on which God wished us to contend. Jesus declared that bad trees bring forth bad fruit, and out of the overflow of the *heart* we do our speaking and acting (see Matt. 12:33–34). It was our hearts God wanted Bill and me to face and He was merely using Bill's alcoholism to get our attention and to show us the underlying dynamics of our marriage and of our relationship to Him.

The first field of battle on which Bill engaged the enemy of his soul was neither his drinking nor our marriage but his relationship with our teenage son, Chris. There was serious conflict between father and son, and Bill felt helpless to resolve it. It was his role as father that he discussed with his counselor, not his role as husband. Bill was angry at Chris because he was refusing to be pressed into the mold Bill wanted him to fill. My husband wanted his son to become a military officer, but Chris didn't want to. It had been Bill's unrealized dream for his own life and he was furious that Chris did not dream those same dreams.

But beneath Bill's anger (as his counselor helped him to see) was the deeper pain of having lost connection with his son because of the continual conflict between them. And perhaps the most powerful and life-changing thing the counselor told Bill was that he had to learn to linger in his pain and not run from it. This was a new concept for him—as it is for all of us. Everything in our nature and in our culture militates against lingering in pain. Whatever works best and fastest to get us away from emotional or physical discomfort is touted as the solution to all our problems.

But Bill discovered over the next several months that instead of focusing his efforts on changing Chris—or even on fixing his relationship with

Chris—he could spend his energy grieving his disappointment in Chris's choices, as well as his disappointment over his own lost dreams. He could choose not to run from his sorrow over not having the intimacy with his son he desperately wanted. Bill's love for his son ran deeper than his anger toward him, and with his counselor's encouragement, he chose to do the hard work of staying connected to Chris, entering the sorrow that lay beneath the anger he so often felt.

Bill's growing willingness to be in pain regarding the loss of his own dreams for his son opened to him a whole new way to see life and to live it. His rages decreased as his grieving increased. Repentance began to replace self-justification more and more. Father and son still struggled to communicate without rancor, but Bill would remind me time and again, "He is a fine boy."

Bill's father-heart had all along been more tender than he had realized, and more damaged by his own father-loss than he had thought. In the process of Bill learning to accept Chris for who he was and not for who Bill wanted him to be, we were able to do a lot of talking together about how he himself had been fathered. His early experiences with his dad had convinced him he was unworthy of love and inadequate to love. God, however, was bent on affirming both Bill's identity as His beloved son and his capacity to love others because of Christ's presence in him. It took some time for Bill to recognize the damaging imprint his father had left on his soul and on his own fathering style, but gradually he began to linger in the pain both of his father's failure of him and of Chris's rebellion against him. He was learning to grieve, and it was profoundly changing his heart.

It wasn't easy for Bill but as he submitted to this discipline of sorrow, he began to repent of his sins against Chris instead of justifying his anger toward him. He told Chris he was sorry for hurting him, naming one by one particular past sins against him as they came to his mind. More than once he acknowledged to his son, "I know you must be angry with me for how I've treated you," and he invited his son to talk about the anger whenever he was ready. He began listening to Chris—really listening to him— and he worked hard to stop trying to control who he was becoming and what he wanted to make of his future. Small steps at a time, this man was repenting well toward the man-child he loved. "A godly father," someone has said, "yearns to lead his son, by quiet example and few words, toward godly manhood."[16] The risks for Bill were huge in this, but his reward was great as well.

For though Bill did not recognize it at the time, lingering in pain for the sake of love is God's own way of being. Jesus stayed on the cross when He could have come down. The Holy Spirit even now "intercedes for us with groans that words cannot express" (Rom. 8:26). And like the father of the prodigal son, our heavenly Father waits longingly with His eye on the horizon to welcome home the sons and daughters who have left Him (see Luke

15:11–32). Bill himself was being conformed to the likeness of his own heavenly Father.

This is but one example of what it looks like for a man to rest in God and risk moving into the terrifying chaos of relationship with only God's foot-lamp as a guide. In the next chapter, the risks that women must take as they seek to rest in God (and in the men to whom they are covenantally bound) will be examined in greater detail.

QUESTIONS TO CONSIDER

1. What "detestable practices" in our present culture remind you of Canaan's defiled culture?

2. What spiritual principle is communicated by God's reminder to the Israelites that it was not because of their righteousness or integrity that they would take possession of Canaan (Deut. 9:4–5)?

3. How can believers fight God's battles against evil and wickedness in their homes, churches, communities, and culture?

4. What kind of "wounds" do today's Christian men endure in fighting spiritual battles, and how can Christian women respond respectfully to those wounds?

5. How can husbands practice the "godly movement" in their homes for which their wives long?

6. Identify some areas of "feminine chaos" and tell why it is difficult for a man to enter that chaos as Christ's ambassador.

Regarding the opening story:

Courageous paternal movement into relationship was missing for Nikki and Eddie. Nikki's father started out with good intentions but through the years was not able to follow through on them.

7. What, if anything, can Nikki's father do to move back into protecting his daughter as he had once promised?

CHAPTER EIGHT

RISK

———

The Price of Feminine Responsiveness

TIM CALLED UP THE STAIRS *to Celia, just as she finished taping and labeling box number 157 in preparation for their move the following week. "Where are the hot dog buns for dinner?" Tim wanted to know. "I have everything else almost ready."*

"I'll be right down," Celia called back, wincing as she gingerly straightened her tired back. This was the hardest move she'd ever prepared for, not just because their three children had added considerably to their volume of "stuff" since they'd last moved but also because she had not wanted to relocate in the first place.

Tim had earnestly said to her, "I really sense God calling me to this new vision of ministry." But Celia had resisted strenuously. She liked her home; the children were in good schools; their church family was supportive—why would Tim want to compromise all that to move them into a city she didn't even like?

Nonetheless, Celia had promised to pray about it, knowing Tim wouldn't force her hand in so important a decision, and secretly hoping God wouldn't tell her to leave the home she loved. "Oh, Lord," Celia had prayed, "You and I both know this move wouldn't be good for our family, and I don't understand what You're trying to teach Tim in this. Make me wise in dealing with my husband."

Then had come God's unexpected question: "My Child, what if I want you to move?" Stunned, Celia had argued long and passionately, naming to her heavenly Father all the reasons why moving would be a mistake. But at each turn God had kindly but relentlessly repeated His question: "What if I want you to move?" No reproaching. No arm-twisting. Just His repeated invitation for Celia to explore what was most deeply in her heart—would she insist on her way or entrust her way to His direction?

Finally, in tears, Celia had conceded: "Lord, if You want me to move, I'll move." In her heart of hearts she wanted to follow the One she loved because He so loved her. "But," she had added, "I can only do this if You promise to go with us." She felt like Sarah, who had left the comfort of Ur just because God had told her husband (not her) to relocate (see Gen. 12:1–9). "At least," Celia consoled herself, "I won't be camping the rest of my life like Sarah had to do. And I have the rest of Sarah's story to remind myself of God's faithfulness."

Drained but resolute, Celia had told Tim the next day, "I'll follow wherever God leads me through you." Then she had started the disruptive process of packing, all the while grieving her approaching loss of familiarity and rootedness with each box she sealed and numbered.

Box number 157 was no exception, but as Celia moved past the stack of completed packing in the hallway and made her way downstairs, an image flashed across her mind of the sequined circus star she had once seen, caught in the suspense between having released her own trapeze bar but having not yet been caught by her partner swinging toward her. "God is my safety net," Celia reminded herself softly as she entered her kitchen's happy confusion of husband and children and slightly burned hot dogs. And from His heavenly vantage point God smiled.

Probably the most difficult risk confronting women who long for godliness is whether or not to give over to God their determined attempts to control the people and circumstances of their lives. Fearful women who wallow in their powerlessness and mistake self-contempt for humility—such women do not struggle to take relational risks. Nor do women who demand their rights and refuse to let go of the trapeze of control.

156

But the woman who, like Celia, is willing to trust God with her life and to receive with gladness the leadership and covering of good men will renounce her strategies of self-protection and take risks of faith to follow what God calls her to do. This risk she will take not without fear, but in spite of her fear. The cost of becoming a responder instead of a controller is sometimes great, but Christ's invitation to rest in Him is rich incentive for any woman who longs for greater connectedness with God and with good men. For she will certainly discover that the risks involved are eminently worth taking.

Outrageous rejoicing flowed through the camp at Gilgal like streams in the desert. The seven days of marching and waiting were over, the walls of Jericho had fallen before the Israelite army, they had carried out God's judgment against evil, and now their tension had given way to an abandon of celebration. Exhausted but jubilant, the warriors had returned to camp, hands empty of plunder but hearts filled with the exultation of victory. Worship abounded, and overflowing joy was exchanged from heart to heart and tent to tent.

Jericho, the first city blocking the Israelites from Canaan, had been utterly destroyed, and God's promise of rest in the land had become more believable than ever. Even Rahab's family outside the camp found reason to rejoice, for though they had lost their old life, a new life with a godly people dawned with hope on their horizon. The battle had been gruesome, but the mental images of carnage did not keep the men from grateful praise for Joshua and for their covenant God. No Israelite wife had been widowed, no child orphaned, no mother made childless. Yahweh was good, and the night was glad.

No doubt most of the Israelite soldiers slept well after the battle of Jericho, their wives and mothers having tended their wounds and bruises and broken bones. Tomorrow they would think about the next battle, but this night was for resting from their labor. It was good to be off duty in the land and to dream of someday trading their tents for houses and their swords for plowshares. Surely God's hornet would precede them in their battle for the next city in Canaan as He had that day in their battle for Jericho. The nation of Israel was yoked to God Almighty, and Yahweh was invincible.

We are not told how long the Israelite army rested between their first and second battles in Canaan. War never proceeds at the pace suggested by movies or history books or even biblical narratives. However, even after victory there is a need for respite. Surely it took some time for the wounded to recuperate, and repairs to weapons and clothing must also have been necessary.

Scripture offers no details about physical or emotional trauma experienced by the soldiers who had done the fighting. War is terrible in any era, and God's people were not immune. Even the women, though they had not participated in or even witnessed the havoc of battle, had to have been affected by the gore of the fighting's aftermath. Gilgal was not that far removed from Jericho that the sound of warfare and the smell of smoke and death had not found their way to assault feminine sensitivities. Everyone in the camp at Gilgal needed to recover from the army's first triumph.

Needing Protection

Scripture is also silent about what it was like for the Israelite women to have waited in their tents while their men waged war in Jericho. They had had no guarantee besides God's promise that their sons and husbands would survive or be unhurt. God's daughters, when they rest in Him, must do the hard, often mundane work of waiting and praying as they care for those they love and prepare havens of refreshment to comfort, encourage, and bless others. To enter God's rest in their own homes in the Promised Land, both the men and the women of Israel had to courageously yoke themselves to God and to His purposes. Such yoking is never without risk.

Does God ever call women to engage in warfare for His kingdom? It depends on what is meant by "warfare." Surely women struggle mightily in prayer on behalf of all who occupy their homes and their spheres of influence. They also must find courage to stand strong for Christ in their homes, their workplaces, their communities, and their churches. But we as women also long to be protected by godly men who will stand strong with us and for us, moving against the forces of evil to make our hearts and our homes safe places in which we can rest.

It is God's intention that husbands in particular protect their wives as Christ guards the purity and beauty of His church. "Husbands, love your wives, just as Christ loved the church," the apostle Paul teaches, adding that men "ought to love their wives as their own bodies" (Eph. 5:25, 28). As a man instinctively protects his own life and honor, so he is expected to be the courageous protector of his wife and children. The same masculine courage is meant to extend toward women and children in church and community as well, giving evidence of a man's submission to the life and character of Christ in him.

Unfortunately there are many women today who have had to become tough because of men's failure to protect and cherish them. When Bill recently underwent an outpatient procedure in our local hospital, one of his nurses came to the waiting room where I was and asked me, "Are you the woman Mr. Groom wants to grow old with?" I smiled and said I was, and as she brought me to Bill she said, "You two have restored my faith in relationships." Later Bill and I talked about how this attractive divorcée must have been badly hurt to have been so impressed by Bill's obvious love for me and by our kindness to each other. We wondered who or what it was that had destroyed her faith in relationships. Both of us guessed it had likely been in her associations with men.

This woman, of course, is not alone. Her number is legion—countless women discouraged and worn out by fighting battles they shouldn't have had to fight, resigned to protecting themselves because no men will come alongside to fight for them. True, some women choose isolation out of hardness of heart or entrenched self-sufficiency (though these choices too have their reasons). But many other women have experienced betrayal and abandonment and have lost the protection they desire and should receive from good men. Do we not need to hear again God's command, "Defend the cause of the fatherless, plead the case of the widow" (Isa. 1:17)? Women will contend for themselves and their children if they must, but God's men ought to be doing it for them.

HATING ALONENESS

From the beginning, women were created to image God not so much in His movement into chaos as in His passionate desire for relationship. God longs for intimate connection—both within the Trinity and with His image-bearers—and there is something about our chosen responsiveness to His initiating love that delights and blesses Him. Women have a similar capacity to bless men with their responsiveness to men's kind movement toward them. We women are designed to receive their strength with pleasure, enjoying their delight in us and nurturing the life their love brings to us.

But what happens when God's male image-bearers don't bring their goodness to us? Because men hate and fear chaos, and because our inner feminine hearts feel chaotic even to us, we fear they will not move toward us and we will be alone. Women hate aloneness—not just physical loneliness but emotional disconnection. Personal isolation feels as much like death to us as personal inadequacy feels to men. This is the legacy that has come to us from our first parents in the Garden of Eden, and every woman has been disappointed by some man at some time in her life. This is the fact of sin. All of us—men and women alike—have inherited the consequences of the fall.

So the question remains (as I asked in a previous book): "What do women do when men disappoint them?"[1] If the men in our lives are not at rest in God, able (in Christ) and willing to move toward us with kind strength, our greatest temptation as women will be to move toward them to demand

159

from them the relational connection we think we cannot live without. If men's fear of chaos keeps them from movement, our own fear of loneliness keeps us from resting in God and being content to invite men to move. It is so often backwards, is it not? Men would rather wait than move so they don't have to risk failure, and women would rather move than wait so they don't have to risk aloneness. Our greatest fears motivate our greatest sins against each other, and neither men nor women end up reflecting God's image as they should.

Nor does either receive what each one most desires. If a man will abandon himself to God and move courageously toward his wife, he may experience the joy of her glad response to his love, which he would never have known if he had been either passive or aggressive. And if a woman will abandon herself to God and wait prayerfully for a good man's willing involvement in her life, she may find the rest in his kindness she would never have experienced if she had tried to be the initiator and upholder of their relationship. There is no guarantee that a man's good movement or a woman's patient waiting will get either of them what they want, for every healthy relationship is grounded in reciprocal freedom of choice. However, his bad movement (or passivity) and her strident demands (or fearful withdrawal) can pretty predictably do damage to them both.

Scripture affords ample evidence of the damage done when a man abdicates godly movement or a woman disdains masculine protection. In the biblical narrative about Satan's seduction of Eve in the Garden of Eden, for instance, we are told that Adam was "with her" during the temptation (Gen. 3:6). However, he said nothing to either Eve or Satan while the entire future of our world was being weighed in the balance of Eve's decision whether or not to eat the forbidden fruit. Unlike God, who spoke into the chaos to create life, Adam refused to speak into the chaos of evil, and the result was death.

Eve, for her part, consulted neither Adam nor Yahweh before her conversational connection with Satan led her to disobedience. Instead of inviting Adam to speak, she invited him to share her sin. Instead of waiting, she moved. Instead of listening for God, she exchanged words with God's enemy. Words wrongly used can be disastrous. Women hate silence and will fill it up with words to avoid loneliness.

Words establish connection and imply a certain level of emotional closeness. God intended exactly that, for the apostle John wrote, "In the beginning was the Word, and the Word was with God, and the Word was God" (John 1:1). This Word was God's communication with His image-bearers, and the incarnation of the Second Person of the Trinity, Jesus Christ, not only connected God to us (by sharing in our humanity) but also connected us to God (through His own atoning death in our place).

160

Words evidence our humanity as distinct from any other aspect of creation and they carry great power to either bless or harm. Adam's silence, therefore, represents a monumental failure to bless Eve and it did incalculable harm. In fact a man's chosen silence toward a woman remains today one of the most violent weapons in his arsenal by which he protects himself against her or makes her pay for something she has done that he doesn't like. His weapon of silence is counterpart to a woman's own weapon of words. Too often we women wield our word-swords without regard to how woundingly disrespectful or ungrateful or emasculating they may be to the heart that receives them. If men are sometimes called to enter their terror of chaos and trust God by speaking, then women are called to enter their terror of disconnection and trust God by more often keeping silent. It is a most appalling risk.

FEMININE RISK

Clearly, the risks we are invited to take as God's children are not always physical, as were those taken by the Israelite infantry under Joshua. Especially for women, the risks we take in obeying God involve our sense of social safety and our feelings of being loved, accepted, and cherished. Men most often take risks with regard to their being adequate or successful, while women's risks are more often about being treasured or connected. Consider, for example, the story of one particular woman in Jesus' day whose reputation for being immoral (most likely sexually immoral) was well known in her community. We know neither her name nor the city she lived in. We don't know many details about her life at all, except that she "had lived a sinful life" in a town where Jesus had been invited to a dinner party at the home of a Pharisee named Simon. This unnamed woman had no connection with a good man, no one who cherished her, no one who protected her safety or honor, no one who delighted in her heart. (The story of the huge risk this prostitute took is recorded in Luke 7:36–50.)

It seems likely from the context in Luke 7 that the fallen woman in this town had encountered Jesus before coming to the dinner party. Her later actions indicate she had heard Jesus' offer of grace and had received His gift of forgiveness. Jesus had no doubt spoken at the local synagogue, and Simon the Pharisee (a highly respected man in the community) had invited Him to a meal so the town intellectuals could discuss theology with Him. The woman had not been invited to the party, of course, for not only were women considered incapable of theological debate, but this particular woman's status as a public sinner had closed virtually all social doors to her.

She was, however, allowed to enter the open courtyard of Simon's home and stand with other uninvited "guests" at a respectful distance away from

161

the central table where Simon's friends reclined to eat. Some came to listen in on the table conversation and learn from the rabbis. Others, the town unfortunates, stood and waited until the invited guests had finished eating and had left the courtyard, for then the "crumbs," or leftovers from the meal, were theirs for the taking. The richer the host, the more extra food was prepared for the poor. It was a fairly workable if somewhat humiliating system for feeding the local down-and-outers.

And down-and-out this woman certainly was. Especially "out," for she had removed herself from respectability and community by having chosen a life of sexual impurity. The social, economic, and religious disparity between this woman and Simon, the Pharisee hosting the party, could hardly have been greater, though both were part of the same Jewish community. Socially and physically, the space separating the invited from the uninvited guests was, by unspoken and mutual consent, never crossed. That is why this woman's actions at the party were so shocking, so unheard of, so unbelievably risky. She would break all the rules imposed on her by her place in that culture.

LOVE'S EXTRAVAGANCE

As Simon's guests reclined on cushioned benches around the central table, their feet extended away from the food, it was obvious to those who had seen Jesus arrive at the dinner party that the rabbi from Nazareth had been snubbed. Certain rituals of honor and the expected amenities of hospitality toward Jesus had been deliberately neglected by Simon, who was probably withholding his approval until he had tested Jesus' orthodoxy. Three basic gestures of Middle Eastern hospitality had been denied Him: the washing of His feet, the traditional kiss of greeting, and the use of fragrant oil to anoint His head, especially as He may have been the guest of honor.

None of these gestures of hospitality had been extended to Jesus, though presumably at least the first two had been offered to all the other guests. The implications of Simon's neglect are explained by Kenneth E. Bailey, a scholar of Middle Eastern peasant culture. He writes, "To omit [the courtesy of footwashing] would be to imply that the visitor was one of very inferior rank."[2] Thus Simon's omission was an intentional insult, as was his refusal to greet Jesus with a kiss. Bailey quotes another scholar, H. B. Tristram, as observing about contemporary Middle Eastern customs, "To receive a guest . . . without kissing him on either cheek as he enters, is a marked sign of contempt, or at least a claim to a much higher social position."[3]

These two public affronts against Jesus were evidently seen by all, including the sinful woman, who had hurried to Simon's home to anoint Jesus with the expensive perfume she had up until that day used to fragrance herself as she plied her trade. Jesus' message of God's forgiveness had given her hope for a new life, and no longer needing the perfume for its illicit purpose, she had planned to honor Jesus with it—another courtesy Simon had failed to show to the invited rabbi.

Though Jesus no doubt felt keenly the sting of Simon's snub, He did not depart in anger but instead went to His place at the table unwelcomed and unwashed. It was the woman who gave way to hurt and anger regarding Jesus' mistreatment. Grateful to have been set free from her life of shame and abuse, and appalled that the One who had forgiven her was now Himself being shamed and abused, she could not hold back her tears of anger and sorrow. Embracing the recklessness of her love for Jesus, she followed her heart and risked what is most important to a woman—her safety from misunderstanding, scorn, and rejection. What social connection she might have had left in that town she was willing to sacrifice for the One who had spoken clean words of genuine love to her. For Him, she would refuse to play things safe.

First, she risked drawing near to Jesus across the space buffering the haves from the have-nots. Coming directly to Jesus' feet, weeping for her own sin and for the insult He had borne, she washed His feet with her tears. But how was she going to dry them? Asking Simon for a towel was out of the question, so the repentant prostitute let down her hair to wipe Jesus' feet, an action described by Kenneth Bailey as "an intimate gesture that a peasant woman is expected to enact only in the presence of her husband."[4] If she had been married, it would have been grounds for divorce, so shameful was the public letting down of her hair.

This passionately grateful woman had, without a word, crossed the barriers between male and female, rich and poor, respectable and shameless. Next, she began kissing Jesus' feet again and again, then reached for the flask hanging about her neck and did what she had come to do: She poured out her love for Jesus in fragrant perfume on His feet, sweetening the air for everyone in Simon's courtyard.

But not everyone there appreciated the aroma of such ardent gratitude from a tainted woman toward the man who had taught her she was a cherished daughter of the King. She had wordlessly declared herself one with Jesus, receiving the rest He had offered and risking everything to give Him thanks. But would Simon and the others believe in her repentance? Would they reward the risk she had taken in breaking through all those unseen barriers to stand in her rightful place as a restored member of their community of faith? Would they embrace her and welcome her back to the synagogue as a forgiven daughter of Abraham?

More important, would Jesus condescend to being yoked to such a woman, a prostitute redeemed but not yet mature in her redemption? Or would He keep her at arm's length until she had proved her faith and improved her life? What is it that ushers us into and preserves us in oneness with God? Is it *our* goodness or His? The answer is crucial to our journey Home.

Reason for Hope

Christ promised to those who come to Him for rest, "My yoke is easy and my burden is light" (Matt. 11:30). We may not always experience it that way, especially as He leads us into our own personal "testing ground" to reveal what is deep within our hearts. Sometimes we pour out our hearts in an abandon of love like the forgiven prostitute but at other times we may lose our passion to follow Him wherever He leads. It is then we must remember that being connected to Him—and *staying* connected to Him— is not about our behavior but about His love. Even our obedience is not about our *doing* but about our *being* His son or daughter and daring to act that way.

Jesus' yoke is easy if we will persevere in resting in His love for us, not ours for Him. Our oneness with Him is confirmed not by what we do but by who He is. He will never be swayed from His covenant promise to be our God, because He cannot change His nature. Jesus has paid the price of our sin by His death and has restored us to Himself by His resurrection, sealing His betrothal commitment by the sending of His Holy Spirit into our hearts. This is a done deal—an *eternally* done deal, based on God's unchanging love from beginning to end. This is our hope, and it is a sure hope because it rests in Him and not in us.

Because of this hope, the priests bearing the ark of the covenant, for example, had been so certain of Yahweh's covenant promise that they obeyed His command to enter the treacherous Jordan River, willing to sink and drown before they would let go of the precious ark. Likewise, the disrupted but passionate prostitute had followed her heart's love for Jesus into a firestorm of unspoken criticism and rejection, having been joined to Him by His forgiveness and by her own responsive gratitude. Peter had wept bitterly at having denied his beloved Lord but he would still remain yoked to Him, because even his disobedience could not keep Jesus from loving him. "If we are faithless," the apostle Paul reminds us, "[God] will remain faithful, for he cannot disown himself" (2 Tim. 2:13). Nor could Peter's disobedience keep him from repenting and seeking restored oneness with his Savior, for though he had denied his Lord, he could not deny his own deep love for Him.

Jesus' yoke is easy because it binds us to Him with the cords of His own eternal and unchanging love. In His love we find the ease of His delight in us exchanged for the dis-ease of our own rebellion or weakness or fear. His rest is easy. What is hard is believing He loves us as much and as faithfully as He does, even when we are loveless or faithless. Resting in His uncon-

164

ditional love in the face of our recurring fear and sinful scramble for safety is our greatest struggle. Do we dare risk trusting His Father-love when we've been disobedient children, or do we not? That is the question of the hour. It is in fact the question of *every* hour.

The Grace of Tears

Surely the forgiven woman who stood weeping in Simon's courtyard had to have believed that God loves sinners unconditionally. What kind of tears did she shed as she made up for the Pharisee's rudeness to Jesus? Surely she was mourning many losses—not merely her own but also her Lord's—His loss of respect and honor, His public shaming. Had she not felt a similar rejection time and again? "He was despised and rejected by men," the prophet Isaiah had declared about Messiah, "a man of sorrows, and familiar with suffering. Like one from whom men hide their faces he was despised, and we esteemed him not" (Isa. 53:3). Surely this rabbi was such a man, acquainted with her grief as with His own. Her tears for Him were tears of mourning.

But it was also this woman's sin that had reduced her to tears. Having repented and been forgiven, she began to see the terrible damage she had done by defiling herself and others and by closing her heart to the grief she was causing her heavenly Father with her own self-contempt. Now yoked to her Father again, she could not but weep for her past waywardness. When we are broken by our wrongdoing, hating our sin and hating what it does, we show forth our truest identity as sons and daughters of God. For only those who are children of Yahweh hate sin—in themselves and in the world—and hate it enough to turn from it and long to be freed from its power. "Lord Jesus, have mercy on us!" we cry, for we know we cannot cast out our own sin. And He offers us mercy every time.

And then, like the restored prostitute, we weep not just tears of sadness and tears of repentance but also tears of gladness. For we taste God's own joy at our return to His embrace. Henri Nouwen describes this intertwining of sadness and joy in his book *The Return of the Prodigal*. "Grief asks me to allow the sins of the world—my own included—to pierce my heart and make me shed tears, many tears, for them," he writes. "This grief is so deep not just because the human sin is so great, but also—and more so—because the divine love is so boundless."[5] When we soften our hearts in repentance, we feel overwhelmed that it is not revenge but love, not rejection but kindness that greets us at our return to our heavenly Father.

These were the tears that cleansed the feet of Jesus, left unwashed by Simon the Pharisee. These tears connected her heart to the One she loved. These were tears of faith, for though she had been disobedient, she had not been rejected by God. Though she had been an outcast in her community,

165

Jesus had drawn her into eternal connection with Himself. Though she had sold her body to simulate love, there was One who had always loved her truly, body and soul, and He always would. This unnamed woman's tears embraced and celebrated these incredible realities, marking her as a woman of great faith. She had responded to the good movement of Jesus into the chaos of her sin and shame, and without words she had shown Him the reverence and newfound purity of life that surely made His heart glad. But what would Simon and the others do? Her heart was clean, but her future was far from certain.

WAITING WITH UNCERTAINTY

I know what it's like to be right with God but uncertain about what He might lead me to next. After Bill had made his decision to stay in the marriage and to seek help in sorting out what was in his heart, we both still had a lot of hard work to do. We stood together on the Jericho side of the river, but the conquest of Canaan was far from complete and we had many questions about how to fight the enemy of our souls.

God's invitation to risk taking an honest look inside would open our eyes to the real enemy of our souls, for there were unseen pockets of rebellion and self-sufficiency in us of which we were dangerously unaware. Oswald Chambers writes, "The great mystical work of the Holy Spirit is in the dim regions of our personality which we cannot get at, . . . [and] there are motives [we] cannot trace." He goes on to declare that if being cleansed from sin by Jesus' blood "means in conscious experience only, may God have mercy on us."[6] That is to say, even the secret sins in Bill and me were covered by the limitless efficacy of Jesus' atonement.

Nevertheless, these secret sins were not harmless, though they were forgiven. For as long as Bill and I remained unaware of them (or believed they were not all that sinful), they maintained their grip on our will and kept us enslaved to their power. Left undisturbed in our souls' dim regions, our unconfessed sin had been used by the evil one to divide us again and again. We had, for example, unknowingly allowed anger to take deep root in our souls, and it had produced in us the bitter fruit of defensiveness and self-justification for our own sin, and unforgiveness for the sin in the other. God wanted to show us what was deeply in our hearts, to bring our hidden wrongdoing and wrong thinking into the light of our conscious thought, so we could deal with each other with integrity of heart.

Slowly, slowly the tension level in our household began to subside, however, and the level of our hope began to rise. Bill's counselor never dealt with his alcoholism, and that disappointed me. But I was encouraged by the changes in Bill's relationship with our son, Chris. Facing this painful issue was breaking up the logjam of anger in Bill's heart, opening avenues for us to talk about what was going on with us too. Besides, I knew if my husband could enter his pain and repent toward his son, God was surely at work, and someday Bill might repent of his love affair with the bottle as well and turn his heart fully back to me. It wasn't easy, but I was learning to linger in my own pain and to wait patiently on God to do His work in the heart of the man I was learning to love again.

What gave me hope during this time? Bill wasn't drinking less; if anything, his drinking was becoming (to me, at least) more obviously compulsive. What gave me hope was not just observing the change in Bill's relationship with Chris but the changes that were going on in myself. For there was something shifting inside me during those waiting years. Even as I watched Bill losing his war against alcoholism, I could more and more recognize it was not *my* struggle. I argued less and less with him, because this was his Jericho, not mine. No longer able to pull me into the fray, he had to do business with God, and now it was more *his* blood in the sometimes turbulent water of our life together than mine. When he became frazzled with the futility of his struggle, I deflected to God the blows of his anger.

In fact even in the midst of Bill's unrest, my heart was increasingly drawn to him with a compassion I'd not felt in a long time. His verbal attacks on me, when they sometimes came, seemed less life-threatening (though they made me sad), and I was able to offer him kindness instead of criticism or self-pity. I waited in the camp at Gilgal, uncertain whether he would survive the battle against his addiction, but increasingly certain I would go on loving him no matter what. Because of God's work in my own heart, Bill could not stop me from loving him. Besides, I knew God would win the war and bring me safely Home at last—whether Bill quit drinking or not.

It felt good to rest in my relationship with God instead of trying to rest in Bill by shoring up *his* relationship with God. Even as the noise and confusion of his fierce fighting assailed me, dismantling my self-sufficiency and my illusions of control over people and events, I received wonderful tastes of God's nearness. I needed Him desperately, and He came to me time and again. And what encouraged me more than anything else was the realization that God was pursuing hard after the heart of His son, and I could see Bill cracking the door of his heart to Him every once in a while.

RISKING REJECTION

Meanwhile, as Bill occasionally opened his heart to God and to me (though he still ran to the bottle when his pain became too great), I was being invited by God to open my own heart to painful memories and distorted self-images I had buried for decades. During those post-Jordan years, God brought me face-to-face with ways I had been harmed by others in my past, particularly by men I had trusted and who had betrayed my trust by being sexually inappropriate with me. Because they were Christian men, leaders in church and in Christian education, their betrayal had thrust me into the double bind of silence and self-blame. There had been no one to tell and no one to blame but myself, I thought. I could not have told my parents, nor could I have acknowledged even to myself the unthinkable possibility that these "good men" had had bad thoughts and had done bad things. It had been easier for me to believe I was bad and did not deserve to be loved. In that way I was able to at least keep alive the illusion of false intimacy connecting me—however inappropriately—to the men whose approval I so desired.

But as my heart began breaking over the losses in my marriage and as I found rest in going to God with the truth about my heart, I began also to recognize and admit that I had been damaged by the very men I had thought cared most for me. In the process of this excruciating crumbling of my illusions, I discovered deep pockets of pain and rage I had never acknowledged to anyone. But now, it seemed, was the time to talk about my secrets. God gave me a few safe people to tell, and I also cried out to Him my terrible anger and disappointment. Amazingly He never turned away, not even when I turned my anger toward Him for not having prevented the damage done to my heart.

In fact the opposite happened. For when I opened the dark and hurting places of my heart to my heavenly Father, I found He loved me more than I'd ever thought possible and I began resting ever more of the weight of my soul in the One who could bear all that was there. My earlier refusal to enter the pain and grief of my losses had hardened my heart into a determined but sterile piety in my relationship with Him. But now my sterility began giving way to tastes of genuine passion toward Him and intimations of deep but carefree joy. It felt scary but also very right.

Then, however, God asked me to take a risk I had thought I could never take. He invited me to tell Bill my stories of pain and sorrow. I argued with Him, telling Him I thought I would die if I obeyed Him in this. Bill would hate me. He would turn away in disgust and never love me again. How could God ask me to risk opening myself up to someone who could hurt me so badly—more badly even than the men who had damaged me as a young woman? How could I risk losing the man who had finally begun moving back toward me? This was suicidal.

But God reminded me of something I had already learned but had almost forgotten. He told me again that pain and death were not synonymous. If Bill turned away from me when I opened my heart to him, I would surely be plunged into an abyss of sorrow and loneliness. But I would not be

168

destroyed, because God is the keeper of my soul and He never lets go of any of His children. The enemy could hurt me, but my life was in my Father's hands, and He loved me more than I loved myself.

So eventually I did what God had asked me to do. I began giving Bill words about my sorrow, sometimes about pain that he himself had caused, and finally about what the men in my past had done to harm me. At a deeper level than ever before I was showing Bill the real me, the wounded and angry Nancy who was loved by Jesus and longed to be loved by my husband as well. This risk of intimate sorrowing felt like death to me.

At times Bill was receptive to my stories and most kind, and I experienced tastes of rest and comfort in his presence that made me hungry for much, much more. At other times he could not hear my heart, and I would end up feeling more sorrowful and alone than ever. But God was right; I did not die, because He never let go of me. And in the process of sharing my real self with the man I loved, I became more and more sure that God's love would sustain me, and more and more willing to risk Bill's disapproval. My knowledge *about* God was deepening into the joy of actually knowing Him, for each risk I took increased my dependence on Him, and He was always there.

Those years held times of risk for both Bill and me, and most of the time we could take only baby steps toward living real with one another. The baby steps never felt like baby risks, of course, for all our risks loom large in the moment. Yet when I reminded Bill that he was God's man and that I enjoyed his good heart, the look on his face was rich reward. And when he surprised me by bringing me to a five-star hotel after an anniversary dinner one year, I laughed out loud in the lobby, and he loved it. On that particular night, as we sat on our hotel balcony wrapped in luxurious robes that were not our own, watching lightning chase the clouds across Biscayne Bay, we forgot for a time that the war wasn't over yet, and we took pleasure in just being together.

The risky steps of trusting God that Bill and I took during those years did much to strengthen our oneness. We were having to live a new way in a new land, and by taking risks we were finding God faithful and learning to follow Him into ever broader experiences of His promised rest.

WISE TRUST

God always invites us to risk when we open our hearts to oneness with Him and allow Him to guide our way. For if we have His Spirit within us, we will join our hearts to others as well, and being hurt will be inevitable because we live in a fallen world occupied by fallen human beings. The risks God calls us to, however, are never an invitation to naïveté or foolish trust. God's sons must move and His daughters must wait, but none of us is asked to endanger our hearts unless God is clearly leading us into that danger for His glory.

Jesus Himself recognized the folly of trusting others too quickly or unwisely. Very early in His ministry, "while he was in Jerusalem at the Passover Feast, many people saw the miraculous signs he was doing and believed in his name. But Jesus would not entrust himself to them, for he knew all men" (John 2:23–24). The omniscient Christ knew intimately the inner hearts of all who claimed to believe in Him, and He knew better than anyone that "the heart is deceitful above all things and beyond cure" (Jer. 17:9). Realizing that some of the Jerusalem converts were false and others were weak in their faith, He would not entrust Himself to them.

We too must be wise in choosing whom to trust. It is no sin for a woman to refuse to risk offering her heart to an unrepentant man who means her harm. Nor should a man risk moving toward a relationship that will do damage to his soul. God doesn't ask us to put our faith in someone whom we do not know or who is unworthy of our trust. We are not to rest our hearts in just anyone, but only in those who have shown they deserve our trust. Christ's own example of testing the trustworthiness of people shows us that we must depend on His Spirit in us, listening for His voice so we can know whom to trust and when to risk.

Jesus did, however, reveal His heart more and more to His intimate circle of Galilean disciples, because He knew they would grow to trust Him only as they experienced more of His trustworthiness. And because Jesus has faithfully proved He deserves our implicit faith in Him, we must continue to grow in our willingness to risk all for Him as He leads our way.

Looking Within

It is not unusual for God to allow disruption into the marital relationship in order to offer us a deeper look at our own individual hearts. What *is* unusual these days is for couples to move beyond their struggle with the surface disruption and into the issues of sorrow and sin within. The wrong done by the other looms gigantic, and when one's strategies to change the other prove fruitless, the only solution that seems reasonable is to protect oneself and leave the marriage, whether physically or emotionally. Especially in our culture of disposable marriages and portable partners, the inclination to stay and do the hard work of learning to love well an imperfect partner is weakened, and we are called fools for not seeking the happiness we "deserve."

But as long as we keep our Jerichos external to the deeper issue of what is in our own hearts, God cannot come in and wage battle with whatever is keeping us from resting our souls in Him. This is no easy task to which He invites us. We are all terrified to look inside at the depth of our sin (which surely would prove we are unworthy of love) and at our helplessness to control our world (which would indict us as incompetent and render us utterly dependent on God). Yet here God was, inviting Bill and me to an inward inspection that would expose me (I thought) as unlovable and expose Bill (he thought) as inadequate. What kind of God was He? How could my revealed unloveliness or Bill's unmasked incompetence be a good thing?

The answer is, only when we face our unloveliness will we look to the One who loves the unworthy, giving us His own worthiness. And only when we are helpless will we ask for help from the Omnipotent God and thereby know ourselves competent because of His Spirit in us. "Christ in [us], the hope of glory" (Col. 1:27), who "[dwells] in [our] hearts through faith" (Eph. 3:17), establishes our beauty and adequacy, for He is beautiful and able. Resting not in ourselves but in His presence in us, and obeying not our own impulses but only and whatever He whispers in our ears—this is the fruit of looking within and confessing what we find there of sin and sorrow. It is by yielding ourselves, in terror, to honesty and grace that we find the soul rest Jesus promised.

THE INTIMACY OF DEATH

Another struggle was to come to Bill and me toward the end of our disruptive years, for Bill's stepfather and then his mother died in 1990 within six months of each other. Sustaining Mama while she cared for her husband, Larry, through the final stages of his fast-growing cancer was heart-wrenching and totally exhausting. But I bonded with Mama as I watched her love to the end a difficult man facing a difficult death. I knew her pain because I had begun facing my own, and my heart became knit to hers. I had no idea at the time that our new oneness would soon cause me great grief.

For Larry's death was only the beginning of sorrows. Within two weeks of his passing, Mama broke her hip in a fall and had to be hospitalized. While waiting for surgery, she was diagnosed with cancer of the lung, the same disease that had just taken her husband.

I was distraught. More than that, I was furious with God. Why had He opened my heart to Mama and then marked her for death? Why had He let me see my own pain so I could see hers, and then call her Home to be with Him? It seemed a most cruel joke, and I was not laughing.

Lost in my own struggle to accept God's yoking in this new loss, I could hardly comfort Bill in his dismay. My heart was consumed with the new risk the Father was asking me to take. All my life I had withheld my true heart from everyone, not trusting that anyone would love me if they really knew the secret me. I'd become expert at giving my hands, however—being cheerful and helpful and kind, making dinners for the sick and baby-sitting for young mothers—but fearing to connect deeply with anyone, even Bill. Now God was inviting me to give my heart to this woman I had come to love, instead of playing it safe by offering her only my hands in her final months. I knew what God wanted me to do, and I knew I would do it. But that did not mitigate the struggle, for habits of self-protection fight long and die hard. The pain of intimacy is excruciating, for if we deeply love, we will also deeply grieve when the one we love leaves us. I chose to give my heart to Mama but I knew it was going to be broken.

After her hip surgery, Mama could no longer stay alone, so she came to our home to live. Within two months' time she had lost almost every significant aspect of life as she'd known it for almost thirty years—her husband, her job, her home, her proximity to friends, her mobility, her privacy, her health. We had fixed up a special room for her and had moved in her things, but there were too many changes for her to assimilate. Her world had gone altogether out of control, and in an attempt to reestablish some sense of balance, she chose to deny her approaching death. This was one loss she would not face.

And in deference to her extremity, we conspired with her to keep silence. Denial was her wall of protection, and we defended it to the end. Alcohol was Bill's wall of protection, for though he could not deny her dying, neither could he face it head-on. And in the loneliness of my own struggle to accept Mama's dying and to face it without Bill's emotional presence, I could sometimes hear the lonely tears of Jesus' own sorrow, so closely did I sense His presence with me. For three months after her coming to our home, together Bill and I helped Mama to live and helped her finally to die.

Few experiences are as soul-shattering as the death of a parent—unless it is the death of both parents. Bill's world was unalterably changed by his being orphaned, and though he dulled his agony with alcohol, he was profoundly undone by this deep and irreversible loss. I knew that even in this trauma God was at work but I was lost in my own sorrow of living through and later remembering those wonderful-terrible days of leading Mama Home.

For I too felt orphaned after Mama's death. Both my parents were still alive, but attending Mama in her dying had bonded me to her, and I could not speak of her without tears for many months to come. Battling her disease had been physically exhausting and emotionally draining for Bill and me. God had been good, and caring for Mama had been a precious privilege. But the yoke of living Jesus' life and seeing with His eyes the suffering of illness and death seemed sometimes heavy indeed. We knew in the end Mama had gone safely Home, but our grieving for her would last a long, long time.

172

When we face our deepest pain and know it won't destroy us, and when we see the worst of our sin and know it forgiven, then and only then does our fear begin to lose its power, for we have nothing to lose but our pretense about our hearts, and this too is rest.

How do we drop our pretense and face the truth about ourselves in the context of our most intimate relationships? What would it look like for us as husbands and wives to enter our terror of exposure and shame and sorrow in order to find the rest Jesus wants to give us? The final chapters of this book will grapple with the answers to these and other questions about what will more and more characterize our lives as we find our rest in Christ, even in the entering of our terror.

 ## Questions to Consider

1. What is your response to the belief that today's women do not need the protection of men?

2. Why do you agree or disagree that personal isolation feels as much like death to a woman as movement into darkness feels to a man?

3. What kind of risks might a wife take in relating to her husband if she were at rest in God's love and knew she could not be destroyed?

4. Evaluate the strengths and weaknesses of whatever guidelines you have for deciding whom you can trust.

5. What would it be like for you to "linger in your pain" of disappointment or loss instead of running from it?

Regarding the opening story:

Celia courageously risked the myriad changes of moving to a new city, confident that God was guiding her life through her husband and that He would never forsake her. When she opened her heart to oneness with God, He invited her to risk.

6. How (and why) might you have handled differently (in your own family, for example) the impasse of Tim's desire to move and Celia's reluctance to be uprooted?

7. What in Tim's and Celia's attitudes seemed right and deserving of imitation by other couples in resolving conflicts?

Part 3

INTIMACY

AS OUR

SHELTERED

PLACE

CHAPTER NINE

GRACE

The Glory of Repentance

IT WAS ONLY A MINOR DISASTER, as disasters go, but it seemed major. Chuck had begun filling the sink with water, had walked to the back porch to finish a quick chore, and had forgotten the running water for five minutes before discovering the flooded kitchen. Chuck's cries of dismay brought eighteen-year-old Nate running to help. Without a word, Nate scooped a stack of dish towels, dishcloths, and even pot holders from the kitchen drawer and threw them on the floor to soak up the water.

"What do you think you're doing?" Chuck hollered at his son. "Go get a mop—you're just making more of a mess!"

Nate hurried off to get the mop and a bucket, and for fifteen minutes father and son worked together on damage control.

But when Chuck turned to thank Nate for his help, a different kind of flood poured out—not from a faucet but from a son's wounded heart.

"You're welcome," Nate began, "but I don't appreciate you yelling at me when I don't do things your way." His voice grew louder as he continued, "I come wanting to help you out, and you make me want to leave and let you do it yourself!"

Chuck tried to protest, but Nate broke in. "No! Don't try to excuse what you did. You've been doing this to me ever since I was just a little kid!"

Chuck was quiet now, listening with a sorrowful gladness. For several years he had been inviting his son to talk about how his fathering style had hurt Nate as a child, and now was the time for him to hear his son's angry words.

For several minutes Nate's anger flowed—a rushing stream of words long unsaid and tears of pain finally released. Chuck received his son's pent-up anger with humility, until Nate had finished. Then the father spoke.

"You're right, Nate. I've hurt you so often and you are right to be angry. I'm sorry for the way I treated you—have often treated you. I was wrong and there's no excuse. I hope you can forgive me."

Chuck's words of repentance in response to Nate's long-suppressed anger gave way to mutual tears and the embrace of forgiveness granted. In heaven, the angels were dancing.

The exchange of repentance and forgiveness is one of the most fundamental ingredients of any vibrant relationship, including our relationship with God. When we recognize and acknowledge personal wrongdoing, renouncing our sin before the Almighty, the divine/human connection is restored and intimacy is strengthened.

The same is true of all interpersonal relationships, and it is especially essential in sustaining the intimacy of marriage. Repentance always opens the door for grace given and received, as it did for Chuck and Nate. And it is grace that alone can revive and nourish any relational connection broken by sin.

The Israelite community, rejoicing after their victory over Jericho, had no inkling of the deadly danger lurking in their midst. The army's conquest of Canaan had begun magnificently, and yoked to Yahweh, they were ready to take on the work they had yet to do. Joshua began immediately to make preparations for their next battle, sending spies to check out the site, which was not far off. Most of the Promised Land was still only a promise, for there remained giants in the land and much wickedness to be destroyed.

The next community in Canaan devoted by Yahweh for destruction was a town named Ai, which in Hebrew means "the ruin." (The story of this battle is told in Josh. 7:1–26.) Though Ai was a small town, it occupied a strategic location in Canaan's hill country. Located north of Jericho and due west of the Israelite camp at Gilgal, Ai controlled access to the much larger and better-fortified cities farther south and inland. That is why its defeat was vital both to morale and to military advantage.

Joshua's heart was no doubt encouraged, therefore, when the spies he had sent out reported to him, "Not all the people will have to go up against Ai. Send two or three thousand men to take it and do not weary all the people, for only a few men are there." The war's timetable could be moved up if the most wounded and weary stayed behind to rest, while those most refreshed went back to war.

So Joshua took the spies' advice, sending only half of 1 percent of his fighting men into the western hills to take the town of Ai. As this small but confident army marched off to battle, the remaining Israelite warriors awaited their return, expecting to add their comrades' tales of conquest to the war stories of Jericho. Anticipation and faith ran high among Yahweh's people.

UNEXPECTED DISASTER

Imagine, then, the shock and terror that must have ripped through the camp when, instead of a victory march, a bedraggled and defeated contingent of armed men came staggering back to Gilgal in total disarray. They had been routed by the men of Ai, chased back down the slopes they had earlier climbed with such expectation of victory. Thirty-six women had been widowed in the battle, their children now fatherless. Suddenly despair reigned where celebration had so recently held sway—soldiers, commanders, and civilians alike plunged into dismay and confusion. What did *this* turn of events mean?

On his face again, this time in grief before the holy ark, Joshua lay with clothes torn and dust on his head, hearing the mourners' wails but struck dumb by his own consternation. The elders of Israel kept company with him, their own garments torn and their heads dusted in abject sorrow. All day the noble leaders lay prostrate in their grief, listening for some word of hope from Yahweh, or at the very least a word of explanation. Calamity had come on them, and they knew not why, nor what to do next.

Finally, late in the afternoon, Joshua broke his silence with a cry of confusion and complaint. "Ah, Sovereign LORD, why did you ever bring this people across the Jordan to deliver us into the hands of the Amorites to destroy us?" It surely seemed God had made a mistake or had broken His promise, and Joshua wanted to know what was going on. Why the Jordan miracle if they could not win this battle?

Perhaps, Joshua thought, it was their own fault for having desired too much. "If only we had been content to stay on the other side of the Jordan!" he exclaimed, yielding to the seduction of resignation. East of the Jordan they had been successful, destroying the armies of Sihon and Og. East of the Jordan they had been safe, protected from the Canaanites by the raging Jordan. If only God had not promised them Canaan! If only they had been able to squelch their God-prompted yearning for rest in this good land! Why had they let themselves be seduced by Yahweh's promises instead of staying dead to hope?

"O LORD, what can I say, now that Israel has been routed by its enemies?" Joshua demanded. "The Canaanites and the other people of the country will hear about this and they will surround us and wipe out our name from the earth. What then will you do for your own great name?" It was God's own fault that His reputation was about to be ruined. As far as Joshua could tell, God had gotten Himself into a terrible bind, threatening His people with extinction in the process. What was Joshua supposed to do with this mess? How could he lead God's people if God was going to betray him and them? What of His covenant?

These are the kinds of questions we often throw up in God's face when the circumstances He allows into our lives are incongruent with our expectations or our understanding of His Word. We are quick to call Him unfaithful, He whose Word is eternally the same. We call Him cruel, the One whose very nature is lovingkindness. We call Him unknowable who has stooped to reveal Himself to us. And we call Him to account, He who is the potter and we the clay. We are all more like Joshua than we want to admit.

JUSTICE REQUIRED

If the news of Israel's shameful retreat had sent shock waves through the camp, imagine Joshua's reaction when God responded to his outcry with these words: "Stand up! What are you doing down on your face?" Mourning his army's defeat and his soldiers' deaths had seemed appropriate to Joshua and the elders of the people. Down on their faces seemed a good place to be, given their circumstances. Are we not right to grieve when we experience losses?

Certainly grieving is the right thing to do when we experience the evil in our world and its consequences in our lives. But in the case of Joshua and the Israelites after Ai, sorrow and dismay about their loss—and the not-so-subtle shaking of the fist in God's face—were *not* appropriate, given what was really going on.

"Israel has sinned," God declared, shedding a whole new light on the situation. This defeat was not the result of God unyoking Himself from His people, but evidence of the Israelites having slipped out from His yoke in disobedience. "They have taken some of the devoted things; they have stolen, they have lied, they have put them with their own possessions," Yahweh informed Joshua. Though it would turn out that only one soldier and his family were guilty of these things, their sin had brought condemnation to the entire community, contaminating all who were yoked to God by covenant. "That is why the Israelites cannot stand against their enemies," God stooped to explain to Joshua. "They turn their backs and run because they have been made liable to destruction."

So that was it! What should have been devoted to destruction—some plunder from the city of Jericho—had not been destroyed. Instead it had been brought into the very camp of God's people, not only dooming the one who had stolen it from God but endangering the entire nation of Israelites as well. "I will not be with you anymore unless you destroy whatever among you is devoted to destruction," God warned. "You cannot stand against your enemies until you remove it."

Now Joshua understood. There was sin in the camp, and the appropriate response was not that the Israelites mourn their military loss but that they mourn the unconfessed disobedience in their midst. Repentance is what was needed, a "deep, radical change of both perspective and commitment, resulting in a moral and spiritual transformation."[1] Joshua was brought abruptly out of ignorance regarding the true nature of the situation so that sin might be revealed, confession might be made, repentance might be evidenced, and justice might prevail.

"He who is caught with the devoted things shall be destroyed by fire, along with all that belongs to him," God instructed. "He has violated the covenant of the LORD and has done a disgraceful thing in Israel!" When God speaks in exclamation marks, it's clear He feels strongly about what He's saying. God meant business: The Israelite who had yoked himself to Jericho's spoils must share the fate of Jericho's spoils. Not only was he thief and liar but murderer as well. The blood of thirty-six comrades was on his hands, and he must die.

Early the next day Joshua convened all Israel to bring justice against the one who had contaminated the people of God. Choosing by lot, Yahweh fingered the tribe of Judah, then the clan of Zerah, then the family of Zimri, and then man by man until Achan, son of Carmi, son of Zimri, was found to be the one guilty of bringing disaster on Israel. Now disaster would come on him, as he stood chosen before Joshua and all the people he had betrayed.

"My son, give glory to the LORD, the God of Israel, and give him the praise," Joshua intoned, solemnly charging Achan to tell the truth and confess his sin to God. In confession, Achan would glorify God by publicly declaring his sin, so that it would be clear God was being just in punishing him.

"It is true!" Achan cried. "I have sinned against the LORD, the God of Israel." Then he described to Joshua and to all of them how he had coveted and taken from Jericho a beautiful robe, along with some pieces of silver and a wedge of gold. Concealing the booty from his comrades, he had buried the items beneath his tent. Perhaps even his family had not known.

Joshua gave word, and the items were quickly retrieved and spread out before the Lord as testimony against Achan. Just before the battle for Jericho had begun, Joshua had warned them all one last time to "keep away from the devoted things, so that you will not bring about your own destruction by taking any of them" (Josh. 6:18). In choosing disobedience, Achan had identified himself with God's enemy, thereby devoting himself and his family to destruction.

The devoted articles, along with Achan, his family, his animals, his tent, and all that he possessed, bore the mark of Yahweh's enemy and were now set apart to suffer the fate Achan himself had meted out in God's name against the inhabitants of Jericho. Joshua and the elders of Israel executed them by stoning, then all that had belonged to Achan was burned as Jericho had been. Their remains were covered with a large pile of rocks, a second and most sorrowful memorial in the land of promise.

"Then," Scripture says, "the LORD turned from his fierce anger" against the sin in Israel's camp, and the war against the sin in Canaan could be resumed.

THE LESSONS OF UNYOKING

Why this swift and ruthless judgment against Achan? Destroying the decadent Amorites who had hardened themselves against righteousness and decency for centuries is one thing. But Achan was a child of the covenant, marked with circumcision and a participant in the Passover celebration. How could God have ordered his death and the destruction of his family? Had not Achan confessed? Shouldn't God have forgiven him?

Sometimes we forget the high cost of our sinning. Long before Achan had stolen from the dead of Jericho, he had known that hardening his heart against God and against His covenant would bring disaster on himself. This was no casual transgression nor a false step made in ignorance or forgetfulness; Achan knew what he was doing and perhaps had even planned his larceny in advance. Moreover, his "confession" had not been voluntary. Achan had hardened his heart, keeping his sin secret until the casting of the lot forced him to admit his guilt. This was not repentance (a heart sorrow for acknowledged sin) but exposure (the shame of being caught). The difference is profound.

Besides, as Achan's countrymen later observed, Achan "was not the only one who died for his sin" (Josh. 22:20). Thirty-six others, along with his own wife and children, went to the grave because of him. Achan's deliberately chosen disobedience did damage to more than just his own soul. The same is true of our own disobedience.

But even beyond recognizing the ripple effect of our sin, we must not forget that *all* sin must be punished by a just and holy God, in keeping with His very nature. Death is always the wages of sin—both physical death and (far worse) spiritual death. Achan and his family suffered the temporal wages of his sin, and only God knows whether or not his confession evidenced a true repentance unto eternal life. But our sin too requires the death penalty, and only God's mercy in executing His own Son in our stead offers us hope for forgiveness and new life in Him. The price God Himself paid to restore us to Himself is exorbitant.

The story of Achan's sin and punishment has much to teach us about the cost of hardening our hearts against God and His Word. When we dull our conscience and indulge our sin, forgetting the One to whom we are yoked and pulling away in directions He does not want us to go, we bring trouble on ourselves and grieve the very heart of God.

Had God stopped loving Achan? Never for a moment. Nor does He stop loving us, even when we wander far astray from His leading. "This is not the way," He warns us (as He had warned Achan). "Come back, come back," He cries out in an anguish of love. How often do we realize God is passionate for our repentance, yearning to reconnect His heart to ours? God "longs to be gracious" to us (Isa. 30:18) and He carries out His judgment against our sin with holy sorrow, intending His discipline as a vehicle of mercy toward us.

Our heavenly Father is evidencing His compassion when He stands in the way of our disobedience, for love and justice are inseparable in the Godhead. If He did *not* punish sin, hating what it does to us, it would prove He does not love us, and that would contradict His very nature. It was for Achan's good that his guilt was confronted, giving him opportunity to repent and be forgiven. Unconfronted, his sin would have taken root and multiplied, in which case his final destiny and that of his children would have been far more terrible than their physical death. Unhindered transgression inevitably leads to rejecting God's yoke altogether, and eternal spiritual death is its final and terrible end.

In addition, Achan's punishment was a reminder to all Israel—and to us—that God takes sin seriously. He is passionate about His holiness, and He designed redemption as His people's opportunity to showcase that holiness so He will be glorified in all things. Moreover, His glory never contradicts His children's good. The Israelites' safety and their rest in the Promised Land were inextricably bound to their faith in God and to their obedience to His covenant. Achan's punishment was meant to yoke Yahweh's people to Himself with stronger cords of trust and submission than ever before.

EVIL REDEEMED

Thus it was with renewed hope that the army of Israel went back to war after bringing God's holy judgment against the sin in their midst. (The story of the second battle against Ai is told in Josh. 8:1–29.) Joshua took not 1 percent but 100 percent of the infantry into battle a second time against Ai, and he followed the military strategy laid out by Yahweh Himself. Amazingly God would use what had been set in motion by Achan's sin and work it not *against* but *for* the Israelites, transforming evil to good.

The plan was to take advantage of Ai's false sense of security from Israel's former disaster and to seduce the men of Ai into overconfidence. To that end, Joshua set up an ambush of the city, situating a secret contingent of his finest troops behind Ai at night and marching the rest of his army into plain view across from the city the next morning. When the warriors of Ai came out to engage the Israelites, God's people feigned retreat, running away as they had before and luring Ai's army to pursue them.

After all the men of the city had rushed to join the pursuit, Joshua signaled to his soldiers behind the city, who rushed in and set the city ablaze. Too late, the men of Ai saw the smoke and recognized their imminent danger, caught as they were between Joshua's main army (which had turned back to the battle) and the Israelite soldiers streaming from the burning city.

Once the army of Ai had been defeated, their city was devoted to destruction as God had said, except that this time, "Israel did carry off for themselves the livestock and plunder of this city, as the LORD had instructed Joshua" (v. 27).

What a fool Achan had been! He had disbelieved God's goodness, thinking Him stingy for withholding riches from His children and grasping to procure treasure for himself. Not only did he forfeit rest in the land, but he forfeited his very life. In contrast, his comrades, who had believed and obeyed, would receive not only the land but its riches as well.

All, that is, except for the thirty-six who had died because of Achan's sin. But God had not abandoned their families, for He had already made provision in His covenant for a regular tithe (tenth) of the Israelites' earnings to be given back to God "so that the Levites . . . and the aliens, the fatherless and the widows . . . [could] come and eat and be satisfied" (Deut. 14:29). God would let stand the consequences of Achan's sin—He would not resurrect the thirty-six casualties of war. But just as the men of Israel had been God's hands to punish Achan for his sin, they must also become God's hands to provide for the victims of Achan's sin. They must see to it that their comrades' widows and children receive their share of the booty of Ai. In this way God through His people overcame Achan's sin so that the evil he had perpetrated would not prevail.

For this also is true: Those who are yoked to God must not only fight for justice and righteousness in the land to make a way for their families to thrive and their worship of God to be enjoyed. They must also be willing to show that God is a compassionate Father, comforting those who mourn their losses, providing for those who have no resources, and even restoring to community those who evidence genuine repentance. This is the burden and the glory of the yoke that binds us to Him, and Him to us. Being one with Him, we must also act as He would act.

HIDDEN SIN EXPOSED

Consider again the prostitute who crashed the dinner party of Simon the Pharisee. (This story continues from Luke 7:36–50.) She had wept tears that evidenced repentance, mourned sin's damage, and celebrated forgiveness. This weeping should have opened wide the door for her reentry to the community of faith, as God's grace had opened to her the door to eternal life.

But when Simon saw this woman of the street wiping Jesus' feet with her let-down hair and smelled the fragrance of her sin-bought perfume, he did not open his heart to his restored "sister" of the covenant, but instead further closed his heart to the One who had restored her, saying to himself, "If this man were a prophet, he would know who is touching him and what kind of woman she is—that she is a sinner." Simon's heart judged both the woman and the rabbi, missing altogether the drama of worship he had just witnessed. For Simon thought Jesus failed to recognize He'd been defiled, thereby invalidating His credentials as God's prophet. The Pharisee's heart was blinded not only to the meaning and the worth of the prostitute's tears but also to the rebuke they carried regarding his own unrighteous behavior toward Jesus.

For the rabbi from Nazareth was fully aware not only of who the woman was but also of what unspoken disdain there was in Simon's heart. For though this Pharisee had not given words to his thoughts, Scripture tells us that "Jesus answered him" as though he had spoken aloud. "Simon, I have something to tell you," Jesus said. These words were not a request to speak but a well-recognized introduction to a public rebuke. Kenneth Bailey explains that this phrase "is used all across the Middle East to introduce a blunt speech that the listener may not want to hear."[2] Simon's reply, "Tell me, teacher," was self-incriminating, for though he called Him "teacher" (or rabbi), he had not treated Him with the respect due a rabbi. Now, however, Simon was opening the way for Jesus to expose his sin, which would mercifully offer him opportunity to repent of his insolence.

The parable Jesus then told Simon was about two debtors, one owing a moneylender about two months' earnings, the other owing the same moneylender about two *years'* earnings. When neither could pay, the moneylender forgave the indebtedness of both, and Jesus' question to Simon was, "Now which of them will love him more?" The Pharisee was caught. "I suppose the one who had the bigger debt canceled," he replied, the logic being too obvious to miss. "You have judged correctly," Jesus said.

Then Christ went on to interpret His own parable by exposing Simon's sin to all who were present. He stunned the circle of respectable, self-righteous men reclining at Simon's table by drawing attention to the woman—one of the most despised and least empowered members of that community—and praising her for doing the very thing Simon himself ought to have done. Jesus' public rebuke of His host was an unthinkable discourtesy in the Middle Eastern culture, and the rabbi from Nazareth was certain to be thought incredibly ungrateful and uncouth in pointing out Simon's social failure. Those who think imitating Jesus means we must be slaves to propriety and never offend others fail to understand the shock His next words caused.

They were words addressed to Simon but spoken directly to the woman at His feet. Kenneth Bailey explains, "Were Jesus facing Simon, we would imagine a tone of harsh accusation, . . . but delivered facing the woman, it takes on a tone of gentleness and gratitude, expressed to a daring woman in desperate need of a kind word."[3] Looking at the repentant prostitute, Jesus asked Simon, "Do you see this woman?" That is to say, Do you, Simon, see her actions as I do? "I came into your house," Jesus said, reminding Simon of his obligations as host. "You did not give me any water for my feet, but she wet my feet with her tears and wiped them with her hair. You did not give me a kiss, but this woman, from the time I entered, has not stopped kissing my feet. You did not put oil on my head, but she has poured perfume on my feet."

Then Jesus, referring back to the parable He had told, concluded His rebuke of Simon's heart attitude with these words, "Therefore, I tell you, her sins, which were many, have been forgiven; hence she has shown great love. But the one to whom little is forgiven, loves little" (Luke 7:47 NRSV). The point was clear: This woman's actions toward Jesus had not been seductive or immoral, as Simon had supposed. Rather, they had been an outpouring of her gratitude for having been forgiven. More than that, her actions had made up for a deliberate deficit in Simon's hospitality toward Him as guest, and, therefore, she ought to have been praised not disdained by him.

Surely this woman had sinned much; this accounts for the greatness of her gratitude and love. But did she really have more sins than Simon or was she merely more aware of them and more willing to repent of them? Consider the list of sins that Simon (according to Kenneth Bailey) needed to confess and for which he ought to have sought forgiveness: "Deep levels of pride, arrogance, hard-heartedness, hostility, a judgmental spirit, slim understanding of what really defiles, a rejection of sinners, insensitivity, misunderstanding of the nature of God's forgiveness, and sexism. The most damaging [of all is] that Simon witnessed the woman's dramatic action and . . . refused to accept her repentance."[4] Simon the Pharisee was a greater debtor than he knew, and his own refusal to see it and to mourn over it meant it was he and not the immoral woman who was refusing Yahweh's yoke. Righteous though he appeared to his community, Simon was inwardly hard of heart and far from God's kingdom.

To this fallen but repentant woman Jesus then said, "Your sins are forgiven." His words created quite a stir, for those at Simon's table, already stunned by Jesus' rebuke of their host, were further offended that He would claim the right to forgive sins, a privilege exclusively Yahweh's. Their reaction did not bode well for either the woman's or the rabbi's acceptance in that community, but Jesus continued to focus His attention and kindness on the restored daughter of the covenant still standing at His feet. "Your faith has saved you," He said gently to her. Then, in the traditional shalom of blessing, He added, "Go in peace."

Under Jesus' peace-giving this weeping woman of sin had become a woman at rest, not because she could rest in her community (they may well have continued to ostracize her) but because she was secure in Jesus' love. A woman at rest in Jesus knows she will not be destroyed no matter what others may do or say. The inner quiet and tranquillity of her soul gives her strength to face the disappointment of rejection and the loneliness of not being cherished. It also protects her from giving way to bitterness or revenge. Such a woman of inner beauty can wait and persevere in her loving, undeterred from using her gifts to bless others and to forgive even those who mean her harm.

WEEPING AND WAITING

This is the life of Christ in us, if we are yoked to Him as the prostitute was. Sometimes the direction He leads us in is pleasant, and we are glad to be led. But at other times we want our own way and hate the restrictions He places on us by His Spirit. And many times we feel both ways at the same time. Ambivalence indeed abounds.

Our greatest struggle, however, is not to eliminate our ambivalence, for until our redemption is perfected in glory, we will be redeemed but imperfect here on earth, caught up in the mystery of grace. Sometimes we will revel in our intimacy with God and sometimes we will rebel against it. The deeper question is how God responds to our ambivalence and the actions that flow from it. Does Jesus throw off His yoke and disown us when we disown Him? Did He love the prostitute when she anointed Him but reject His disciple when he swore he didn't know Him? Did His love for Bill and me as Mama lay dying vacillate according to our ability to accept this loss at any given moment?

Considering our inherent tendency to want to strain against Christ's yoke when it is dangerous or inconvenient or asks more of us than we want to risk, can any of us truly enter the rest Jesus offers? And once there, can we stay? When we fear and run from grace to follow our own self-sufficient path to happiness, how does God respond to our resistance? Those who refuse to repent, like Simon the Pharisee, cannot receive Christ's forgiveness, for they have closed themselves off from the grace and comfort of His gentle yoke. It is no wonder they remain restless and can find no peace.

Even those who *have* received Christ's yoke sometimes pull desperately against it in times of fear or crisis. "Restless" and "without peace" can hardly begin to describe the apostle Peter's inner distress as he stumbled out of Caiaphas's courtyard into the night, weeping bitterly over his denial of Jesus. That look—those eyes—would he ever be able to erase the image seared on his soul? He who had been so brash, so verbal, so brave—how could he have been so naive about the depth of sin waiting to ambush his own heart? How could he ever face his Lord again? Worse than that, what if he never *could* face his Lord again? What if Jesus died with this monstrous betrayal between them? How could Peter live knowing his terrible sin and not knowing his terrible sin forgiven?

Judas Iscariot faced a similar remorse. He, too, thought death would be preferable to bearing the weight of his guilt, especially after he'd been unable to reverse his decision by returning the silver the Jewish leaders had paid him. Along with the eleven other disciples, he had been intimately yoked to Jesus for three years, hearing His truth, watching His miracles, dispersing His funds—albeit sometimes to his own pocket (see John 12:4–6).

What had possessed Judas to betray the rabbi he served? Scripture says that "Satan entered into him" (13:27), but had Judas given Satan an open door of some kind so his soul had been easily entered? God alone knows. But Judas's suicide because of his overriding guilt reveals the strength of the grip Satan had on his heart, for nothing but stubborn hard-heartedness in disbelieving God's love for us can keep us from being forgiven by Christ's death in our place. Not until we get Home will we know whether Judas repented before he hanged himself, but if he is not in heaven, it will not be because Jesus was unable or unwilling to forgive him.

We do know, however, that Peter refused the option of suicide. His heart was broken, to be sure, for he had deeply hurt the Lord he deeply loved. Even if Peter during those next terrible days remembered Jesus' teaching regarding His own resurrection, how could he be certain Jesus would receive him back to His heart after he had publicly denied Him three times? The anguish of Peter's sorrow must surely have intensified to the point of despair when the following day Jesus was led to Golgotha and crucified in open shame. This cruel death and the gaping wound in Peter's own heart must have shaken his soul and his faith to the core.

RESTORED TO ONENESS

That is no doubt why, when the women on the third day after Jesus' death brought the disciples word that Jesus' body was no longer in the tomb,

Peter and John raced to the burial garden with such haste. Perhaps it also explains why, when they found there Jesus' undisturbed grave clothes but not Jesus, Scripture says that John "saw and believed" that Jesus had risen (John 20:8), but Peter "went away, wondering to himself what had happened" (Luke 24:12). Peter's guilt had gotten in the way of his faith, even in the presence of Jesus' empty tomb.

It is often the same with us. When we sin, the accuser of our souls finds ample data for casting doubt on our faith. We may wonder if we were ever genuinely yoked to Christ in the first place, for our faith in ourselves is shattered by our rebellion. And so it should be, for even our most fervent resolve, like Peter's, can give way before unexpected terror. Those who imagine the Christian life will be an uninterrupted journey from faith to more faith, from glory directly to more glory, have not yet plumbed the depth of their own capacity for sin. "The heart," Jeremiah reminds us, "is deceitful above all things and beyond cure" (Jer. 17:9). It is a grace that God reveals our sin to us, for faith in ourselves was never His intent.

But often our disobedience shakes our faith in God too, for we wonder how He can forgive our failure and take us back again and again, even when we repent. In fact the more we love and want to serve Him, the more we feel His pain at our sinning. Like Peter, we have seen the eyes of sorrow and have known it was our sin that brought the sorrow there. The more we know of His heart toward us, the more we feel His heart broken by us. This is the most unbearable cost of love—the knowledge that we have deeply wounded the One we deeply love. This is the cost Peter bore for three agonizing days, and his agitation was most surely occasioned by the knowledge that Jesus died more alone than He had to be. Thus is our sin the more terrible as we love the more passionately.

It is the same with those whom we love and by whom we are loved on earth. Jill Briscoe tells the story of her rebellious teen years when her friends were urging her into behavior she knew went contrary to the standards her missionary parents had taught her to observe. Taunted by a friend saying she was just afraid of what her father would do to her if he ever found out, she replied that she was more afraid of what *she* would do to her *father* if he ever found out. This desire to please the ones we deeply love is what motivates us to bless and not harm them. But this same desire causes us incredible pain when our frailty or selfishness or revenge or self-protection causes us to hurt them. Love is a two-sided sword in our hands.

Imagine, then, what a leap of hope and dread must have exploded in Peter's soul when he heard the women repeat the angel's words to them at Jesus' tomb, "But go, tell his disciples and Peter, 'He is going ahead of you into Galilee. There you will see him, just as he told you'" (Mark 16:7). Go tell His disciples *and Peter!* Then the reunion with Jesus would include him too not just the other ten! He would see Jesus again—oh, glorious day! He

189

would look into His eyes once more—but what would he see there? A holy fear contended with unspeakable joy in the torn soul of this repentant man.

The intimate details of Peter's first encounter with Jesus after His resurrection are not recorded in Scripture. Even the usually outspoken apostle never disclosed the words that passed between them before Jesus even revealed Himself to the other ten disciples. We only know that the men who had been with Jesus on the Emmaus road were told, "It is true! The Lord has arisen and has appeared to Simon [Peter]" (Luke 24:34). The apostle Paul reaffirms Peter's private meeting with Jesus, writing that after the resurrection Jesus "appeared to Peter, and then to the Twelve" (1 Cor. 15:5).

What did Jesus say to the man who had publicly denied even knowing Him? And how had the disciple responded? What words did Peter offer to express his sorrow and repentance? Did their tears mingle as penitent and Savior conversed together? Having heard Peter's confession, did Jesus repeat His invitation, "Come to Me, My heavy-burdened friend, and I will give you rest"? Peter had not thrown off the yoke he had shouldered in oneing himself to his Lord, but what chafing it had caused when he had jerked aside in sudden opposition to Him! And Jesus' shoulders were bruised in the jerking too, for though He and the angels in heaven rejoice at His children's repentance and return, His body bears the marks of our sin—His pierced head and hands and feet and side—even into eternity. This is the mystery and the wonder of grace. Someday we will see for ourselves and we will give way to an abandon of worship and joy.

Nothing is ever bland or tidy with God, but always mystifying and passionate. He is ever in the process of bringing moral order out of the chaos of our lives but He never despairs that our chaos may win. He always wins. He will make a fool of the enemy in the end, for He alone can take our worst sin and turn it to good if we will repent.

Moses the murderer oversaw the death of every Egyptian firstborn to bring Yahweh glory. "I have raised you up for this very purpose," God told Pharaoh, "that I might show you my power and that my name might be proclaimed in all the earth" (Exod. 9:16). Rahab the barren prostitute became Rahab the fruitful princess, named in the genealogy of God's own Messiah. Achan's sin caused Israel defeat, but it set the stage for Ai's overconfidence and eventual destruction.

So it was with the immoral woman at the Samaritan well and the one in Simon's courtyard—tainted women, the least believed and least respected of all, becoming evangelist and ardent worshiper, praised by Jesus Himself. Every time God brings good out of evil and life out of death, we can celebrate by spitting in the enemy's face, turning back on him the shame he meant for us. Thus is the invincible justice of God revealed against sin every moment of every day, foreshadowing that great day when Satan will be overthrown at last and death will never threaten God's children again.

190

That is why there is nothing more crucial to living the Christian life than the continuing and continual repentance of the individual believer. In the recurring chaos of our moral failure, we must again and again open our heart's door so God can move to restore order by inviting us to rest in Him. What opens the door to His coming is our repentance—acknowledging and turning from our sin every time it overtakes us. When there is sin in the camp of my heart, I must deal with it ruthlessly lest it contaminate and ultimately destroy me. The transgression may appear slight, but any forbidden thing, no matter how small, will grow to overwhelm me if left unrepented.

In their fantasy book, *Tales of the Kingdom*, David and Karen Mains tell the story of Amanda, a princess who found and kept a dragon egg in Great Park instead of turning it over to be destroyed. She knew she was wrong, but when the baby dragon hatched, she became more and more attached to it and more and more unwilling to give it up. So she kept it hidden and avoided going to the Great Celebration where she would see the King and he would see her sin. Repentance would mean both seeing his sorrow and giving up her forbidden thing, and so she refused to repent.

But the dragon did not stop growing and soon it was no longer cute, no longer harmless, no longer manageable. Finally, when it threatened to destroy her and all of Great Park with its full-grown ferocity, she had to decide: Kill the forbidden thing or be killed by it. Neither the decision nor the task was easy, and her wounds from the battle were many and deep. But deepest of all was the wound to her pride and to her perceived worthiness of being loved by the King. Would he receive her back and dance with her again at the Great Celebration? She did not find rest for her soul until she finally not only turned her back on her sin but also returned to look in the eyes of the King to see his love shining toward her.[5]

Restoration of our hearts to the heart of our heavenly Father is always the intention and end result of our repentance. The legitimate shame we feel for having harbored or indulged what is forbidden can only be banished in the encircling arms of our Creator-God who made us for Himself. This is His passion, He who "is patient with [us], not wanting anyone to perish, but everyone to come to repentance" (2 Peter 3:9). "For God did not send his Son into the world to condemn the world, but to save the world through him" (John 3:17). This is God's good news, the gospel offered to all who will receive His gift of repentance.

GLORY IN FORGIVENESS

What, then, is the meaning and purpose of repentance? According to Webster's dictionary, to repent means "to turn from sin and dedicate oneself to the amendment of one's life," or "to feel sorrow, regret, or contrition for."[6] But when the apostle Peter calls the Jerusalem Jews to recognize they had killed their own Messiah, he says, "Repent, then, and turn to God, so that your sins may be wiped out, that times of refreshing may come from the Lord, and that he may send [again] the Christ, who has been appointed for you—even Jesus" (Acts 3:19–20).

Thus the call to repentance according to Scripture requires that we turn from our sin, but not toward a greater effort at self-improvement. Rather, we are to "turn to God" so that our "sins may be wiped out" by the blood of Jesus, not by our own dedication to amending our lives. Moreover, our repentance will result in "times of refreshing [that] come from the Lord," for God always nourishes us with His grace when we acknowledge our sin and ask for His forgiveness. Did not the tax collector "[go] home justified before God" when he beat his breast and prayed, "God, have mercy on me, a sinner" (Luke 18:9–14)? The Holy Spirit always blows His refreshing wind on hearts distraught by the recognition of personal and particular transgression.

In fact repentance itself reflects God's glory, for it is His gift to us in the first place. The apostle Paul challenged believers in the early Roman church with this question: "Do you show contempt for the riches of [God's] kindness, tolerance and patience, not realizing that God's kindness leads you toward repentance?" (Rom. 2:4). Compassion and not condemnation is the motive behind the Holy Spirit's work of conviction in our hearts. If He never showed us our sin, we would never address the heart issues that keep us far from God. But because of His kindness, He leads us to repentance, the doorway to His grace.

And when we do repent, God always cleanses exactly what He has shown us needs cleansing. When Isaiah stood exposed before God's throne, he cried out, "Woe to me! I am ruined! For I am a man of unclean lips, and I live among a people of unclean lips, and my eyes have seen the King, the LORD Almighty" (see Isa. 6:1–8). Then the lips that Isaiah knew to be unclean were cleansed at once by one of the angels, who took a burning coal from God's holy altar and touched Isaiah's mouth with it, saying, "See, this has touched your lips; your guilt is taken away and your sin atoned for." Repentance (acknowledging and turning from sin) brought Isaiah the refreshment of knowing his sin forgiven and his relationship with a holy God restored.

But Isaiah's repentance was not horrifying to him. His *sin* dismayed him, but he had seen the King and would never be the same again. Rather than run from the holy God he had encountered in his vision, he longed to stay connected to Him and to do whatever He wanted him to do. When the voice of the Lord sent an invitation abroad to use lips (once unclean) for holy purposes by asking, "Whom shall I send? And who will go for us?" (i.e., Who will speak words of truth in the name of the Triune God?), Isaiah was quick to respond, "Here am I. Send me!"

This was not duty but zeal, not penance but passion, not begrudging the effort but begging for a chance to obey this One he now desired more than anything else in his life. Even when Isaiah was told that no one would listen or respond to his words of witness on Yahweh's behalf, he did not hesitate—he would speak what he was sent to speak, even knowing his words would go unheeded and his "ministry" would fail by earthly standards. Obedience is all God asks. The consequences are always up to God to do as He sees fit. This is the passionate rest of being sold out to God when once we have been in His presence and have tasted His love and grace.

TRUSTING GRACE

What am I trying to say? Just this: Repentance is a friend—the best friend we can have, spiritually speaking. We have heard Jesus' words: "Be perfect . . . as your heavenly Father is perfect" (Matt. 5:48), and too often we have dedicated ourselves to amending our lives to bring our behavior in line with God's law. But consider what else Jesus said in this same passage: Anger is the same as murder; lust is as bad as adultery; our behavior must exceed the righteousness of the most fastidiously religious among us; we must love our neighbors *and* our enemies (see Matt. 5:20–48). In this context, Jesus' call to perfection seems sadistic and cruel, for surely He knew no mortal man could measure up to this standard.

But in fact Jesus' admonition to "be perfect" is the kindest call of all, for it invites us to admit we have *not* measured up as perfect. Someone else's perfection must cover our own imperfection, and this is the gospel—that our repentance is everything because God's grace is everything. And it is our repentance that invites us to the banquet of His grace if we believe Jesus' righteousness is our own through faith, and we walk into God's kingdom of rest through Christ, who is the door.

Rest is never exemption from struggle, but an invitation into struggle. However, it is the struggle to believe God's love, not to try harder to earn it; it is the struggle to admit our sin instead of striving to cover it up; it is the struggle to stop pretending we're strong and instead ask God for His strength in our weakness. Sometimes we fear rest, because it inevitably requires that we face our helplessness against the deep hold sin has on our hearts and we are left with only our imperfection, neediness, and weakness to recommend us to God. How much we would rather bring our goodness to Him—our accomplishments and spiritual victories and ministry successes. How odd that He prefers our failure—and even at times precipitates our failure—so that we will cling to Him until He blesses us.

And what does this have to say about our intimate relationships? Are they not dependent on repentance and grace far more than on perfection and performance? Far too often we make our list of expectations and requirements of each other and then we evaluate one another against them. We think if we repeat our demands often enough (or sweetly enough or persuasively enough or threateningly enough) that success will follow—the other person will change and conform to our list. And the fact of sin (we will always fail each other in some way at some time) we see as an insurmountable obstacle to our rest, necessitating our guardedness, our refusal to trust, our willingness to settle for no-hassle, our stinginess with forgiveness—lest the failure be repeated and we be hurt again. The other's sin thus has unlimited power to hinder our rest, and we think it craziness to live any other way than defensively and on duty.

Yet that is not how Jesus lived, nor is it how His Spirit in us desires to live out Jesus' life in us. How did He deal with relationship "failure"—when others failed Him or refused to receive His love?

First, He entrusted Himself to no man, for He didn't need to be told that the heart of everyone is deceitful (see John 2:23–25). That is to say, He lived in reality about mankind's fallenness and refused to demand that anyone "come through" for Him, though He often *asked for* their faith, their obedience, and their prayers. We too must recognize that every relationship will disappoint us sooner or later, and our trust in any person cannot be absolute. We can and should, however, risk trusting those who consistenly show evidence of the work of God's grace in their relationships—the grace to repent, the grace to believe in God's forgiveness, the grace to offer forgiveness to those who have sinned against them. The reason I rest in Bill as much as I do is because I have seen him repent and forgive time and again, and I trust the grace of God I see at work in his heart.

And at those times when Bill does not repent, I must keep my own line of connection to Jesus open enough to allow the Holy Spirit as much time as it takes to work His forgiveness into my heart. I must also continue desiring Bill's repentance and become ready to express my forgiveness if and when he does repent, so that our marriage can be more fully restored. What Oswald Chambers calls "the enormous leisure of God"[7] in working out His purposes allows all of us time to persevere and grow in our faith, moving steadily in the direction of forgiveness and reconciliation, for that is the direction in which Jesus always moved. Particularly with His chosen disciples Jesus entrusted as much of His heart as they were able to bear (see Mark 4:30 and John 16:12). And as their trust in Him deepened, their intimacy with Him flourished as well.

Jesus also always moved to offer whatever was needed to express love to the other. Because He was God, He was always right in deciding what was needed in any given situation. Because we are not God, we must listen carefully for His voice in us to show us what is the right way to love another at any given moment—whether to confront or to comfort, whether to speak or to keep silence, whether to act or to wait. As we pray for the other, we must take God's cue as to how to respond, and then respond that way ourselves.

194

Because we are not God, however, it goes without saying that we, like Simon Peter, will also have to repent of our own sins as the Holy Spirit reveals them to us, and we will have to ask forgiveness from the person whom we have harmed by our sin. This we must become willing to do regarding every sin, no matter how "minor" it may seem (especially in comparison to the other person's sin against us). My sin is always mine to repent, whether Bill's wrongdoing seems greater than mine or not and even whether he ever repents of his or not.

Thus our rest in God is dependent not on our circumstances but always on grace—His grace to each of us individually and His grace to us overflowing to others, especially our spouses. Our trust can never rest fully in ourselves nor in our friends nor in our spouses, but in the power of Jesus Christ to spread His love abroad in our hearts until it becomes a river of grace overflowing its banks to refresh those who don't deserve it. How else can we live with and love another fallen human being except the way Christ lives within and loves us? If we would receive His grace, we must be willing to dispense it as well.

THE RELIEF OF REPENTANCE

Repentance—for both men and women—requires humility to acknowledge our sin as the Spirit reveals it to us and to ask for the grace of forgiveness time and again. Our continual immediate response to the Spirit's chafing keeps our relational yokes easy to wear and our burdens of sin from weighing us down. Of course one mark of being yoked to Him is that even if we don't want to repent, the chafing will continue to irritate and invite us back to His heart until we finally yield to His love.

Sometimes, however, we must struggle long with a larger chafing, an entrenched and stubborn pulling against the Spirit who yokes us to God and to His purposes. This habitual rebellion calls for repentance, to be sure, but we may need to turn to Christ for mercy in pulling our sin out by its roots, no matter what the cost. This is what Bill and I came to need as we arrived at a sort of standoff in our marriage during the months following Mama's death. We had recommitted ourselves to our marriage. We had seen God work in each other's hearts. We had known His grace and His presence during the months of bringing Mama to her Home-going. But after her death, when our life resumed an outward semblance of greater normalcy, we found that the mighty earthquake of death had dislodged significant pillars that had previously sustained our inner lives. Old habits of addiction and control began rearing their ugly heads more strongly than ever, and these strongholds had to be revoked at an even deeper level if our marital oneness was to survive and thrive.

For me, what was at stake again was whether I should exert pressure on Bill to deal with his alcoholism, which he had used to numb his pain during Mama's dying. Therefore, the month after Mama went Home to be with Jesus, I took a week away from my own home to be with Him at a prayer retreat. I needed the quiet to grieve and pray but I also had another agenda. Two years had passed since Bill and I had recommitted ourselves to our oneness, and he was still drinking. Was it time to force the issue?

I needed to draw aside to listen for God's voice telling me what He wanted me to do. The final day of the retreat was to be a day of silence, and that is the day I'd set aside for making my decision. Before daybreak I made my way to the chapel to pray and wait for God's word to me. Sitting on the floor before a lit candle, I confessed my sins before Him so I could hear His voice clearly. Finally, I was ready to ask, "Shall I insist that Bill get help? Yes or no?"

Quietly I listened. For many minutes there was no answer. I searched my heart for more sins to confess, then waited some more. Still there was no answer. For a long time I prayed and listened, but my heart found no rest in either a yes or no from God. I left the chapel unenlightened and disappointed. God had assured me of His presence, but He had not told me what to do. How was I supposed to find rest in His silence?

The next day I told a friend about my experience, and she asked me point-blank, "Does your struggle have anything to do with your own self-image?" Instantly I remembered a conversation I'd had months earlier when a woman had asked me after a talk I'd given, "Is Bill still drinking?" I had answered "Yes," and internally I had added, "But if I were doing things right he probably wouldn't be."

My illusion of control over Bill's choices was more deeply entrenched than I had thought. This quandary over whether or not to force Bill's hand had in reality been a control issue all along—my desire to make him change by taking things into my own hands. For this I needed to deeply repent—and to let go of the control.

This is not to say that confronting an alcoholic with hard choices is always wrong; sometimes it is the only right and loving thing to do. But God made it clear to me in that moment of truth that He wanted me to rest in Him and wait for Him to carry out His own timetable with the man I loved. Though I hated the thought of Bill's continued drinking, the realization that God was in charge meant that I could go off duty about the alcoholism. What a relief to confess my sinful control strategies and let them go! If Bill never quit, I would still be God's daughter, and He could still use me to show His love to the man of my vows. I could return to the comfort of Jesus' yoke and become once again a woman at rest in Him.

Thus I entered a new level of rest in God, having nothing to hide about the sin in my heart, nothing to prove about my own goodness, and nothing ultimately to lose, because of Jesus' presence with me. I began to look more and more to my heavenly Father for the nourishment of His grace toward me, and less and less to Bill, yielding more and more my demands that he change his life or that he never let me down.

And an amazing thing took place in my heart in the following months as I lived in the relief of not having to have Bill be different in order for me to love him. Not only did I fight him less, but I began to respect him more. I could see he was just a man, struggling to know how to live, pursuing a self-sufficiency I knew would not work, but subject to the same blindness and stubbornness of heart that I saw in myself. My growing respect for my husband surprised me, and so did my growing desire and willingness to submit my heart to him. He was an unfinished vessel not yet fully given over to the Potter's design, but so was I. And as I trusted my life to Christ, I also longed to rest my heart in Bill.

In the next two chapters we will explore some differences between what it looks like for men and women to rest in Christ. Chapter 10 will deal with the suffering required of men as they lay down their lives for the women under their care, and chapter 11 will concern itself with the glory of a woman's submissive spirit.

QUESTIONS TO CONSIDER

1. Tell about a time when, like Joshua, you felt God had let you down without reason or explanation (as far as you could discern). How, if ever, was the situation resolved?

2. When have you been harmed because of someone else's sin? Describe your process of learning to forgive the one whose sin did you damage.

3. When has someone else been harmed because of your sin? Describe your process of seeking to heal the relationship.

4. What are the greatest hindrances to your own repentance?

5. Explain why you agree or disagree with this statement: "There is nothing more crucial to living the Christian life than the continual repentance of the individual believer."

6. Give an example of how our repentance is related to our rest (with God or with others).

Regarding the opening story:

Chuck's willingness to ask forgiveness of Nate is more crucial to their intimacy than his earlier attempts to justify himself or to never sin against him again.

7. What usually prevents us from listening, as Chuck did, to the anger and hurt someone else feels because of something we did?

CHAPTER TEN

SACRIFICE

The Suffering of Love

JIM HAD THOUGHT it would feel more exciting, this renewed wooing of his wife, Denise. They had struggled for the last year of their nine-year-old marriage, and the counselor had challenged him to "court" her again, to pursue her heart, and to make sacrifices to show her his love. The men in Jim's accountability group—Christian men wanting to improve their marriages—had been a real encouragement, but after ten weeks of trying to live more sacrificially, none of them felt particularly heroic either.

Then Larry, Jim's counselor, met with the group one evening to help them assess their progress. "What changes have you made in your marriages that reflect Christ's suffering for the church?" he asked.

The men glanced sheepishly at each other, then at Larry. No one had thrown himself in front of a truck or fought off ruffians to save his wife. Had they been deceiving themselves? Were they nothing but well-intentioned failures? No one felt qualified to say a word.

"Okay," said Larry, "let's try a different approach. What have you done for your wives in the past two months you never would have done two years ago?"

That being an easier question, several men spoke up. George, usually a miserly type, had taken money from a savings account to buy a diamond bracelet for his wife's birthday. His friends smiled and nodded—this was a major shift for George. Lee, the "macho" one of the group, told how he had confided to his wife that a Boy Scout leader had molested him as a boy. The men's silence was a mixture of self-consciousness and respect.

After a moment, Fred, a Type-A personality, broke the silence. "Last night," he offered, "I didn't yell at my wife when she was fifteen minutes late getting ready to go out for dinner. In fact I even complimented her when she finally came downstairs. Frankly it wasn't easy, but the look on her face made me feel pretty good."

Frank said he'd felt the same way when he'd actually changed the baby's diaper without being asked—not just once but four times in the last two weeks. John, the accountant, had ended an argument with his wife without having to prove he was right, and Carl, the unassuming newcomer, admitted with a shy smile, "Yesterday I did the opposite—I told my wife I thought she was wrong— usually I just give in to her."

Jim grinned with the rest of the men, then told his own story of how quick he'd always been to criticize Denise for not being neat, and how last week he had instead pitched in to help her straighten the house after work to get ready for company.

None of the stories were heroic, but all were stories of sacrifice. No one had received a medal, but each had had a taste of acting like the good man he was because of the presence of Christ in him.

Perhaps, Jim said to himself, I can do this, after all.

The suffering of love occurs far more often in the context of the ordinary than of the extraordinary. When men obey the apostle Paul's admonition to love their wives "just as Christ loved the church and gave himself up for her to make her holy" (Eph. 5:25–26), they seldom are called to physical death as Christ was. They are, however, called to the less sensational imitation of Jesus' daily interactions with His followers.

Christ still treats every disciple according to his or her own need in the moment, so that all of us can know ourselves loved with strength and kindness into righteous living. Men who long to love their wives as Christ loves the church—like the members of Jim's accountability group—will find great joy in the little sacrifices that make up the larger sacrifice of changed hearts, revealed in incremental changes of behavior. In repenting of former pride or selfishness, of thoughtlessness or even abuse, a husband can discover and meet his wife's particular needs, thus imitating the sacrificial love of Christ Himself and extending His kingdom in important, though nonspectacular, ways.

The solemn procession had started at dawn, several Levites leading the way. On their shoulders they bore the sacred weight of the ark of the covenant, symbol of God's presence with His people. Masses of people followed—men, women, and children, including the non-Israelites living among them—moving purposefully from their tents in Gilgal, west into the valley separating Mount Gerizim from Mount Ebal. The long-anticipated day had come, and each family made its way to the position assigned to its tribe—six tribes on the south toward Mount Gerizim, six tribes toward Mount Ebal on the north, the priests and the ark in the valley in between.

It took some time to convene almost two million people, but this was in accordance with what Moses had prescribed before his death. "When the LORD your God has brought you into the land you are entering to possess," he had told them, "you are to proclaim on Mount Gerizim the blessings [of obeying God's commands], and on Mount Ebal the curses [of disobeying God's commands]" (Deut. 11:29). In compliance with Moses' instructions they now filled the valley on this holy day of assembly.

At last each tribe stood in its appointed place, and all eyes turned toward the north as Joshua stepped up to the huge slabs of whitewashed stone set up on Mount Ebal. The towering pillars could be seen by all those present as Joshua wrote on them the words of the law Moses had been given by God Himself. Then Joshua read the law aloud in the hearing of all the people, reminding them of their covenantal responsibility to remain yoked to Yahweh by observing His commands. Obedience, as they knew, was integral to the cost of their covenantal yoking. (This incident is described in Josh. 8:30–35.)

COVENANT VOWS

Every covenant has at least two parties, each party promising to do whatever has been agreed on. The covenant between Yahweh and Israel stipulated that Yahweh would be Israel's God and that the Israelites would be and act like His people, living holy lives by obeying the commands Joshua had just declared across the valley to all the people.

When Joshua had finished, the people announced to one another across the valley the many blessings of keeping the covenant and the dire consequences of violating the covenant. From Mount Gerizim resounded the voices naming the promised blessings that would flow from obedience:

You will be blessed in the city and blessed in the country.

The fruit of your womb will be blessed, and the crops of your land and the young of your livestock. . . .

You will be blessed when you come in and blessed when you go out.

The LORD will establish you as his holy people, as he promised you on oath. . . . Then all the peoples on earth will see that you are called by the name of the LORD, and they will fear you.

DEUTERONOMY 28:3–13

The blessings continued, echoing across the valley: The Israelites and their land would be fruitful and they would be honored among the nations. But they would have to forsake all other gods and remain yoked in obedience to Yahweh alone.

Then from Mount Ebal came loud cries of stern warning—the curses that would come on God's people if they disobeyed and worshiped other gods.

You will be cursed in the city and cursed in the country. . . .

The fruit of your womb will be cursed, and the crops of your land, and the calves of your herds and the lambs of your flocks.

You will be cursed when you come in and cursed when you go out.

The LORD will send on you curses, confusion and rebuke in everything you put your hand to, until you are destroyed and come to sudden ruin.

DEUTERONOMY 28:16–66

The curses went on, terrible and terrifying. If the Israelites broke the covenant, they would lose their rest, becoming aliens again in a land of captivity among a people who knew not Yahweh and who would abuse them ruthlessly.

It was too beautiful a day to consider such heinous possibilities as were voiced from Mount Ebal in dire warning. Surely those who heard were well aware of their own proclivity to sin. How could they hope to avoid these called-out curses? No doubt the terror of bringing calamity on themselves stirred in every heart present as God's people considered the consequences of their inevitable sin.

FESTIVAL OF FORGIVENESS

Perhaps that is why God included one other event in the agenda of this day of sacred assembly. Halfway up Mount Ebal, the mount of cursing against lawbreakers, Joshua built an altar, using uncut fieldstones. This was not an altar of human accomplishment situated on Gerizim, the mount of blessing for obedience. No, this was an Ebal altar on the mount of God's just cursing—a necessary altar of divine grace for those who were making a vow of obedience they would all someday break.

On this unhewn altar would be sacrificed the burnt offering that fore-shadowed the death of Messiah, the Lamb of God who would take away the sin of the world. On behalf of all the Israelites, someone brought for-ward a flawless bull, laid hands on its head, then killed it on the north side of the altar, its blood pouring out against the altar as payment for the peo-ple's sin. Then the entire animal was burned on the altar, signifying the Israelites' complete surrender to and dependence on Yahweh to forgive their sins if they repented. Putting their trust in Yahweh's forgiveness (bought by the shedding of blood) was their part of the covenant when their obedience failed.

Finally, the day now far gone, the Israelite parents brought their weary children back to their tents. Reminded again that they were Yahweh's treas-ured possession, forgiven because of the shed blood, they would rest their souls in His love and rest their bodies in preparation for what still lay ahead. As they had done with Moses some years earlier, they now had reaffirmed once more their commitment to obedience. "This day I call heaven and earth as witnesses against you," Moses had said, "that I have set before you life and death, blessings and curses. Now choose life, so that you and your children may live" (Deut. 30:19–20).

Once again, they had chosen the Lord, had chosen life, had promised obedience, had repented of their sin, and had trusted the efficacy of the sacrifice on Mount Ebal. What lay ahead were battles yet to fight, terri-tory to take and hold, and long months of anxious waiting in their Gil-gal tents. From holy celebration in the valley they returned to conse-crated living in the camp, encouraged to live out their gratitude to God through renewed devotion to His commands. Yahweh's promise of fruit-fulness in the land no doubt rang joyously in their hearts, and hope ran high that their children after them would choose life as they themselves had just done.

But the rest in God's Promised Land for which they hoped would exact a price—not of perfection but of faith, not of works but of grace, not of ease but of suffering. The Ebal altar was more central to their hope than they knew, for the One whose death its sacrifice prefigured would also offer a yoke of oneness with Himself that would bear rich fruit, though not with-out cost.

YOKE OF SUFFERING

For like the Israelites of old, all who shoulder Jesus' yoke will not find it easy nor His burden light unless they have yielded fully to His leading. Two animals yoked together can accomplish much fruitful work, but only if they pull together. Opposing each other will harm them and compromise their productivity. When we take Jesus' yoke, we must let Him set both direction and pace for our lives. "Take my yoke upon you and learn from me," He said, "for I am gentle and humble in heart" (Matt. 11:29). What does His gentleness and heart-humbleness have to teach us? And what will be its price tag?

When Jesus described Himself as gentle and humble in heart, He was referring not to His personality type but to the posture of His heart, both toward His Father and toward His beloved, the church. Christ was continuously responsive to His Father as His head, and whatever the Father told Him to do on behalf of His Bride, He did. It is this level of intimacy with God to which Jesus invites us if we will shoulder His yoke. We are to learn from His example how to so fully rest in our heavenly Father that we can relate to others with gentle strength and sacrificial humility in any circumstance or distraction.

But Jesus was also describing His heart toward the church when He said He was gentle and humble in heart. And when He took the role of the lowest servant in washing His disciples' feet, He told them that such humility would be the cost of their discipleship as well, the price they would pay in being His yokefellows for the work of realizing His Kingdom on earth. "I have set you an example that you should do as I have done for you," He told them (John 13:15). That is to say, if menial tasks were what Jesus was willing to do as Lord of the church, such acts of service must characterize the disciples' lives too—and our own as well.

In theory we know this to be true, and some have even followed Jesus' example by physically washing the feet of fellow believers. But when humbling lessons come on us unexpectedly—when we are blindsided by criticism or are overlooked despite our best efforts or remain unappreciated when we've sacrificed much—when these hurts come, our instinct is to bolt from the servant position and demand better treatment. We know we're right, so we clamor to prove the other wrong. Someone else gets the praise, and we smolder with envy. No one else will do the dirty work so we do it, but with a grudging and self-righteous spirit. We may have felt noble agreeing to follow in Christ's footsteps, but it feels painful to be rejected or misunderstood.

In moments such as these, what is really in our heart leaks out. God allows the spirit behind our behavior to be tested, so we can discover whether or not it resembles Jesus' gentle and humble spirit. Unfortunately what is often revealed in us is deep anger—toward others for having wounded us and toward God for having allowed us to be wounded. We reject these sword thrusts of the Spirit, His gracious assault against our stubborn resistance toward obeying our Father's will no matter what the cost. We want to win the war for the land but we demand that we not be bloodied in the process.

It is repentance we need then and grace to follow our Lord anew despite our fear and our inclination to rebel against the pain. Someday our major Gethsemane test will come, and we will need the discipline of having repeatedly yielded ourselves to the foot-washing tests of dying to self-delusion (regarding our goodness) and self-protection (from suffering pain). These daily dyings are practice runs that keep us repentant and dependent. We have more to suffer than we think.

LOVE'S HUMILITY

Suffering is always the cost of discipleship, enduring the large and small humblings that identify us with Jesus. It is a call for both men and women, for pain and loss are burdens we all must experience if we are to be inwardly conformed to the image of Christ. But the apostle Paul is specific to name husbands as the ones in the marriage relationship who are to bear the burden of suffering and sacrifice for the sake of their wives. We women struggle to gladly yield ourselves in chosen submission to our husbands' leading (the topic of the next chapter), but men are called to lay down life. "Husbands, love your wives," Paul taught, "just as Christ loved the church and gave himself up for her to make her holy . . . and to present her to himself as a radiant church" (Eph. 5:25–27).

Christ's oneness with us as His Bride means He treasures us as His own body, having given Himself fully in order to endow us with His own holiness. And that is how a husband is to approach his wife—with a willingness to give himself up for her so that when he sees at last her real essence in heaven, he will be overjoyed that his love for her had so enhanced her inner beauty.

In what ways did Christ give Himself up for the church? What did He suffer that a man must also become willing to suffer for the sake of revealing Jesus' own spirit toward his wife? There is perhaps no passage in the New Testament that more concisely records the extent and cost of Jesus' "gentle and humble" spirit than the description of Christ that the apostle Paul recommended all believers imitate. "Let Christ Jesus be your example as to what your attitude should be," he wrote. "For he, who had always been God by nature, did not cling to his prerogatives as God's equal, but stripped himself of all privilege by consenting to be a slave by nature and being born as mortal man. And, having become man, he humbled himself by living a life of utter obedience, even to the extent of dying, *and the death he died was the death of a common criminal*" (Phil. 2:5–8 Phillips, emphasis added).

What will characterize the movement of godly men toward their wives as they obey Paul's instruction to let Jesus be their example? Three aspects of sacrificial servanthood on the part of a believing husband are suggested in this passage: The chosen yielding of his prerogatives, a respectful movement into his wife's "world," and the humility of "dying" in repenting of his wrongs (especially toward her).

Yielding Prerogatives

If a person is to yield his or her rights in any given situation, it is imperative that he or she recognize ownership of those rights before trying to give them up. Describing Jesus, Paul said, "he, who had always been God by nature, did not cling to his prerogatives as God's equal" (v. 6 Phillips). In other words, Jesus knew and believed that He was God's equal but He did not cling to His heavenly glory nor insist on being treated like the divine Being He was.

Similarly, a redeemed man must believe he has been adopted into God's family and must confidently live out of his new identity—i.e., the sonship bestowed on him because of his faith. When a man embraces his identity as a son of the great King, then the suffering of a gentle and humble spirit can also be embraced, for nothing can alter who he truly is. A crucified king is still a king; a mistreated prince (or princess) is still royalty. A godly man can move with kindness in his world because his true, regal identity is established forever.

Nor is his essential manhood in question. Many times a man will doubt that he has what it takes to be a godly man, able to love his wife well. But God never calls anyone to a task for which He has not already equipped him or her. How to be manly in any given circumstance may be a mystery to a husband, but he need not search for something external to himself to give him guidance. Rather, he must look within to find what God has already placed in his heart to image Himself. "There is no missing piece to my soul," declares Don Hudson, "that must be reapplied the way a severed limb is reattached to a body. The real problem is not that which I lack, . . . [but] my refusal to live out that which is most true about me."[1]

It is in fact Christ's own presence in a man through His Spirit that can give him courage to risk living out of his redeemed heart. And in the strength of his identity as God's man (not in an attempt to assert it or to prove it or even to earn it), a man can give up his demands that his wife treat him in any certain way. Though she is instructed by the apostle Paul to respect him as her husband (Eph. 5:33), he can move toward her with kindness even when she does not respect him in the way he would like, because his identity is not at stake. This yielding is not passivity (which is rooted in fear of failure) but a gentle strength flowing from the person he knows himself to be, having spent time in God's presence. He has tasted his Father's strong love and he does not forget it, not even in the midst of disrespect or chaos.

206

Moreover, such a husband has the confidence to free his wife from his control, not demanding her obedience or submissiveness (which Christ never does), but demonstrating that he can be trusted by persevering in showing himself trustworthy. For a man to comply with the spirit of Jesus' servant leadership, he must create an atmosphere in which his wife not only is free to submit but is glad to submit, because she knows her husband's heart is bent toward her good.

Moving Humbly

"For [Jesus], who had always been God by nature, did not cling to his prerogatives as God's equal, but stripped himself of all privilege by consenting to be a slave by nature and being born as mortal man" (Phil. 2:6–7 Phillips). What unfathomable humility for the King of kings to vacate heaven and enter our world, consenting to be not just mortal man but a slave by nature! And what a challenge such humility presents to the husband who desires to be like Him.

For as a husband becomes rooted in his redeemed identity in Christ, he is invited to move with kindness into a willing involvement in the spiritual, physical, and emotional life of his beloved, opening his heart to listen to her and to cherish her special beauty. He must relinquish his preoccupation with success and embrace instead Christ's own focus on serving the Bride He loves. Many a man is intimidated by the chaos of a woman's world, preferring to remain on the fringes of it. He will be glad to toss her tidbits of advice but he is loathe to feel whatever she is experiencing. Yet a husband is invited by Christ's own example to risk moving into his wife's world by initiating conversation with her (as Jesus did with the woman at the Samaritan well), by entering her chaos (as Jesus did when Martha was upset), and by resisting whatever in her life is not in her best interest (as Yahweh removed Rahab from her destructive Jericho lifestyle). God's sons can connect with God's daughters in wonderfully redemptive ways. This is kind movement into a woman's world on her behalf and for her good.

Perhaps no suffering a man does for his wife is more important than the suffering he does in praying for her. His call to love his wife as Christ loved the church involves spiritually nourishing and protecting her. That is to say, he is not merely to care for her physical well-being, but he is to imitate Christ, who "loved the church and gave himself up for her to make her holy, cleansing her by the washing with water through the word, and to present her to himself as a radiant church, without stain or wrinkle or any other blemish, but holy and blameless" (Eph. 5:25–27).

No man can cleanse his wife's heart from sin; only the blood of Jesus can do that. But this passage implies that a man must care for, nourish, and protect his wife's spiritual life. It is not clear exactly what this might mean in terms of a couple's personal or corporate worship. There is, for example, no biblical formula for them to follow in their devotional time together—who does what or how or how often. Each couple must work out those things in their own marriage according to the spiritual gifts and inner leading of the Spirit in each of them.

But a man's willingness to suffer in prayer for his wife reflects not only his concern for her spiritual well-being but also the intercessory passion of Christ Himself. While on earth Jesus prayed for all His disciples (see John 17), particularly for Simon Peter. "Simon, Simon," He said, "Satan has asked to sift you as wheat. But I have prayed for you, Simon, that your faith may not fail" (Luke 22:31–32). The writer of the Book of Hebrews says that Christ prays always for all believers at His Father's throne (see Heb. 7:25). I know a few men who have been kept awake at night by God to intercede in spiritual battle on behalf of their wives. I earnestly desire that their number grow. Women desperately need and long for the prayers of their husbands and of good men in their churches.

Why does a woman desire her husband's intercession for her? Not because she cannot pray herself—God never turns a deaf ear to any of His children. But as Christ's intercession as head of the church is somehow vital to our well-being as believers, so a husband's intercession for his wife is important to her, offering her encouragement in her faith-walk and reinforcing the Holy Spirit's protection from the enemy's attack against her soul. Her husband's Spirit-empowered movement to nourish her spiritual life and gifts will afford her a place where she can become more and more the holy and blameless Bride of Christ, made radiant with the knowledge of being loved.

It is a task any redeemed man can accomplish. I once heard a teacher tell a group of men, many of whom were new Christians, that they were called to be spiritual leaders in their families according to the instruction of the apostle Paul in Ephesians 5. When some balked at the task because they felt inadequate, being young in the faith, the teacher said, "You can pray for your wife starting today—no one needs training for that."

He was right. And as a man prays for his wife in the spirit of Christ's own passion for His Bride's spiritual well-being, she can learn to be at rest in his kind covering. I know of few godly women who do not desire this kind of humble movement by a good man.

It will require patience and humility for a man to involve himself spiritually and personally with his wife instead of running from her, to listen to her concerns and not "turn her off," to allow her feelings to mingle with his own, to be gentle toward her without caving in to her. It will surely take much time and energy to pray for her and to think creatively about how to love her well. But when he recognizes the impact he can have on her for good and sees in her eyes the gladness of receiving his kindness, something in his very soul will resonate with joy, and he will taste something of what it means to live as a strong and godly man.

Repenting Wrongs

"And, having become man, [Jesus] humbled himself by living a life of utter obedience, even to the extent of dying, *and the death he died was the death of a common criminal*" (see Phil. 2:5–8 Phillips, emphasis added). How could the apostle Paul instruct believers to "let Christ Jesus be your example as to what your attitude should be," when he himself also declared, "All have sinned" (Rom. 3:23)? Even if a husband in imitation of Jesus risks moving into his wife's world (as Jesus stooped to ours), how can he live a life of "utter obedience" to God (as Jesus did) in his relationship with her?

Paul knew the gospel well enough, of course, to know that in learning from Jesus how to be humble and gentle, we must practice not just obeying Him but also repenting when we don't obey Him. If we are willing to live at the dread mercy of grace, we will find that repentance is part of the yoke Jesus asks us to take. The weariness and burden of trying to obey perfectly is exactly the burden Jesus wishes us to bring to Him in exchange for His own yoke of forgiveness and rest.

In our pride and self-sufficiency we are like Simon the Pharisee, sure of our goodness, judgmental of others, unaware of our deep sin, and confident we can keep the law perfectly enough to please God. This burden of self-delusion we are invited to exchange for the yoke of humility and gentleness that Jesus Himself wore—humility to depend on the Father as He did, gentleness to love the unrighteous in imitation of Him.

For not only are we to receive His grace, but we are to offer it to others as well, pulling alongside Jesus Himself as He bends His own strength to the yoke we bear with Him. His grace to us becomes His grace through us, because yoked to Him, "we become his partner as he shares his strength with us, easing the weight we once had to pull alone."[2] This is the dance of grace, the unforced rhythm of godly sorrow, divine forgiveness, and a renewed passion to obey.

Most especially is forgiveness required within the yoke of marriage, for here we are reduced by our vows and by our fallenness to a most inescapable necessity for grace given and received. Both husband and wife must embrace the discipline of repenting toward one another, for it alone swings open the door for the exchange of forgiveness.

It is a daily thing, this need for mutual repentance and grace, which calls not for continual introspection but for a practiced attentiveness to the subtle chafing of Jesus' yoke against the shoulder of our conscience. The Spirit quietly highlights our relational wrongdoings, those instances when love has failed on either side of oneness. Yet we find repentance difficult to countenance—men, because many think it unmanly to admit being wrong, and women, because they fear being seen as foolish or weak. Asking forgiveness is an invitation to the kind of humility repulsive to us but intrinsic to Christ's relationships during His incarnation.

Nevertheless, we can learn to recognize both our need for repentance and the particular sins for which we need to ask forgiveness. A man, for example, can see the hurt in his wife's eyes if he will look, or catch the despair in her voice if he will listen, or observe the anger underlying her response if his heart is attuned to hers. And he can attend to those things instead of ignoring them. He can also perceive the sin in his own words or glance or attitude, and he can become willing to hear how he has done damage by word or deed or by omission of word or deed.

Larry Crabb writes:

> One of the great tragedies of life is that no man fully sees the damage that his unmasculine style of relating does to others. Those that get a glimpse descend to the depths of brokenness and contrition. And it is from those depths that genuine repentance arises. . . . [Then the] hope of actually *blessing* others—nourishing his wife, positively influencing his children, encouraging his friends—grows stronger than the terror of entering darkness. And good movement begins . . . [but never] naturally; there is always a fight against powerful urges in the other direction. Good movement always begins in repentance over bad movement.[3]

And nothing draws a woman to the heart of a man like his willingness to admit he is wrong. His fear that she will disrespect him if he repents is almost always unfounded if his repentance comes from honest sorrow and not from cowardice. When a husband's repentance is genuine, his wife's respect for him will likely increase, because she knows that only a man confident in his identity as God's son can embrace the humility of godly sorrow for his sin. My husband, Bill, has my deepest respect in this, for he is quick to feel the chafing of Jesus' yoke and quick to make things right with me. May his tribe increase!

From Jesus' perspective, nothing was more important than laying down His life for His Bride in obedience to His Father, though it cost Him a criminal's death. He invites us to rest in His completed work, and in imitation of Him, a husband must by his Christ-like spirit invite his wife to rest her heart in his strong but gentle love. It will take many "dyings" on his part, for love is always a death sentence. He will have to endure the death of his pride and aloofness, of his ease and self-justification, of his pretense and impatience. But if he will endure these "dyings," he may know the pleasure of experiencing his wife resting in peace in his presence.

Most wives dearly desire such rest, though few believe themselves loved well enough to take the risk of resting in their husbands. Yet it is a risk worthy of a woman's courage, for she too must experience many "dyings" to reflect Christ's humility (as the next chapter will describe). And the risks both she and her husband take will be richly rewarded.

For all who sacrifice themselves to love others according to Christ's example will one day be known for who they really are, even as Christ Himself will one day be revealed to all as Lord of all because by His death He became servant to all. In concluding his instructions to "Let Christ Jesus be your example as to what your attitude should be," the apostle Paul writes of Jesus,

> Therefore God exalted him to the highest place
> and gave him the name that is above every name,
> that at the name of Jesus every knee should bow,
> in heaven and on earth and under the earth,
> and every tongue confess that Jesus Christ is Lord,
> to the glory of God the Father.
>
> PHILIPPIANS 2:9–11

Christ's sustained yoking to the will of His Father yielded not only the fruit of our redemption but the revelation of His own and His Father's glory as well. Such fruitfulness out of suffering is the new paradigm that must replace any illusions we might cherish of our entitlement to happiness or of belief in our own goodness. Striving for either success or perfection will never yield God glory nor bring us the soul rest for which we long. Only our submission to Christ and our obedience to the promptings of His Spirit in our hearts can produce fruit that will invite and refresh others into kingdom living. All else we do will end up as field stubble, fit only for the fire. If our lives are to bring glory to God the Father, we must be willing to suffer and grieve the losses of living in a broken world as we become servants to the least of God's children. Daily we must follow the path to this cross.

WAITING AGAIN

In some parts of our world today, the cross borne by believers is physical—that is to say, their suffering is of bodily persecution for their witness to Christ. Such persecution was also intrinsic to the yoking experience of

211

many first-century Christians, especially the leaders of the early church. Some of them paid for their faith with their lives. Jesus had prepared His disciples for this, telling them before His own crucifixion: "If the world hates you, keep in mind that it hated me first. . . . If they persecuted me, they will persecute you also" (John 15:18, 20).

The apostle Peter had been present to hear these words of Christ, but in the terror of confrontation in Caiaphas's courtyard, he had forgotten them altogether. By denying Jesus he had mitigated the world's hatred and had sidestepped persecution. But in saving his skin he had damaged his Lord— and his own soul, as well. His repentance and private meeting with Jesus after His resurrection had bridged the personal gap between them. But Peter still lacked an essential ingredient needed to prepare him for entering instead of evading the coming persecution Jesus had predicted. Peter must face his terror of public exposure, and Jesus would walk him through the process. The apostle John tells the story and he was there. (This story is recounted in John 21.)

The event occurred sometime after Jesus' resurrection and it happened in the context of the disciples' becoming restless in the aftermath of glory. Something surprisingly distressful often happens to us after God has revealed Himself to us in some spectacular way, for we must then go back to living our lives as we had lived them before. What, we ask ourselves, are we going to do with the inevitable letdown? How can we fill the void left by the glory's departure?

The Israelites who had experienced Yahweh's dread presence on Sinai, for example, became bored when Moses was gone for a few weeks. Having been slaves with never any free time, their new leisure no doubt felt purposeless and unproductive, like retirement come too early. Perhaps this emptiness contributed to the golden calf debacle, their orgy an attempt to dull the restlessness they felt. Tired of waiting and impatient to act, they had led even their wives and daughters into lascivious and idolatrous revelry.

A similar dilemma faced the disciples after Jesus' death and resurrection. They had ridden the emotional roller coaster of agonizing grief at His death and outrageous joy at His resurrection. They had seen Jesus alive again but they still faced a future with no clear direction, no guarantees, no timetable regarding the coming of Messiah's kingdom. They had obeyed Jesus in going to Galilee and now they were just waiting—safer than they'd been in Jerusalem but without anything to do.

Finally, Simon Peter could no longer bear the inactivity. "I'm going out to fish," he announced. "We'll go with you," said the others. Doing *anything* was better than doing nothing, and at least fishing is what they knew how to do. Climbing into their boat, they made their way to a spot about a hundred yards offshore and fished all night.

But their nets came up empty after every cast, and the long night ended in a dawn empty of success. Unproductive work is always discouraging, but now it felt like salt in an open wound to the recently unemployed disciples. These displaced fishers of men weren't even good fishers of fish anymore. And then, to make matters worse, some man standing on the shore in the sun's early light exposed their failure, calling out, "Friends, haven't you any fish?"

"No," they answered. And then some unasked-for advice: "Throw your net on the right side of the boat and you will find some." The voice didn't sound scornful or condescending. Maybe he could see something from shore they couldn't see from the boat. It was worth a try.

And then fish, fish, and more fish—too many to haul up, too many to manage, too many for the net to safely hold. At least they could make a little money from this haul of . . .

Wait a minute! John, catching Peter's eye, shouted over the commotion, "It is the Lord!" And without answering, Peter grabbed his garment, jumped in the water, and swam toward shore—let the others take care of the fish; he wanted to be with Jesus!

The boat followed, slowed by the laden net being towed behind. Then, when Jesus said, "Bring some of the fish you have just caught," Peter scrambled *back* to the boat to help the others drag the net ashore. In his unexpected joy he simply could not stay focused.

Fruitful work had become fruitful indeed—enough fish to augment the treasury depleted by Judas's betrayal. But more important, Jesus was with them again and had prepared them breakfast on the beach—barbecued fish and fresh bread to reward their night's work. Jesus served them the bread and fish as He had served them the bread and wine at Passover, and as He had once distributed to them enough bread and fish to feed a multitude.

THE SUFFERING OF RESTORATION

After breakfast Jesus proceeded with the rest of His agenda. Peter's joyous leap from the boat had not escaped His notice, but He and this fisherman had business to conclude. In front of the other disciples Jesus wished to reinstate Peter to full status as loyal yokefellow. Peter's public three-time denial must be countered with a public thrice-repeated covenant affirmation.

"Simon son of John, do you truly love me more than these?" came Jesus' first question. He was facing Peter with his earlier brash boast that his love for Jesus exceeded the other disciples' love. "Yes, Lord," Peter replied, "you know that I love you."

"Feed my lambs," Jesus said, naming Peter as future shepherd of His flock of followers

213

Then again, Jesus' query: "Simon son of John, do you truly love me?" Surely Peter wondered why He was calling him Simon and not Peter, the new name He'd given him months earlier? Was He withdrawing His words that he, Peter, was a rock—in fact *the* rock on which He would build His church? "Yes, Lord, you know that I love you." Couldn't Jesus see his heart? Why this second challenge?

"Take care of my sheep," Jesus said, affirming Peter's leadership position once again. And then, a third time, "Simon son of John, do you love me?"

Now Peter could not hide his hurt, though probably by now he had caught the implication of being asked three times to publicly disavow his three public denials. "Lord, you know all things," Peter passionately declared. "You know that I love you." Was he reminding Jesus of something he'd said in their earlier meeting after the resurrection?

Jesus did indeed know all things and He had prayed for this man, that Satan's sifting of his heart would not result in his falling away from faith beyond the reach of grace. "Feed my sheep," Jesus said one more time to this thrice-humbled, now thrice-commissioned, disciple. The fisher of men would shepherd Jesus' flock, for the painful price of his public restoration had now been paid in full.

However, Jesus went on to tell the humbled fisherman, "When you are old you will stretch out your hands [in crucifixion], and someone else will . . . lead you where you do not want to go." And John adds in his Gospel, "Jesus said this to indicate the kind of death by which Peter would glorify God."

What effect did this prediction of his martyrdom have on the impetuous Simon Peter? Did he become depressed and morbid, brooding on the inevitability of some horrible death? Or did he instead feel a certain freedom in knowing that his death, though unwished for, would glorify God? Sometimes looking death square in the face settles the soul. If we can rest in God being sovereignly in charge of our lives, we can live with nothing to lose in being wholeheartedly God's man or woman. Since the last page of our life's book is already written, we can be off duty about what happens on the pages in the middle.

Finally Jesus invited Peter again as He had years earlier, "Follow me!" The disciple's hurt at Jesus' questions had given way to the inner rest of having nothing left to hide or anything to prove. His sin was public knowledge, and now his forgiveness and restoration were too. He would therefore be more useful to the Kingdom, for he had experienced in a deeper way both his own frailty and his Lord's love. The restored fisherman would be loyal because he recognized his own capacity for disloyalty. He would be strong because he knew his own weakness. He would become bold because he knew even his death would bring his Lord glory. Though persecution would come and his martyrdom was a sure thing, his relationship with Jesus was secure, and that made all the difference.

How does a fallen image-bearer move from terror to boldness? By knowing he or she is loved, forgiven, restored, and empowered by the Holy Spirit of Jesus to live a life of abandoned worship and obedience. Only love, God's unparalleled love, is able to cast out even our greatest fear. This unschooled, ordinary fisherman, having been loved by an extraordinary rabbi, would risk everything in moving confidently to establish and strengthen the Kingdom of his Lord. Caiphas's courtyard no longer held any power to shame or cripple him, for Jesus had rescued him and set him on a rock—Peter "the rock" set firm on Christ, the rock of our salvation.

This is the gospel, and Peter, the redeemed coward and traitor, would proclaim it boldly until the day came for him to die in its defense.

ENTERING GRIEF

Jesus had relentlessly led Peter into the suffering of exposure for the purpose of restoring him not just to his community but to his commissioning. But when Peter had turned to ask Jesus about what would happen to his friend John—would he die a martyr's death too?—Jesus rebuked him, asking, "If I want him to remain alive until I return, what is that to you? You must follow me." That is to say, everyone's story is unique, and God's purposes for each person will be uniquely accomplished in His own time and way.

I had heard Christ saying a similar thing to me when He refused to let me force the drinking issue with Bill. *What I do with him is My business,* He told me. *You follow Me, and I'll take care of him.* And so I had had to let go again, sorrowing at Bill's emotional absence even as I grieved Mama's physical absence. It was a heavy burden, but yoked to Jesus, I wasn't bearing it alone.

Meanwhile, Bill continued to struggle in his own yoke, unable to run far enough from his grief, but also unable to rest or linger long in this new and most exquisite pain. He was angry at God and told Him so yet he feared his anger would destroy his only hope of seeing Mama again. And so this burdened man wrestled with God back and forth, repenting and grieving and shaking his fist and drowning his sorrow and waking up to find it still there.

This battle lasted for six months after Mama died. Then it was with unexpected joy that I greeted Bill's return from a men's retreat one weekend, and he showed me with tears his first AA token, signifying that he had attended a meeting of Alcoholics Anonymous and was committing himself to sobriety.

What had happened there to bring about what I had long prayed for but had never been able to make happen? Bill and I have talked much about the dynamics of that weekend, and though there remains deep mystery about the working of God's grace in his heart, there were events that led to Bill's willingness to attend an AA meeting, events God used to win him to Himself. This man's heavenly Father was passionate to bring a lost son home to His own heart.

The purpose of this men's retreat was to invite the twelve participants to enter both their anger and the underlying grief sustaining that anger regarding trauma in their childhood. All had sustained abuse and shame in their relationships with their parents, and all had chosen a pattern of running from the pain of that brokenness into adult addictions to alcohol and drugs. Because the dynamics of rage and grief that fueled their addictions were largely unconscious, the retreat's agenda was to individually bring each man's rage to conscious expression and then to surround him with the comfort of the other men as his rage gave way to weeping over his loss of parent-child love.

It was, to say the least, a powerfully emotional experience for these men, who bonded together in the intimacy of shared sorrow. There was healing in their tears, release of long-held bitterness in the letters they wrote their fathers, and comfort in the presence of other men who understood and did not shame them for their grieving. And in the context of this masculine mutuality of shared anger and sorrow, Bill found a safe place to acknowledge his own rage and the deep, deep sadness beneath it of having been abandoned young by his father and more recently by his mother.

Not being fathered with love and involvement does enormous damage to the masculine soul, and the loss must be grieved if the rest of a man's relationships are to thrive. The beginning of Bill's grieving that weekend dislodged something angry and isolating in his soul, and when two of his new-found buddies invited him to go with them to an AA meeting, he went. In heaven the angels were having a party.

Ninety AA meetings in ninety days would follow Bill's decision, strengthening not his resolve but his dependence on God for daily grace, daily empowering. The stronghold of his addiction to alcohol was shattered not by his own will nor by my intervention but by the supernatural working of God's Spirit in him. The war wasn't over, but this battle had been won, not by his strength but by his repentance and his acknowledged need for God's grace.

And as Bill opened himself to the anger he had always felt toward his father, he also began to embrace the inescapable truth of his love for his dad—a love his father had not lived well enough nor long enough to receive and reciprocate. Columnist Ana Veciana-Suarez, in an article about the impact of her husband's death on their teenage sons, describes what she calls "the grief of absence" created by father-loss. Her children were fortunate, she says, because

> they cling to wonderful memories of their dad, memories embellished with details and polished by love. . . . But other fatherless children are not so lucky. An abusive father leaves behind only fear and bitterness, a view of the world as a dangerous, traitorous place. And a father who abandons his family

bequeaths a sad legacy of loneliness and rejection. Moreover, the lives of fatherless children revolve around the vacuum created by that absence. Even abused children long for that protective, powerful, precious adult male to nurture them, teach them, endow them with a sense of self, a feeling of worth.[4]

Bill, like all children, had always longed for a good father, and beneath his anger against his dad for having abused and abandoned him, there resided a deep love for him that had never found expression beyond a few moments atop his father's casket. But as Bill began to acknowledge and grieve this unrequited love, he became more able to forgive his father for the harm he had done. He also became more able to embrace the truth that, because he himself had repented and had yoked himself with Christ, he could consider himself a good man and a good father in spite of his imperfections. I loved affirming these things in Bill, and though it was slow and sometimes painful work, his sobriety allowed him to believe them more and more.

As always, repentance yoked Bill and me again to God's grace and brought new hope and new life into our marriage. Far from solving all our problems, however, this entry into a different phase of our yoking would lead us to even greater challenges of trusting and obeying the God who had brought us this far. Our suffering was not over, but we were learning how to grieve it and we would now learn to grieve it together.

THE SORROW OF LOVE

It always hurts to love. Ask Mary, the mother of Jesus. Ask the woman whose tears washed Jesus' feet. Ask Peter, who cried and cried and cried. Ask Moses, who got sick and tired of baby-sitting God's children. Ask the soldiers who were circumcised, the wives who were widowed, the woman at Sychar's well, the sisters of Lazarus. Ask Jesus. All who love must enter sorrow. Even God. Especially God.

For does not Scripture teach us that God Himself suffers because He loves? Jesus, God's Son, does not just know *about* our suffering. Rather, He knows it personally and intimately, for He suffered death, even death on a cross! But the Father suffered too, for Father and Son are One and the pain of the Son draws tears from the Father. The Holy Spirit also suffers as He "intercedes for us with groans that words cannot express" (Rom. 8:26). Part of trinitarian oneness is the sorrow they endure within the Godhead on our behalf. The curse of our covenant-breaking always and continually costs them much pain—even in this very moment. This is the passion of our God.

Perhaps the clearest biblical portrait of the grieving heart of God over His children's rebellion is found in Jesus' parable of the prodigal son (Luke 15:11–32)—more accurately, the parable of the waiting father. In this story the father (who reveals what God is like) longs to restore his two sons to his embrace. Both had left him, the younger going to a far country and squandering his father's money, the older working in his father's fields at home but scorning his father's love.

Loving his two lost sons cost the father greatly, both in time and anguish. Like Yahweh, he waited yearningly for his prodigal son to return. The boy's motive did not matter to him—let it be hunger that impelled him home, just so he came! Even the wasted money didn't matter, only his son. Grieving the prolonged absence of his son, the father in Jesus' story kept watch, his eyes straining along the sliver of horizon for the merest glimpse of his son's silhouette against the sky.

We seldom imagine our heavenly Father watching for our hearts' return with such longing. No doubt that is why Jesus told this parable, especially for the Pharisees who were listening to Him. From their perspective, the father should have been glad never to speak to the boy again. Even allowing him back to pay off his debt (with interest) would have stretched the limit of credibility. But running to embrace him when he finally straggled home, even giving him gifts and throwing him a party—Jesus was a crazy man to tell such a story! No respectable Middle Eastern father would *ever* exceed the bounds of propriety in such a shameless way!

Not even many fathers today are willing to acknowledge, let alone reveal, the ardent love for their children that swells beneath their decorum. But even more disconcerting than this father's passion for the prodigal is his passion for his older son, who refused to welcome his brother back. This older son had been the good kid, the obedient one, the one who locked his true feelings inside and faithfully went through the motions of sonship, never making waves nor humbling himself to ask for anything. Committed to earning his own way through his good behavior, he had experienced no more intimacy with his father than had his far-off brother, even though he did enjoy the approval of the entire community.

At least he enjoyed their approval until he found out his reprobate brother had been welcomed home with a party thrown in his honor. Then his well-camouflaged resentment at having felt forced to do everything right finally erupted. Furious at the perceived injustice of the prodigal's undeserved restoration, the older son refused to attend the party, bringing shame on his father with this public dishonor.

And for the second time that day, the father humbled himself, offering grace to the son who believed he needed no grace. He came out to beg him to join the celebration, for he loved this self-righteous young man too. The sorrowing father wanted both sons back, for he had missed the heart of his pharisaic son as much as he had missed the heart of the one for whose return he had daily strained his aging gaze.

Because God's very nature is to love, no sin in us is beyond His forgiving, no distance we have run from Him is beyond the reach of His passionate desire for our return, no damage to our souls is beyond His healing. Even if we have stayed home, like the estranged older brother, or if (as Al Andrews describes his own prodigality) we have traveled to "a land of safety" and have served "the gods of predictability and passionlessness,"[5] God woos us back, having placed deep within us an insatiable hunger for intimacy with Him. Anxiously our Father-God waits for our response, longing to feel His arms of love thrown about our necks, His kisses of welcome on our faces, His hand of blessing on our heads, His robe of covering over our shoulders, His ring of belonging on our hand, His sandals of provision on our feet.

And we want that too, far more than we know, far more than we are accustomed to admit. Something in us fears grace, for it is the enemy of our self-sufficiency, and our competence feels safer than being on the needing end of forgiveness. Yet our inescapable desire for restored intimacy with our heavenly Father runs deeper than our fear. Our ache for connection with Him is as intrinsic to our nature as His love for us is intrinsic to His—are we not made in His image? Deep calls to deep, and our hearts—His and ours—yearn for oneness. This in truth is who we *really* are, for all children pine for intimacy with their fathers and with their heavenly Father. It is both the basis and impetus for the gospel.

Surprisingly, Jesus ended His parable without ending the story. Perhaps He wished the listening Pharisees (and us) to create an ending of our own. Would the older son admit he desperately wanted his father's love, and would he receive it from him? Did this stay-at-home rebel reenter the family community, partying with the brother he had formerly disdained? To do so he would have had to recognize how deeply he had hurt his father by his grudging allegiance and his proud refusal to ask for anything. He would have had to embrace the brother he had scorned. He would need to repent of his legalism and humbly receive the same grace his brother had received with such astonishment. The call to redemption comes to us all through the tears of our waiting Father.

We tolerate so meager a perception of God's anguish as He watches His image-bearers fall prey to the enemy. The apostle Peter reminds us, regarding Christ's return, that "the Lord is not slow in keeping his promise, as some understand slowness. He is patient with you, not wanting anyone to perish, but everyone to come to repentance" (2 Peter 3:9). Even now God waits yearningly to gather every believing son and daughter to Himself so Christ can come to claim His Bride and take her Home. Meanwhile He collects our tears and accompanies us through our pain. He makes ways of escape when we're tempted and prays for us when Satan sifts us. He grieves when we disobey and longs for our return when we neglect or run from Him.

All these things and a myriad more God suffers every moment, watching us with delight in who we are in Christ but also in grief when we ourselves forget. This is the kind of suffering Father we have, though it is seldom the Father we think we have. "Man of sorrows"—that is what Isaiah called the prophesied Messiah (Isa. 53:3). Like Father, like Son. And in imitation of Him, bearing His name and His likeness, we too must suffer, weeping at sin and brokenness and rejoicing with Him at every lost child who comes home to Him.

How painful is love in all its many manifestations! How searing is its sorrow, how piercing its beauty, how exquisite its tenderness, how irresistible its invitation! And how precious its worship, for when we love others out of the fullness of God's love for us and for them, we worship before Him in song and dance, and even the angels join the celebration.

This is the sweet sorrow of our intimacy with Christ, our head and Bridegroom. Its cost is great, but not too heavy to be borne. For connected intimately to Him, our lives will bear much fruit—in our hearts and for His Kingdom—and this is joy indeed.

The yoking itself brings us joy, for our oneness with Him as we submit to His leading offers us rich tastes of our own Homecoming celebration. In the next chapter we will consider the nourishment we receive through our submission to His love and the ways in which God's daughters uniquely image the glory of that submission in their marriages.

QUESTIONS TO CONSIDER

1. How is the spiritual meaning of the altar on Mount Ebal central to our hope for rest in our intimacy with God and each other?

2. Tell how a marriage might be renewed by the husband's movement in the areas of: (a) yielding prerogatives; (b) moving humbly; or (c) repenting wrongs.

3. Describe an incident you know of in which, like Jesus on the beach with Peter, God restored to community someone who had sinned. How does God reveal His nature through such experiences?

4. Decide which character from Jesus' story of the prodigal son you most identify with and tell how that might reveal what your rest in God is like.

5. What keeps men from expressing their fervent love for their sons or their fathers? Can (or should) this reticence be overcome?

Regarding the opening story:

Jim and the men in his accountability group connected with their wives and risked what was uncomfortable for them.

6. Which marriage relationship represented in the accountability group most resembles your own or your parents' marriage?

7. How did you react internally to the sacrifices described by each husband in the group?

CHAPTER ELEVEN

TRUST

The Nourishment of Submission

"SUBMISSION," BARBARA WROTE *in her journal before turning in for the night, "has always repulsed me. Now it scares me—yet somehow comforts me too—how strange. And how far I've come in the past several months." Pen poised as her mind wandered back in time, Barbara recalled how she had resented her mother's version of submission:* Suffer insults, hide your pain, don't deal with your husband's infidelity, cry and pray alone, and always act like everything's fine, especially at church. Then, when the children are finally grown, divorce him.

Barbara had rebelled as a teenager—against her mother's passivity, her mother's faith, her mother's values. She had determined she would never be mistreated the way her mother had been. She would be strong, and she would find a man who would be good to her.

And Duane had *been good to her*—at least at first. He was a quiet but charming man who hated conflict and seldom raised his voice. Nor did he want Barbara to raise her voice, and she was glad to comply—at least at first. But after a few years, Duane's pattern of returning to work after supper every night began to gnaw away at Barbara's confidence in his fidelity (though he would always supply reasonable explanations), and before long, she'd found it impossible to hold her tongue. It had been unpleasant for both of them.

Then, after Joey was born, Barbara had found herself unable to ignore her suspicions regarding her husband's absences. She'd begun spying on Duane—checking his wallet and his car, calling his office at night to see if he was really there, and even following him to the airport when he traveled. She'd hated what she was doing—it was so much like what her mother had done—but her fear of divorce had made her desperate to keep Duane faithful, no matter what it took.

Lowering pen to paper again, Barbara continued writing: "If it hadn't been for Lauren (what a good friend!), I would never have broken the vicious cycle begun in my childhood. I'm so glad she encouraged me to come back to church again, but what a difference this time! Now I know Jesus died for my sin and I've become God's precious daughter—imagine me, a princess!

"And for once in my life I want to do what God tells me to do, even when it's hard—like submitting to Duane tomorrow. Facing the truth about his unfaithfulness has been excruciating, but I've faced some pretty unlovely things about my own self too. Of course Duane won't see my confrontation of his sin as very submissive—I never would have thought so, either, until I came to see how his infidelity has harmed not just me and Joey but his own soul too. Telling him he must make a choice between me and his mistress is really the most loving thing I can do for him—it will be my invitation for him to repent and be forgiven.

"It's a good thing I'll have people praying for me as I stand in the way of Duane's sin. I pray my spirit will be right and I hope he chooses to stay with me and seek counseling. It's amazing how much I have come to love him now that I know he can't destroy my soul. If he leaves, though, I know God and my friends will walk through this with me.

"Tonight," Barbara's journal entry concluded, "I read Isaiah 30:15 again: 'In repentance and rest is your salvation, in quietness and trust is your strength.' I've repented of my fearful attempts to control Duane's behavior and I'm resting my hope for the future in God. Tonight my spirit is quiet, and I have greater strength submitting my will to God than I ever did in trusting myself or Duane.

"Thank You, Lord Jesus, for Your presence with me!"

222

Barbara closed her journal and put it with her Bible in the drawer of her nightstand. Turning out the light, she waited with only occasional twinges of anxiety for Duane to finally come home from work. Tomorrow would be an important day.

Trust in God is foundational to our submission to Him, just as trust is essential to obeying the apostle Paul's instruction that wives submit themselves to their husbands "as to the Lord" (Eph. 5:22). Satan seeks always to undermine a woman's trust in God, and unless she learns to rest in and submit to His leadership and protection, she will struggle mightily to submit to her husband with humility and strength.

Like Barbara and her mother, many churched women misunderstand what Scripture teaches about submission, and their resistance to yielding their hearts to their husbands is both caused by and results in a failure to trust God as well.[1] Even when a husband does not "deserve" his wife's respect for his leadership, her submissive spirit toward God can govern her attitude choices regarding her husband and his sin. She can learn, like Barbara, to find God's salvation by repenting of her own sin and finding her rest in His love. Then, in the context of trusting Him, she can exercise her God-given strength in dealing shrewdly and lovingly with the man to whom she is covenantally bound.

The process will no doubt require time, prayer, patience, and the wisdom of godly counselors. But any woman who seeks hard after God can learn to replace destructive relational habits with Christ-honoring choices, particularly toward men. Submission is always a trust issue, and that is the topic with which this chapter grapples.

The war was over at last, the fighting finally finished. No more sounding of shofars, no more battle cries, no more marches or wounds or exhaustion or images of dying enemies. After the covenant had been reaffirmed in the Gerizim-Ebal valley, the Israelites had, over a period of several years, successfully completed a military campaign to the south and another to the north, conquering thirty-one kings in all and destroying the people over whom those kings had ruled. Scripture summarizes in these words: "So Joshua took the entire land, just as the LORD had directed Moses, and he gave it as an inheritance to Israel according to their tribal divisions" (Josh. 11:23a). The conquest of Canaan was complete, evil had been routed, and God's justice had been established in the land. After years of combat and bloodshed, both Israelite army and the land itself "had rest from war" (v. 23b).

The Israelites yoked to Yahweh under Moses had moved from slavery to wilderness and from wilderness to the banks of the Jordan River. Then

223

under Joshua, God's people had moved from wilderness to warfare, destroying wickedness and idolatry in Canaan so that a freed land could receive Yahweh's freed children. Now they had moved at last into rest from their enemies, settling into the land promised to their distant ancestor Abraham some five hundred years earlier. In His own time and way God always keeps His promises.

Not that there would be no more battles. Pockets of resistance against Israelite resettlement remained in various areas throughout the land. Some towns assigned to the tribe of Manasseh, for example, could not be occupied by the Manassites, "for the Canaanites were determined to live in that region. However, when the Israelites grew stronger, they subjected the Canaanites to forced labor but did not drive them out completely" (17:12–13). "Rest from war" signified the end of the united military campaigns under Joshua, but it did not mean there were no more battles left for individual tribal clans to fight. Dividing the land, defending its borders, occupying its towns, making foreign houses into kosher homes, destroying pagan temples and detestable shrines in town and countryside—the work of transforming Canaan into Israel would take years to accomplish. Though "the LORD gave [His people] rest on every side, just as he had sworn to their forefathers" (21:44), much labor would yet be required of them.

What then does it mean that Yahweh's promise had been fulfilled: "My Presence will go with you, and I will give you rest" (Exod. 33:14)? The rest given by God to His people obviously signifies something different from easy living or getting something for nothing. What did "rest" mean to the Israelites, and what does it mean for us today?

THE MEANING OF REST

Scripture tells us that "after a long time had passed, . . . Joshua, by then old and well advanced in years, summoned all Israel—their elders, leaders, judges and officials—and [spoke] to them" his parting address. (This address is found in Joshua 23–24.) He reminded them that the rest God had given them had not been based on their efforts but on the work He Himself had done on their behalf. Nor were their new homes the result of their own work, but the labor of countless Canaanite farmers and builders who had provided them places to live for which they had not had to pay sweat equity.

Then Joshua warned the people, "Be very strong; be careful to obey all that is written in the Book of the Law of Moses, without turning aside to the right or to the left." Along with their territory, the Israelites had inherited the covenant call to remain faithful to Yahweh by keeping His commandments. Centuries later another "Joshua"—Jesus of Nazareth—would remind His disciples of the same truth, saying, "If anyone loves me, he will

224

obey my teaching" (John 14:23). One of our greatest needs in being a people at rest is that we know what God requires of us and that we long to obey what He commands.

But as important as our commitment to obedience is, we must never forget the significance of the altar on Mount Ebal. The shedding of blood for the forgiveness of sins is absolutely central to our rest, for without it we would face despair because of our inevitable disobedience. Must we submit to God's commands? Absolutely. Will we obey perfectly? Not in this life. Jesus' perfect obedience and substitutionary atonement is our only hope, and His the only true rest. Our obedience—which is always God's will for us—will then flow from hearts of gratitude, not from a self-imposed duty to perform well.

To substantiate God's call to obedience, Joshua next recited for the Israelites all that God had done for them in the past, beginning with His call and promises to Abraham and concluding with the observation that the Israelites had now inherited those very promises. Our present rest in God is always strengthened by memories of His past faithfulness—not sentimentalizing about "the good old days" but remembering the character and sovereign power of the One in whom we rest. Rest and trust are inseparable, and delighting ourselves and each other with the stories of what God has done to demonstrate His trustworthiness will refresh our understanding of who He is and center us once more in who we are as His beloved sons and daughters.

Finally, Joshua challenged the people with this choice: "If serving the LORD seems undesirable to you, then choose for yourselves this day whom you will serve, whether the gods your forefathers served beyond the River, or the gods of the Amorites, in whose land you are living. But as for me and my household, we will serve the LORD" (Josh. 24:15). Everyone worships someone or something, and we must choose carefully the object of our worship, for it will set the direction not only for our life but for our eternal future.

Rising to Joshua's challenge, God's people emphatically reaffirmed their covenant commitment, declaring, "Far be it from us to forsake the LORD to serve other gods! . . . We too will serve the LORD, because he is our God."

"Then Joshua said, 'You are witnesses against yourselves that you have chosen to serve the LORD.'

"'Yes, we are witnesses,' they replied."

So Joshua "took a large stone and set it up there under the oak near the holy place of the LORD.

"'See!' he said to all the people. 'This stone will be a witness against us. It has heard all the words the LORD has said to us. It will be a witness against you if you are untrue to your God.'"

God's rest, though a gift, must be continually received and reentered, and each time we must bring more of ourselves under His direction and grace. He wants us sold out to Him so that, like Jesus, we do only and always what He bids us do. Abandoning ourselves to His love and leading will deepen our experience of being off duty with Him and on call to obey whatever He says.

What, then, is true rest? *Rest is God's gift of intimacy with Himself, won for us by Jesus' shed blood, which causes us to trust His good intentions toward us as beloved children and which results in our passion to glorify Him through glad obedience to Him and unselfish love for others.* This gift of intimate rest in God is indeed free, but as we receive it, we find that we must relinquish everything in exchange for it. This is the paradoxical economy of God.

"Then Joshua sent the people away, each to his own inheritance." The Israelites' conquest of Canaan and their entrance into rest had been accomplished at last.

FEAR AND SANCTUARY

Central to and flowing from the Israelites' walk of faith as they inhabited this new land, land they themselves owned at last, was their submission to the terms of the covenant they had reaffirmed with Joshua. Surely that submission meant they agreed that God's commands were right and that they desired to follow those commands. But they also had to submit to the humility of receiving God's provision for forgiveness through bloodshed when they failed to obey out of weakness or rebellion—the terms laid out by God Himself. Their willingness to call Yahweh the potter and themselves the clay was the heart of their relationship with Him. It is for us as well.

For it is our willingness to let God be God in our lives that sustains our walk with Him, and this submission alone allows us to find our rest in Him. We are to fear His holiness but we must not forget that His holiness embraces us and shields us from the enemy. "The LORD Almighty is the one you are to regard as holy, he is the one you are to fear, he is the one you are to dread, and he will be a sanctuary," Yahweh told His prophet Isaiah (Isa. 8:13–14). When we trust in God's goodness and submit to His leading, even our dread of Him will open us to rest in Him as a sure sanctuary.

On the other hand, to refuse to submit our hearts to this fearsome God is to invite disaster on ourselves. The people to whom Isaiah spoke unfortunately did not respond to his message with repentance and faith in Yahweh's forgiveness through the shed blood of their animal sacrifices (see Isa. 6:8–13). They saw no need to repent because they thought they had no sin. And to those who refuse to submit themselves to God regarding the reality and desperateness of their wicked hearts, God would be not sanctuary but avenger. Here is what He said to Isaiah about how His rebellious and unrepentant people would experience Him: "But for both houses of Israel [God] will be a stone that causes men to stumble and a rock that makes them fall. And for the people of Jerusalem he will be a trap and a snare" (8:14).

Those who fear God and submit themselves to obey His Word, who regard Him as holy and who worship Him with glorious dread—they will find He is a safe place where they can rest and be secure in His protection. But for those who refuse to repent, who do not show awe at His holiness and who are unafraid to disobey Him, thinking He does not see their sin— for them God is a stumbling block, and their irreverence toward Him will trip them up and keep them from His rest. Submission is of the essence in our covenantal relationship with God.

SUSTAINED BY SUBMISSION

The necessity of submitting ourselves to God in order to remain in intimate fellowship with Him is not true merely of us as created image-bearers, however. Jesus, the eternal Son of God made flesh, declared His own utter dependence on His Father for all things. "I do nothing on my own," He admitted, "but speak just what the Father has taught me" (John 8:28). In many similar passages Christ, the Second Person of the Trinity, expressed His freely chosen submission to His Father, the First Person of the Trinity, saying, for example, "I did not speak of my own accord, but the Father who sent me commanded me what to say and how to say it" (John 12:49). "For I have come down from heaven not to do my will but to do the will of him who sent me," Jesus also said (John 6:38). "I tell you the truth, the Son can do nothing by himself; he can do only what he sees his Father doing, because whatever the Father does the Son also does" (John 5:19).

It was Jesus' submission to His heavenly Father that sustained His very life. "My food," He had announced to His disciples at the well of Sychar, "is to do the will of him who sent me and to finish his work" (John 4:34). Trusting His Father was so intrinsic to Jesus' very nature that He found nourishment in doing whatever He heard the voice of His Father telling Him to do. It was like food to Him; He needed to obey in order to survive.

This picture in Scripture of Jesus' submission to His Father within the "community" of the Godhead is congruent with other biblical texts. For example, Jesus told Nicodemus the Pharisee, "God did not *send* his Son into the world to condemn the world," indicating His Father's prerogative to direct His will (John 3:17, emphasis added). Christ's submission to His Father certainly did not imply His inferiority, of course. Rather, it revealed the chosen yieldedness of an equal so that the purpose ordained by Triune unanimity in the courts of heaven before time began could be accomplished.

Submission is intrinsic to the intimate love relationship within the Trinity—the eternal plans of God mutually agreed on and gladly implemented by Father, Son, and Holy Spirit. Though we most often associate the Father with the work of creation, the Son with the work of redemption, and the Spirit with the work of sanctification, God's work is always—because of the indivisible nature of the Godhead—a "group activity."

All three Persons, for example, collaborated (co-labored) in creation—the Spirit brooding and breathing, the Father speaking into the void, the Son participating in bringing forth shape and life (see Genesis 1 and John 1). All three collaborated in redemption—the Father sending the Son, the sent Son dying, and the Spirit sent by Father and Son to draw the hearts of sinners to faith in the Son's sacrifice (see John 14:16, 26; 15:26; 16:7). And all three collaborate in the work of sanctification—the Father setting and maintaining the Kingdom agenda (Matt. 24:36; 1 Cor. 15:24–28), the Son upholding all things and interceding for us before the throne (Col. 1:17; Heb. 7:25), and the Spirit reiterating Jesus' words to us and empowering the lives of the saints (John 16:13).

Is not this mutuality of work and being within the Godhead where we see clear evidence of the essential submissiveness pervading God's nature? God was under no compulsion except His own divine prerogative to create anything—He was "content" within the Trinity and needed nothing more. We owe our very existence to the Triune choice to bring to life beings who would image God but yet not be God. Who can comprehend the sublime humility of our God in bending to earth and "getting His hands dirty" in the stuff He Himself had made in order to form beings who could choose for or against Him?

More than that, did not the Father submit His own eternal, ineffable love for the Son to the precious end of redeeming His fallen children? Similarly the Son submitted gladly to the Father's will with an abandon of love for Him and for us that danced within the Triune will. And the Holy Spirit submits unreservedly to the sending by Father and Son, as well as to our own need as believers—how else could the impossible chasm between our sinfulness and God's perfect holiness be bridged? The Holy Spirit graciously submits Himself to our frailty by making the preeminent God immanent within us.

Who can comprehend or ever adequately appreciate the submission of the Triune God, both within Himself and toward us, His image-bearers? This is mystery indeed, holy and awesome and altogether beautiful. And the mystery holds within itself something we too must learn as we enter our terror of intimacy, especially as wives.

SUBMISSION AND TRUST

Submission is always an issue of trust if it is to be a chosen thing. The Israelites, of course, had not consented to being subjugated by their Egyptian taskmasters, and their submission to them had been bitter and embittering. There was no trust between master and slave, because the one was able to demand a forced obedience from the other.

But when submission is freely chosen—as it has always been within the Godhead, for example—it is rooted in mutual trust and love. This kind of surrender to the will of another is always a response to the goodwill and trustworthiness of that person. Such surrender is dependent on those qualities if it is to survive. For that reason, we are without excuse when we refuse to place our full trust in God, for He is totally reliable and utterly trustworthy.

Within the Trinity, submission is completely understandable, and even our submission to the Triune God is eminently reasonable (though usually reluctantly given—most of us come kicking and screaming). But among human beings, the trust required in submission may not seem sensible at all. It is precisely the prospect of trusting an imperfect person that makes yielding our will to the will of another so discomfiting. *Is that person trustworthy?* we demand to know. *Would I be foolish to trust that one with my submission?* we wonder fitfully.

Especially is this an unsettling difficulty within the intimacy of marriage, regarding which the apostle Peter enjoins, "Wives, in the same way [as Christ submitted to the Father] be submissive to your husbands" (1 Peter 3:1). We can appreciate Christ's submission to His perfect Father. But how dare the disciple (who himself almost drowned for lack of trust in Jesus) tell us wives to trust our imperfect husbands enough to submit to them? How can we choose to put our faith in someone who is *not* always trustworthy when we, like Peter himself, even have trouble trusting the One who *is?*

Submission in today's cultural milieu is considered abhorrent, particularly when it applies to the marriage relationship. The values of contemporary society, in which people have made a fetish of independence and individual rights, run counter to the revealed nature of the Godhead and of humankind's required submission to the Godhead. Our Western values move us in altogether different directions: Finding oneself is more to be desired than finding God; even those who find Him want to remake Him in their own image; submission is unthinkable for a woman today.

Yet it is the very submissiveness intrinsic to the relationship within the Trinity that a woman is invited to image forth in the world—first toward Christ as her Lord, and also toward her husband if she is married. Just as she trusts herself to the headship of Jesus, she is to desire and model a similar willingness to bring her life under the covering and leadership of her husband—not as evidence of her weakness, but as evidence of the gentle and humble spirit Jesus invites us to learn from Him as we yoke ourselves to Him (see Matt. 11:29).

For this is the very thing to which the apostle Peter urges us as wives—that we become women of inner beauty by nurturing a quiet and gentle spirit toward our husbands—not nagging or complaining or correcting them but giving up our control strategies and showing them the respect of responding to their leadership. What an opportunity we have to bring joy to their hearts by trusting confidently that God will lead us through them (see 1 Peter 3:1–6).

The woman in Scripture who best modeled this, according to Peter, was Sarah, wife of Abraham, who became a woman of beauty by submitting her spirit to her husband. It wasn't easy for her. Submission never is easy, at least not since the fatal incident in Eden. Sarah learned her gentle spirit the hard way. Consider the cost of her beauty treatment. (The following stories of Sarah are found in Gen. 11:27–21:7.)

AN EXPENSIVE MAKEOVER

First, Sarah chose to follow Abraham in leaving the comfort of civilized Ur and the relative security of the family community in Haran, into a nomadic life in Canaan. Imagine a lifetime of camping—pulling up tent stakes time and again, never any neighborhood to settle in, no church to attend (only altars), no family reunions to enjoy—just transience and unpredictability, the things most women can *least* tolerate. All this because her husband had heard God's call and she believed him.

Well, at least her husband was a godly man, we might say. But that was another loss Sarah had to endure, for Abraham was just a man, prone to weakness and self-protection. Though God had appeared to him and had given him rich promises, Abraham yielded to fear when he fled with his family to Egypt to escape a drought in Canaan. "I know what a beautiful woman you are," he told his wife as they traveled toward Egypt. If he had stopped after this compliment, it would have comforted her heart, but Abraham went on to say, "When the Egyptians see you, they will say, 'This is his wife.' Then they will kill me but let you live. Say you are my sister, so that I will be treated well for your sake and my life will be spared because of you."

So much for masculine protection and courageous movement into danger and chaos! Unwilling to create a safe place for Sarah where she could find rest even in the unfamiliar "campground" of Egypt, Abraham instead required that she make a safe place for him, forgetting that God had already committed Himself to being his God. And in leaning on his wife instead of on Yahweh, Abraham in the end gave her over to the danger of Pharaoh's pagan court, getting rich because everyone thought he was her brother. God Himself had to intervene on Sarah's behalf so the pharaoh would give her back to Abraham. No wonder Peter tells us she "put [her] hope in God" and not in her husband (1 Peter 3:5).

But what enhanced Sarah's beauty most was the loss she most grieved— the absence of a child to call her own. God had promised Abraham (why had He not told *her?*) that a nation beyond counting would come from him. But many years passed, and eventually Sarah became too old to bear a child. Finally, tired of waiting for God to come through with what she had long been begging of Him, she decided to take things into her own hands.

"The LORD has kept me from having children," she announced to Abraham one day, not without bitterness. "Go, sleep with my maidservant; perhaps I can build a family through her" (Gen. 16:2). If God wouldn't build her family, she would have to do it herself.

What words might Sarah have wished to hear from Abraham regarding her suggestion? A beautiful young woman can make a man feel good about himself, especially if he's helping God out in the process. But did Sarah feel good that without hesitation and without any words to her, "Abram agreed to what Sarai said" and took Hagar, Sarah's handmaiden, to bed? What a difference it would have made to Sarah if Abraham had stood firm in trusting God. Then he could have calmed his wife's despair with words of encouragement, gently but firmly refusing her "solution" and reaffirming his cherishing of her.

And what a difference Abraham's refusal would have made for every generation since then, even in our world today, sparing us a most pressing political dilemma. For Ishmael, the fruit of Abraham's intimacy with Hagar, is the father of the Arab race, which wages warfare even now against the Jewish nation, the descendants of Isaac, Abraham's later son of the promise through Sarah.

Surely Sarah suffered much from the consequences of her impatience and disbelief in God's trustworthiness. But in those painful years of watching Ishmael grow in strength and in the love of his father, Sarah was thrust again into putting her hope in God—not in her husband nor in herself— and waiting for His sure promises to be fulfilled according to His own timetable.

And when at last she overheard God tell Abraham that she would herself bear a child at the age of ninety, though she laughed at the prospect, she also yielded herself to the miraculous ardor of her one-hundred-year-old "master" (or husband), receiving the gift of new life from him and from God. She had developed "the unfading beauty of a gentle and quiet spirit, which is of great worth in God's sight," because she had done "what is right and [had not given] way to fear" in the end (1 Peter 3:4, 6).

Sarah's beauty treatment had been long and expensive but she stands today as the prime example of a woman of faith for having persevered in struggling to submit herself to God and to her imperfect husband. Her life evidences the hope that when a woman's longing to be fruitfully connected to a good man is transformed by her intimacy with God, she can move beyond merely using him for her own purposes, and she can learn to respect and follow him. For this we are designed as women, and in this we can persevere as spiritual daughters of Sarah.

SUFFERING AND PONDERING

A woman's suffering to submit herself to an imperfect husband is part of the process in her becoming intimately connected to God. If she is to obey His call in this, she will need an ongoing oneness with Him to carry it off. All who commit themselves to follow God's leading will bear losses, even those highly favored by God—in fact, *especially* those highly favored by Him.

Imagine a woman, no longer young but not so very old, climbing a flight of narrow stairs in Jerusalem, retracing her steps to the room from which she and the others had earlier spilled out into the busy streets below. (This story is not from Scripture but it includes events described in Matthew 2, 11–12; Luke 1–2; John 2, 19; and Acts 2.) She could still hear the muffled sound of the Galilean fisherman's strong voice made bold by the strange intoxication that had seized them all. It had happened so suddenly and was so contrary to what they had expected. She felt almost too tired for this most recent astonishment. As with the earlier wonders, she needed some time alone to ponder.

Entering the room, she returned to the spot where she had been when the glory had fallen on them. Gently lowering herself to a cushion with the caution dictated by protesting joints, she settled into a position she could tolerate and closed her eyes for some deep breaths. As the familiar inner quiet began to return, she let her mind go back, back to when this had all begun.

The habit of reflection had kept the memory clear, as had the telling of the story more than once. Not everyone had ears that could hear of angelic appearances and words from Yahweh, but she had confided to some, beginning with dear, dear Elizabeth. How old Elizabeth had seemed back then (actually not too much older than she herself was now) and how safe it had felt to be with her. The angel Gabriel had disrupted both their lives with news of conception, but at least Elizabeth had been married, if too old. News of her own pregnancy would not be received so joyously.

How gracious of Yahweh to have given her three months to be comforted by Elizabeth before returning to Nazareth and to Joseph. She would never forget the older woman's agony at her birthing of John, for even in her pain Elizabeth had offered her words of advice and encouragement. As an unwed mother-to-be she had needed those words, for she was alone when her own time had come upon her in a strange place with no familiar women at hand. Her closed eyes winced ever so slightly at the memory. It had not been easy being God's handmaiden.

"I am the Lord's servant," she had earlier acknowledged, yielding herself to the angel's words. "May it be to me as you have said" (Luke 1:38). Mary pondered again those words that had changed her life forever. She was so young to have yoked herself so unalterably to His will, so naive about what this high privilege of birthing the Messiah would cost her. "Highly favored" the angel had named her, but he had not told her about the suffering. That she would discover later.

Her first inkling of a coming sorrow had occurred when she and Joseph had taken the baby to the magnificent temple for circumcision. There the ancient Simeon had sung his song to the wee Christ, after which he had spoken stunning words to her, saying, "This child is destined to cause the falling and rising of many in Israel, and to be a sign that will be spoken against, so that the thoughts of many hearts will be revealed" (2:34–35). *Spoken against!* she had marveled in dismay. *Who would possibly speak against Messiah?* And then those penetrating words she had not fully understood until just recently, "And a sword will pierce your own soul too."

Long and often she had pondered Simeon's dire prediction. When Gabriel had announced she would be queen mother of Israel's anointed King, he had said nothing about a sword. Of course there had been the stares and whispers when she'd returned home after visiting Elizabeth, three months with child. And Joseph—gentle, upright Joseph—the hurt and bewilderment in his eyes still pierced her heart when she remembered those early days. But these sorrows she had borne, along with the death of her wedding dreams, her isolation at Jesus' birth, and the lonely, anxiety-ridden exile years in Egypt protecting the child from Herod's crazed paranoia. These were but thistle-pricks compared to the wounding of the later sword.

From Loss to Rest

Lost now in thought as she leaned back against the wall, Mary's face responded unconsciously to the snatches of painful memory playing across her mind like shadows cast across a room by morning light. There had been the teenage crisis when their missing man-child, finally located in the temple talking theology with the rabbis, had declared allegiance to His heavenly Father's call on His life. Why had dread shot through her soul at His words? What intimation of approaching loss was Yahweh preparing her for even then? And Joseph—how had he endured being reminded he was not father to this child? These were the first glancing blows struck by Simeon's prophesied sword.

Later to follow were Jesus' words distancing Himself from her own maternal authority. At the wedding in Cana had He not said to her, "Dear woman, why do you involve me? . . . My time has not yet come" (John 2:4)? Of course He *had* met the crisis by changing water into needed wine but He'd made it clear it was not her urging that had motivated His decision.

And later still, when she and His brothers had come to force Him home—He wasn't taking care of Himself, after all—He had asked, "Who is my mother, and who are my brothers?" (Matt. 12:48). Those words had hurt, coming as they did after all she had suffered to follow Yahweh's yoking. Would she not always be mother to Him? Family is what most deeply roots us in who we are—how could He dismiss her motherhood so lightly in preference to His disciples? Even now her Son's words stung, for they reminded her of the sword that had split her family in two.

But the worst piercing was yet to come, the sword gleamingly unsheathed and lethal. How could the joy of the recent Passover have been so eclipsed by the monstrous wound to her heart? "Crucify him! Crucify him!" The words still resounded in her ears, in her soul, in her worst nightmares. How could Messiah die? Why did He have to? Could not the One who had miracled His birth also have prevented His death? And if He did have to die, dear God, did He have to die that way? They had stripped Him naked and nailed Him up for everyone's scorn. How could a mother bear to see it?

Surely this wounding had been almost too much for her. How had she managed to stay on Golgotha's hill as He suffocated in agony and shame? She thought of His laborious effort to name John as the one to care for her, and her heart broke again as it had when His heart had given out at last. Simeon surely had been right. Even now, even having seen Him alive again, tears traced the wrinkles on her cheeks as she pondered His dying. Lost once again in her sorrow, she did not bother to wipe them away.

"Come to me," He had said (someone had reported the very words to her). "Take my yoke upon you," He had invited. But she had already yoked herself in acquiescence to the One who had come upon her and whose power had overshadowed her, as Gabriel had foretold. Now *that* was a sweet piercing she could not forget, the wondrous coming upon her of the Holy Spirit, the overshadowing of the Most High—

Yes! That was it! That was the connection her mind had been searching for! Eyes open now and sitting up, she almost said it aloud: "It is the same One, the same Spirit—come upon me then and come upon me today! The quickening is the same—His new life in my womb, and now His new life in my spirit!"

At last her heart began to be eased, her suffering abated, her pondering rewarded with this fresh realization. Her Son, her Savior, her Comforter— He had come again, this time to stay forever, not in her womb nor by her side but within her heart, not unborn infant but infinite Lord. The sword of Simeon's vision had indeed pierced her heart, but she had not been destroyed. Instead, she had been given at last not only rest but a taste of joy unspeakable and full of glory.

234

Then quiet worship broke out in the upper room, one woman alone singing again her song of adoration:

My soul doth magnify the Lord,
And my spirit hath rejoiced in God my Savior.
For he hath regarded the low estate of his handmaiden: for, behold, from henceforth all generations shall call me blessed.
For he that is mighty hath done to me great things; and holy is his name.

LUKE 1:46–49 KJV

The song went on and worship flowed as Peter's sermon drew to an end outside and three thousand new believers from around the world prepared to receive Jesus' rest and take His yoke on themselves. The celebration of Pentecost, festival of the harvest's firstfruits, would never be the same again after that memorable and most wondrous day.

THE TERROR OF LOVE

The cost of discipleship, of receiving and wearing the yoke Christ offers His followers, will not be exactly the same for all believers. All are called to pay the price of obedience and repentant faith in Yahweh's grace, and all will have to endure the humbling of rebuke and correction when they strain against their yoking. Certainly the life of Jesus' mother teaches us we all must experience the sword-pierce of countless woundings if we give God freedom to have His way with us. No two lives will bear the same sorrows, but all will pay the cost of being yoked to Him.

There is, however, one other price believers must pay, and that is the paradoxical suffering brought about by our fear of being loved. Strange as it may seem, the love for which we yearn—the very love that casts out our fear—is itself what we also most greatly fear, though it is our only hope for finding the rest for our souls that Christ promised. This is mystery, to be sure. Why is love so unsettling, so frightening? And why are we so ambivalent about it?

We fear love because we who have tasted it know our own helplessness before it. Designed to need and desire it above all else (studies have shown that babies cannot thrive or even survive without love), we despise being at the mercy of what we cannot procure for ourselves. Can anyone be forced to love another? Is not love by its very nature freely given? It cannot be coerced, for then it is not love.

We are caught in a quandary, especially when those who ought to love us (like our parents or spouse) do not love us or do not love us well or have betrayed us in a significant way. Our anger flares and we find ourselves

235

deeply resenting the one who does not love us. But beneath our rage and resentment remains our passion to be loved by that very one. It is this passion we dread and try to kill, for we think if we can kill our desire for love, we can mitigate our anguish at being unloved.

Abandoned or abused children, for instance, sometimes feel shame for their unrequited longing for their negligent parents, though God gave them that longing and they are powerless before it. All children love their parents, with whom they are bonded before birth by blood and (at least maternally) by a most intimate proximity. Even those children whose parents have hurt or abandoned them and have not repented do not cease longing for restored relationship with them. Beneath their anger, deeper even than their refusal to enter their desire for connection with an abusive mother or father, there exists the parent-child bond of love that can never be obliterated.

In a similar agony of self-contempt many divorced spouses or cast-aside friends call themselves fools for having loved someone who spurned their hearts. They forget (or have never been taught) that it is never a sin to love. In fact love for the unlovely is the closest thing on earth to God's *agape* love for us, who are intrinsically imperfect. A person's shame for having loved the undeserving is misplaced; it is those who will *not* love or who refuse to receive love who are behaving like fools.

Fear and self-effacement exist in our relationship with God as well. We are designed to deeply long for connection with Him, our hearts restless (as St. Augustine says) until we discover rest in Him. Yet our sin keeps us from loving Him, and our fear often keeps us from receiving His love. We are well aware of our deep bentness and we cannot comprehend how or why, on our behalf, the eternal Father poured out His hatred of sin on His eternal Son at Calvary. And because we can't understand it, we are prone to disbelieve it. God Himself then becomes suspect, and our only hope becomes our greatest terror.

Even when we receive grace to believe God delights in us as His children, we still remain afraid. We balk at yielding ourselves to love, hating to admit we want it and have always wanted it and have even gone so far as to delude ourselves that we had it when we really didn't. Our terror is that if we open our hearts to longing for love, then we will be undone by the loss of love—real or perceived, past, present, or even future. What if God changes His mind? What if there's a kink in our lifeline to Him and His love stops flowing to us because of something we've done? What if, after all, we can lose His love? Our grief, we think, will unravel our souls and we will never know ourselves knit together again. Better to never submit to our desire for love—God's or anyone else's—than to love and lose being loved. Better even to pretend we were (or are) loved than to face that we weren't (or aren't) and to die of sorrow. We'd rather be safe but sterile than alive to our desire and profoundly bereaved. It is a fearsome thing to love and be loved.

Yet we must never forget that though our fear is real, it is not the ultimate reality. God is the ultimate reality, and we must push into our fear (not around or away from it) and through our fear (engaging it and facing it down to what is the worst thing that could happen to us), and then see whether or not God is bigger than what we fear. Can He do what is best for us? *Will* He do what is best for us? Will we believe that "in all things God works for the good of those who love him, who have been called according to his purpose" (Rom. 8:28)? And are we willing to embrace that purpose by being "conformed to the likeness of [God's] Son" in the process (v. 29), no matter what the cost?

Submission—even submission to being loved—asks much of us all, but we have God's promise that His love will never fail us. As the apostle Paul exulted, "I am convinced that neither death nor life, neither angels nor demons, neither the present nor the future, nor any powers, neither height nor depth, nor anything else in all creation, will be able to separate us from the love of God that is in Christ Jesus our Lord" (vv. 38–39). Such words are enough to rouse our most ardent passion for submission.

STOOPING TO ASK

And because genuine submission, modeled after the glad oneness within the Trinity, must always be freely chosen, wives must search their hearts to know whether or not they even want to be conformed to Christ's likeness in the matter of submitting to their husbands as Christ submits to the Father and as the church submits to Christ. The desire to obey God must always flow from Him and not from ourselves, for in our own hearts there are hidden pockets of resistance to His bidding that we may not even realize.

For years I did many of the "right" submissive things in my relationship with Bill, saying suitable words and trying hard to act submissive (whatever that might mean). But my spirit was far from respectful of Bill's leadership, for I did not trust him nor did I know how to be honest with him. Even when God began confronting me with the disrespect of my heart toward my husband, though I knew to repent and to ask for Bill's forgiveness, I still wasn't sure what to do differently. Nowhere could I find a set of rules that would lead me into appropriate biblical submission.

What I eventually discovered instead was that my struggle was always more with God than with Bill, for only my heavenly Father could subdue my willful spirit and replace my hard heart with a soft heart reflective of His own kindness. I had to continually do business with God, bending my will to His and pleading for a similar longing to honor Bill with my heart as well. Sometimes His answers to my prayers about how to treat my husband were very specific.

I remember an occasion before Bill had quit drinking when I attended a Christian conference where I was scheduled to speak the following day. I was talking with one of the other speakers, who happened to say in the course of our conversation, "Did you ask Bill to pray for you about your speaking tomorrow?"

Embarrassed that I hadn't even thought about it, I tried to let myself off the hook by saying something about how I wished Bill would have thought of doing that himself.

"But," the man persisted, "did you ask him to pray for you?"

"No," I had to admit, "I didn't."

However, I did go straight from that conversation to the phone in a nearby hallway to call home. Fortunately Bill answered the phone, and I had the opportunity to confess my spirit of pride and self-sufficiency and to request his forgiveness. I also asked him to pray for me, which he did immediately and, I think, gladly.

Since that day I have never spoken to any group of people without receiving Bill's prayers on my behalf—that God would give me His words, that the enemy would be restrained from harassing me or my listeners, and that I would remember that both he and God would always love me, however well or poorly I might do. This man's words in my ears and his hands on my head never fail to make my heart rest, and I am always glad to submit to my need for his prayers and to his kind spiritual movement on my behalf—as was true even in the years before Bill had attended his first AA meeting.

SOBER AND REAL

So often we find in retrospect how we have refused to ask for what we need, preferring to protect ourselves from love and its danger. We see how we have built our illusions and have dulled our disappointments and have run from our pain and have tried to control what other people do and say. We have made safety our paramount priority—until God breaks in, as He did to me that Sunday afternoon when Bill came home after his first AA meeting, a man determined to trust God for his sobriety.

Everything changed for us that day, and not all of the changes were pleasant. It wasn't long before Bill and I discovered we had some soul-rocking challenges facing us as we began to live without alcohol influencing our relationship. I had been twenty years praying for this to happen, and now that God had done it in His own way and time, I began to hope I could finally rest my heart in this redeemed, now sober man.

But rest in Bill is not what I found—not at first, anyway. My suffering— and Bill's—was far from over. For being at rest in God does not mean being free of pain and sorrow. The Israelites were not problem-free, even after they

238

had finally taken the land and had moved into the territory assigned by Joshua through the casting of lots. They were finally in new homes, but they were not yet Home. Neither are we, this side of Jesus' second coming to our earth.

And while we remain here, no matter how long we have been yoked to the One who offers us His rest, we will find it is often painful to stay yoked to Him, following His example of loving the imperfect, oftentimes unlovable people nearest to us. What happened to Bill and me happens to all who experience a major change in a significant relationship. We had to learn to live a new way in an unfamiliar place. Old habits, though deeply ingrained, had to gradually and painfully give way to new and better habits. We had to switch from surviving in the desert and from doing battle in Canaan, and instead enter the daily grind of planting and weeding and keeping house in the promised land. Our work had just begun.

A major shift happened when Bill yoked himself to Jesus in sobriety. Now that neither Bill nor I had the alcohol to protect us, he had to face his pain unnumbed, and I could no longer use his drinking to justify my self-protection. We were invited by his sobriety to enter realms of risk we had not entered before, following the Spirit's yoking into patches of pain we did not want to enter.

Mama's death, for example, became more real to us both as we faced it without the anesthesia of alcohol. Now that I was entering the "safety" of Bill's sobriety, I had to finally look at my anger toward him because of his emotional abandoning of both Mama and me when we needed his presence desperately. And together Bill and I both had to struggle again with our anger that God had taken Mama from us before we were ready to let her go (are we ever really ready?). Six months after Mama had gone Home, we entered our grieving again.

THE DISCIPLINE OF GRIEVING

To open oneself to sorrow in the presence of someone else requires a kind of trust Bill and I had not yet reached with one another. Now, as we began feeling more safe in our relationship, we dared to begin processing together the damage we had done to each other's hearts, and a new kind of fear faced us both. It was clear that our heavenly Father intended to heal deep wounds in our souls.

For it is when we ignore and refuse to grieve our losses that our souls are most greatly harmed. Sins perpetrated against us that remain ungrieved and unrelinquished retain their power to cripple us emotionally, spiritually, and often physically. Our past often retains a stranglehold on our present lives.

The harm to our souls is not merely the result of hidden pain, of course. We also must face and repent of our hidden sin, for we have pursued strate-

239

gies for managing our lives, minimizing our sorrow, and protecting our hearts from others, even God—strategies utterly contrary to the rest Jesus longs to give us. Therefore, our process of healing will call forth from us not just tears of sadness but tears of repentance.

Past abuse, of course, is never healed in the sense that it is no longer remembered. The Israelites never forgot their Egyptian bondage; the annual celebration of Passover required by God reminds Jews to this day of the abuse from which Yahweh delivered them. Their abuse certainly is not the point of their celebration; their deliverance is the point. Nevertheless, remembering the abuse is the vehicle by which they both grieve the bitterness of Egyptian cruelty and celebrate God's salvation from it. The memories of our own personal histories must be similar vehicles for both sorrow and praise. In this way God's redemption shines brightly against the backdrop of pain, and His name is glorified for having thwarted the evil one's wicked intent to destroy our lives.

That is why the Holy Spirit in us calls us to sorrow over our losses—not so that we become self-focused or self-pitying, but so that we can move through the grief process into a willingness to forgive those who have harmed us. This process is neither easy nor hasty. We must follow the disruptive course of consciously facing the offense, sorrowing over its damage, repenting our own wrong ways of responding, refusing to avenge ourselves, and learning to rest in Christ's love for us and His forgiveness. It may take a long time, and it surely will cost us considerable suffering, but it will be a suffering that brings healing, both for our own hearts and for those whose lives we can touch with the kindness wrought by our brokenness before God.

This suffering Bill and I enter more and more willingly (if not always joyfully) for the good of our marriage. We do not want to waste our years of marital turmoil, which God allowed into our lives so we would be disrupted into greater dependence on Him. Like Moses, whom God disciplined in the desert for forty years to prepare him for useful service, Bill and I want our suffering to count for God. We want our oneness to reflect more and more the unadulterated love and oneness within the Trinity.

To that end, Bill and I have chosen to embrace the suffering of love, seeking to offer as much of our hearts to one another as we can, by asking the Spirit to reveal as much of our hearts to us as we can humanly handle at any given moment. As we then share both our pain and our shortcomings with each other, we practice the exchange of forgiveness and healing grace back and forth, and God's glory shines in and through us.

Strangely enough, though there is sadness in naming our pain and repenting our sin toward one another, this sorrow of grieving and humbling ourselves draws us together as nothing else has ever done before. Suffering carries within itself the potential for connecting people with each other in a deep way, for sorrow is the environment in which intimacy grows best. Early in our marriage the secrets of unacknowledged sin drove deep wedges between Bill and me. Now, as we open our hearts to one another, we do battle for our marriage, mutually and continually repenting before God and each other so that unwon territory of the heart can be claimed and given reciprocally. Our passion for one another carries the price tag of openness and suffering. We both think it's a bargain.

More than anything else, Bill and I want our marriage to showcase the glory of the Father's grace and forgiveness, made possible through Christ's death and resurrection and made available to us by the Holy Spirit's presence in us. If trinitarian love can shine through us, we will consider our lives fruitful indeed.

Now and Not Yet

Sometimes, however, we lose our focus without even knowing it. We return to some destructive habit we thought we had conquered, not recognizing how deep was its power to disrupt our souls. Sins confessed and forgiven we find ourselves doing again, and we live baffled by our own hearts and by the hearts of others.

It is then we need to quiet ourselves again in God's presence, retreating (if only symbolically or internally) to the mountain to be alone with our Father, as Jesus so often did. If we wait for Him, He will come, though we can never predict nor control when or how He comes. Nor can we expect Him to give us clear answers for solving our immediate dilemma. For if ambiguity is the perfume of God (as someone once said), then our presence with Him may offer us more encouragement than direction.

In the midst of a recent struggle to know how to deal with a particular sin of Bill's that had done harm to me, for example, I cried out to God in my sorrow and confusion, "How do I live in a fallen world when what I long for from Bill I don't receive? How do I forgive without letting him off the hook?"

How do I do it with you, My child? I heard Him ask. *I have promised never to leave or forsake you, but do I ignore your sin? Would that be good for you? Do I not love you enough to show you My heart of sorrow when you fail to love? My sorrow at your sin does not mean I don't love you—it proves I do.*

Do not suppose, He continued, *that sorrow and delight cannot exist simultaneously in Me. In you they are often either/or, but in Me they are both/and. My Son's scream of forsakenness echoes always in the chambers of heaven, but so does the laughter of pure joy. Do not err in divesting joy of sorrow, nor sorrow of joy. One does not cancel out the other, though in your heart one or the other may predominate at any given time. Love does not keep score but it is also neither surprised by sin nor complacent about it.*

241

What is difficult for you, My precious daughter, is to confront the sin, especially in Bill, My son. You fear he cannot handle your honesty—is this not a recurring disrespect in you, My dear? You fear his anger and you want to protect him from having to look at hard things, at deep strongholds of My enemy in him. Do not protect him and do not fear his anger, for this is his battle with Me, not with you.

But do not minimize the damage done to you by this sin, either, My child. My sons must be called to the holiness of sacrifice, especially the sacrificing of their sin—their damaging rage, their absence or passivity, and the "back doors" they leave open for themselves to indulge their addictions. When you overlook their sin, your heart is not beating in rhythm with My own. You must ask much of My men.

And ask much too of My daughters—that they not pretend and also that they not get even. This is their call to holiness—that they sorrow over the sin done and being done to them and that in the midst of their pain they offer kindness even to the unrepentant. They fear being hurt and they fear inflicting hurt, for either holds for them the potential of death—the death of either attack or abandonment by men.

But remind them too that I have defeated death. Though My enemy uses the threat of death to terrorize My image-bearers, I use it to draw My children to Myself and to usher them into My presence. My love is the only reliable antiterrorist protection available, but you must face your fear and not hide, for hiding is futile, unless it is in Me.

Though I received no directives about what to do or say in my relationship with Bill, I was comforted by the words of my heavenly Father. I stood in His presence on holy ground, and He spoke to me. It was enough. I entered His rest.

THE COMFORT OF SUBMISSION

I don't presume to know very much about what it means to be a godly, submissive wife. I know it is not about performance. I'm sure it has nothing to do with self-contempt. I have found that my "right words" can be a mask behind which I hide my true heart. I recognize that my mood and inflection are more important than what I do or say.

But submission of heart and spirit are far more elusive. Even with the best of intentions I can disrespect Bill in a heartbeat. I do not trust the overflow of my heart because there is yet so much of pride and self-centeredness hidden there, and it can leak out at the slightest provocation. At times I find great joy in trusting Bill, for he is a good man and quick to repent. At other times (especially when the dark side of his own heart is showing), I run from him and determine to live emotionally on my own without ever asking anything of him again. My ambivalence confounds even me.

Nevertheless, this much I can say with integrity: I long to rest in God and in Bill more and more. I know God intends to bless my life through my husband, and I want to go wherever He leads me through this redeemed but fallen man. I want to evidence toward him the responsive attitude I am nurturing toward Christ in my best moments. In submitting to Bill, I know I can help him accomplish God's work by providing him encouragement and refreshing as he does whatever God calls him to do. I also look to him to make a way and a clear path for me to respond to God's call on my life.

This respecting and submitting I want to do especially as together Bill and I seek to know and follow God's leading for us in our retirement years. I encourage him, trying not to control. We discuss God's will, but I cannot hear God's voice for him. I affirm his gifts and his strengths, but I cannot tell him what God wants him to do. I can follow where he leads, but I must not be the leader. I refresh him when he becomes work-weary, but I cannot do his work for him.

In these ways I model the church as Christ's Bride, loving my husband and waiting to bring forth the fruit of oneness as he moves to bring his love to me. My submission to his leadership does not imply I am less than he. Rather, it affirms that I am equal to my head, yet deliberately willing to follow the man to whom I am covenantally yoked. As Bill yields his will to Christ's leading, I find comfort in accepting his leadership, even as Christ found nourishment in yielding His will to the will of His Father.

The more I understand and experience submission in my marriage, the more I have come to love it, for it expresses as can nothing else in human intercourse the essential nature of intimate love among the three Persons of the Triune God. The mystery of oneness in marriage somehow mirrors the glorious exchange of love and joy and mutual submission that ever swirls within the Trinity.

Of course no wife can perfectly respond to her husband in the way that Father, Son, and Holy Spirit dance with intimate gladness. Nor can she relinquish her heart to him with the extravagance with which the church will one day abandon herself to Christ (see Eph. 5:22–27). However, when a woman rests in God, she can respect her husband, encouraging his obedience to God and refreshing his heart with her responsiveness to his love. She can become willing to wait for a place opened up and made safe for her by the covering of her husband if she is married, or by other good men (especially in her church) if she is unmarried. She can exchange her need to control men for a greater willingness to ask for and trust their goodness on her behalf. She is able to face her terror of loneliness, knowing that even in the suffering of being alone, she can believe herself to be precious and beloved by the kindest Lover of all, even Jesus. This submission any redeemed woman can practice in the strength of Christ's own submission to her need for tender cherishing.

MUTUAL SUBMISSION

Not long ago, as Bill and I were discussing the issue of a wife's submission to her husband, he asked, "Who submits to the wife?" I stared at him, uncharacteristically speechless for a moment. "Her children?" I guessed.

"I don't think so," Bill replied. "I think her husband submits to her by sacrificing himself for her."

Of course. How could I have missed it? Husbands are to model servant leadership in their relationships with their wives. Once when the disciples were arguing about who of them would be most honored in Christ's coming kingdom, Jesus rebuked their pride and selfish ambition with these words: "You know that the rulers of the Gentiles lord it over them, and their high officials exercise authority over them. Not so with you. Instead, whoever wants to become great among you must be your servant, and whoever wants to be first must be your slave—just as the Son of Man did not come to be served, but to serve, and to give his life as a ransom for many" (Matt. 20:25–28). A husband must serve his wife by laying down his life for her as Christ did for the church, thus accomplishing the mutual submission the apostle Paul called for in Ephesians 5:21.

Both men and women are to model Jesus' submissive spirit, especially in their marriages. We as wives teach our husbands what it costs for the Bride of Christ to abandon herself to her Bridegroom, and our husbands teach us about the wooing and sacrificing Christ does for the church. As we submit to them, and as together with them we submit to our Lord, Christ Himself will one day "be made subject to him who put everything under him, so that God may be all in all" (1 Cor. 15:28). Then will be made perfectly clear the words of Paul to the Corinthian believers: "Now I want you to realize that the head of every man is Christ, and the head of the woman is man, and the head of Christ is God" (11:3). For in that day the glory of submission—our own and Christ's—will be made manifest, to the eternal praise of our great and most wonderful God.

The next and final chapter will examine the ways in which our rest in God, especially as husbands and wives, will give way to a passionate love that will bear rich fruit for Christ's kingdom.

QUESTIONS TO CONSIDER

1. Which aspect of the definition of rest, found on page 226, has been the most difficult for you to live out in your relationship with God?

2. What in your past or present circumstances hinders you from trusting God's kind intentions toward you?

3. To which of the "submission struggles" of Sarah or Mary (Jesus' mother) do you most relate?

4. How has grieving your losses (both large and little) contributed to your experience of resting in God?

5. What specific relational changes might a spouse make to live out a more Christ-like submission—i.e., a husband to serve more sacrificially, a wife to be more respectful and responsive to leadership?

Regarding the opening story:

Barbara's mother's notion of submission had been to ignore her husband's sin and to say nothing. Barbara rejected that notion but did her best to control her husband's behavior until God intervened in her life.

6. Describe the difference, if any, between what you believe Scripture teaches about a wife's submission to her husband and the version embraced by Barbara's mother.

7. What do you consider biblical and/or unbiblical regarding Barbara's plan to confront Duane's sin?

Chapter Twelve

Rest

The Joy of Passionate Abandon

THE ACCIDENT HAD CHANGED EVERYTHING, *and on this night, five years later, Todd was glad for the changes. Lying on his side so he could watch his wife, Lynne, as she slept, Todd resisted the impulse to touch her one more time. A warm glow lingered after Lynne's passionate response to his lovemaking, and Todd, unable to sleep, wanted the moment to last.*

How different things had been before, Todd thought—before the crash and Lynne's long coma, before the many months of therapy and the struggle to manage her pain. He had always enjoyed their marital intimacy during their thirty years before the accident, but almost losing Lynne had permanently altered the way he approached her now.

Maybe it was Lynne's new fragility that evoked this deep tenderness in him and made her more precious. As he watched her sleeping peacefully beside him, Todd thought back to the many weeks he'd kept tearful vigil over her unconscious body, praying she would awaken to speak his name once more. He'd been unable to hold back his words during those tormenting days—words of sorrow for having taken her for granted, words of gratitude for all she'd done

247

for him and the children, words about how God was revealing Himself to him during that agonizing season of waiting.

Later Lynne had told him she remembered hearing some of those words, but at the time he'd just needed to say them to stay connected to her. A sudden gladness warmed Todd's heart as he recalled the first words Lynne had said when she awoke from her coma. "Are you okay?" she wanted to know. How like her to think first of him and not of herself!

The injuries from the accident, of course, had slowed Lynne down in every way, and Todd had slowed his own pace to coincide with hers. Nowhere had this been more difficult for them than in their lovemaking, but nowhere had it been more rewarding either. The new gentleness Todd felt for his wife had expressed itself in his patient passion toward her, even when she could not fully respond. "I can wait," he would assure her. "We have the rest of our lives to finish what we've begun tonight." Then she would rest, certain of his love.

And wonderfully, Todd's patience had over time released in Lynne a willingness to abandon herself to his love in ways she'd not been able to experience before. Never had she felt more treasured as a woman, and never in all of his sixty years had Todd felt more fulfilled in his manhood. Tonight, as he lay quietly beside the woman he loved, he couldn't seem to get enough of drinking in her beauty.

A soft sigh interrupted Todd's reverie as Lynne opened her eyes and smiled in response to his tender look. "Mm," she murmured, "I love you so much."

"And I love you, my dear," Todd whispered as he reached to draw her close. "You cannot know how much."

Tragedy of any kind—by which Satan always intends to destroy our souls—can instead become God's kind intervention to bring us to Himself and change us from the inside out. When our circumstances drive us to greater dependence on our heavenly Father, He will capture our hearts and transform our wills into an abandon of obedience that will make our lives an integral part of His larger story of grace and salvation. Todd's God-dependence, for example, had enabled him to become the kind of lover God always intended he should be. As we yield ourselves to God and join in His passion for His own glory, our small and self-centered goals will more and more give way to cooperating in His eternal plan to overcome evil with love—which is possible only in His strength, not our own.

Our gracious God continually entices us into oneness with Himself—the oneness made possible by Jesus' atoning death—so that we may enjoy the pleasures of passionate abandon to Him in love. Like Lynne's response to Todd's tender movement toward her, we as believers can choose to risk giving ourselves wholly to God in receiving His love. To this intimacy we are invited, and for this gift we will offer Him everlasting praise, for we will have found in Him that for which we'd always longed: a place to rest.

"As for me and my household, we will serve the LORD," Joshua had said, and the people had responded, "We too will serve the LORD, because he is our God" (Josh. 24:15, 18). And they had kept those covenant vows—at least as long as Joshua and the current elders of Israel remained alive. "After Joshua had dismissed the Israelites, they went to take possession of the land, each to his own inheritance. The people served the LORD throughout the lifetime of Joshua and of the elders who outlived him and who had seen all the great things the LORD had done for Israel" (Judg. 2:6–7).

But the next generation of Israelites and the ones after that—those who had not seen with their own eyes the Jordan River held back or the walls of Jericho crumble into dust—those third- and fourth-generation Israelites were less awed by Yahweh and less faithful to His Word. They "knew neither the LORD nor what he had done for Israel" (Judg. 2:10), not because they had not heard the stories of Yahweh's mighty deeds, but because they had not joined their knowledge about Him to faith in His love for them.

And because these latter-day unbelievers were not personally yoked to Yahweh, they began to wander from His Word. Idolatry crept into their culture, and intermarriage with the neighboring Canaanites corrupted their worship and their morals. Finally, there was war in the land again, only this time the Israelites were the ones being attacked. Yahweh was graciously allowing His people to be punished by the surrounding pagans, calling His children back to the yoke that would protect and bless them once again.

For three hundred years after Joshua's death, God's people repeated a destructive, repetitive cycle of disobedience, punishment, repentance, deliverance, renewed obedience (as long as the deliverer was alive), then disobedience, punishment, repentance, deliverance, and so on—again and again. During all that time Yahweh never unyoked Himself from the people He had chosen to love, but they strained mightily against His yoking time after time, always to their own great detriment.

AN UNLIKELY YOKING

Then a calamity struck that no one had anticipated. (This story is told in 1 Samuel 4–6.) Influenced by the superstitious mentality of the surrounding peoples, the Israelites, losing a war with the idolatrous Philistines, decided to carry the holy ark of the covenant into battle with them. Surely, they thought, this "good-luck charm" would assure them of Yahweh's blessing, and they would be able to defeat their enemies.

Unfortunately, however, the Israelites lost that battle, and with it the ark of the covenant that for close to four hundred years had symbolized Yahweh's presence among them. In triumph the Philistines brought Yahweh's sacred ark home with them and set it up in their pagan temple beside Dagon, their god of fertility.

Had Yahweh left His people? No, they had left Him. Was He still yoked to the Israelites? Yes, and His ark would be returned to them, but not by their own efforts or shrewdness. God Himself would bring it back—evidence not only of His commitment to them (despite their unworthiness) but of His jealousy for His own name, which was above every name—even Dagon's.

For the morning after the ark had been set up in the Philistines' temple, the shrine priests arrived to discover their god lying facedown in front of the ark of Yahweh. Distressed, they righted their god, but the next morning it happened again, only this time Dagon was found not only facedown but headless and handless as well. Only the idol's body had been left intact.

Then disaster struck the people of the Philistine city where the sacred ark had been taken—a devastating plague, transmitted by rats and characterized by tumors in the groin area. Much alarmed, the elders of the city eventually transported their Israelite trophy of war to another Philistine city. There a similar plague broke out, killing many and causing a panic among its citizens. The elders of that city tried moving the ark to yet another city, but the people there panicked when they saw it coming, for death from the tumors was already among them, and they wanted nothing to do with this foreign God or His deadly ark.

In desperation the leaders of all five Philistine city-states convened to resolve this crisis. On the advice of their occult diviners, they decided to put Yahweh to a test. They wanted to determine if this seven-month plague afflicting thousands of their people was His judgment against them for having captured the ark, or if the onset of the plague at that particular time had been merely a coincidence. So they built a brand new cart, large enough to carry both the ark and a wooden chest. In the wooden chest they placed a guilt offering to appease Israel's God: five gold rats and five gold models of the deadly tumors, one of each for the five Philistine rulers.

To this cart bearing the ark and the conciliatory offering to Yahweh, they hitched a yoke of animals that would be *least* likely to bring the cart and its cargo back to Israelite territory: a pair of cows that had never been yoked before and that had just birthed their young. Knowing the unlikelihood of these animals pulling together in their unfamiliar yoking, and knowing also that milk cows would go straight for their newborn calves if given a chance, the Philistines penned up their calves in a place *opposite* from the territory

250

of the Israelites. Then they released the cows hitched to the cart and watched to see what they would do.

"Then," says Scripture, "the cows went straight up toward Beth Shemesh [in Israel], keeping on the road and lowing all the way; they did not turn to the right or to the left. The rulers of the Philistines followed them as far as the border of Beth Shemesh" (1 Sam. 6:12). The plague had not been coincidental.

COMPELLED TO OBEY

How ironic that those milk cows were more obedient to Yahweh than His chosen people had been. "Obey God's law without turning aside to the right or to the left," Joshua had said, but God's people had forgotten his words and had wandered far from the path of obedience. In contrast, the two milk cows, lowing all the way in abject grief for their left-behind calves, could not help but submit to Yahweh's yoking, turning neither to the right nor to the left, but going straight along the road to Israel.

What does this story teach us? For one thing, we see again the power God possesses for accomplishing His purposes when His yoking prevails. The two milk cows acted contrary to their very nature—both in their pulling together as yoked draft animals (which they weren't) and in their abandonment of their bawling, hungry calves (which violated their every instinct). Through this revelation of His mighty power, not only did Yahweh affirm His greatness to the Philistines, but He also blessed His covenant children by returning to them the ark signifying His presence among them.

The people of Beth Shemesh were harvesting wheat when the cart bearing the sacred ark came to a stop near a large rock, and they were overjoyed. They stopped gathering the fruit of their labors and celebrated this fruit of God's labor on their behalf, chopping up the cart to build a fire on which to sacrifice the two milk cows in gratitude for Yahweh's return to His people. Worship was the only appropriate response, as it always is when we stand in His presence.

But we must not miss another instructive aspect of this story. The two cows keeping on the road in submission to Yahweh's yoke obeyed God, "lowing all the way." Lowing is the mooing sound cows make when they need to be milked, and the inclusion of this auditory detail in the biblical narrative indicates the suffering these animals endured to do what God was compelling them to do. Sometimes our own obedience to God's will also militates against our instincts to avoid pain or to remain in control of our lives. But when we embrace suffering in order to do what He calls us to do, we reveal our hearts of passionate love and worship toward Him.

For it is this chosen suffering that expresses the life of Jesus in us. We long to have others see Him in us, and so we enter with Him into the sor-

251

row in our world—weeping at death, showing compassion to the sick and hungry, touching the untouchable, unbinding the death-bound, being persecuted unjustly without complaint, and walking daily the way of the cross. For suffering is the fruit of Christ's Spirit in us, brought forth from our yielding to His yoke of love. The apostle Peter wrote, "If you suffer for doing good and you endure it, this is commendable before God. To this you were called, because Christ suffered for you, leaving you an example, that you should follow in his steps" (1 Peter 2:20–21).

When we obey God with the single-mindedness of the Philistine milk cows, moving in spite of pain to respond to His call, we bring glory to Him and good to His Kingdom. In all our dealings with God, even in our conflicts with Him, He reduces us to a fervency of desire for Himself and His will. This is the mystery of being compelled by the gospel to abandon ourselves to the One we cannot help but love and obey.

DARKNESS AND REST

Yet how often we, like the Israelites in their war against the Philistines, simply use God for our own purposes instead of serving Him with an abandon of love. We live our lives far removed from Him, employing our own strategies for successful living and forgetting He wants our hearts. Too late we recognize that our broken oneness with Him has scattered our rest, and we have lost His presence, for the enemy of our souls thinks he can carry Him off to a distant land. Having taken our eyes off the One we cannot yet see, the storms around that we *can* see have caused fear to intrude into our hearts, threatening to undo us. Obedience then seems too hard or too painful, and Satan is able to convince us there is an easier way to live life. It is how he tempted Christ and it is how, in a myriad of disguises, he tempts us today.

For it is true that there are easier ways to live. The rest Jesus gives is not without struggle. What He offers is not the absence of problems but rest in the midst of those problems. "Sometimes God calms the storm," someone once said, "and sometimes He lets the storm rage and calms His child." That is what Christ does for us, being present with us in all that we must face. "Fear not," Yahweh said to His people, "for I have redeemed you; I have summoned you by name; you are mine. When you pass through the waters, I will be with you; and when you pass through the rivers, they will not sweep over you" (Isa. 43:1–2). Centuries later, Jesus' request to His Father on behalf of His disciples was this: "My prayer is not that you take them out of the world but that you protect them from the evil one" (John 17:15).

For the enemy remains very active in our world and in our hearts, waging continual, unseen warfare against all oneness—every joining of human to Yahweh or husband to wife or parent to child or neighbor to neighbor.

252

Satan abhors connectedness and seeks always to alienate, divide, and isolate, whereas God is One and moves always to reconcile, unite, and bring together. Satan hates families; God Himself is a "family," and we are His family too. Is it any wonder that our warfare against the ancient serpent must also be continual?

Yet God can use even the darkness of evil—and our own fear of that darkness—to make His light shine ever more brightly in our world. It is in darkness that we most need light, and in the face of great evil we are most in need of a goodness greater than ourselves. As the darkness of uncertainty and chaos threatens to overwhelm us, we are driven to need God as never before.

When Bill was working as a railroad engineer, he used to run a mile-long freight train at sixty miles an hour along a stretch of uninhabited north Florida timberland that was pitch-black except for the engine's headlight illuminating the ribbon of rail ahead. And when it was foggy and visibility was almost zero, Bill said, he experienced what it was like to live by faith—having to trust that the wayside signals alongside the tracks were reliable and that there was nothing dangerous on the shrouded track ahead.

When our lives seem as uncertain as that stretch of foggy forest, when even the light of our best resources and common sense cannot pierce the blackness of uncertainty or evil—*that* is when we will either look to God in faith, trusting Him in the darkness, or we will put our lives in emergency stop and refuse to go on until the fog lifts. If we will turn to God in our darkness and watch for His heart-signals along our path, He will give us glimpses of Himself that will encourage us to keep on going.

Do we hunger for God enough to engage in the struggle and enter the risk of uncertainty in order to see His face? If our deepest desire is for Him, nothing will matter more to us than connecting with Him and doing what He commands, whatever the cost. If, on the other hand, our demand for personal happiness or relational safety or financial security or anything or anyone else takes priority over a passionate desire for doing what He tells us to do, we will live our lives self-protectively and miss the joy of abandoning ourselves to His promised rest.

ABANDONED TO OBEDIENCE

The consuming desire to live life obedient to God despite any risk is the legacy left us by Peter, the impetuous fisherman who became an impassioned apostle of the risen Christ. "Do not leave Jerusalem," Jesus had said, "but wait for the gift my Father promised" (Acts 1:4). And so they had stayed and they had waited, receiving at last the baptism of the Holy Spirit on Pentecost, the Feast of First Fruits. It was Peter who preached that day to the Jewish pilgrims from around the world, three thousand of whom repented of their sin and were baptized in Jesus' name.

253

It was also Peter who shortly afterwards healed in Jesus' name a crippled beggar at the temple gate, Peter who announced to the gathering crowd that their repentance would lead to "times of refreshing . . . from the Lord" (3:19), and Peter who, with the apostle John, was thrown into jail for preaching the resurrection of Jesus. (These and the following stories about Peter are told in Acts 2–5.) How did this man who had trembled in Caiaphas's courtyard, denying he even knew Jesus, become willing to go to prison for Jesus' sake and astonish the Jewish leaders "when they saw [his] courage"?

Surely Peter's newfound boldness was grounded in Jesus' private meeting with him after His resurrection to restore their personal relationship. Breakfast on the beach with Jesus and the other disciples had also strengthened Peter's courage, for the apostle's place of leadership in the church had been once again publicly reestablished. But it was Peter's willingness to wait for the Holy Spirit that united him most intimately with the Lord he loved. After Pentecost Jesus was not just *with* him but *in* him, and he was a changed man.

"If anyone loves me," Jesus had said, "he will obey my teaching. My Father will love him, and we will come to him and make our home with him" (John 14:23). God Himself had moved into Peter's heart, setting up housekeeping there and setting a new agenda for Peter's life. Jesus' love had utterly won him over, and obeying his Master's voice became the ruling passion of his life. That is why, when the Sanhedrin "commanded [Peter and John] not to speak or teach at all in the name of Jesus," they replied, "Judge for yourselves whether it is right in God's sight to obey you rather than God. For we cannot help speaking about what we have seen and heard" (Acts 4:18–20). Regardless of threats, they *had* to obey Jesus' command to give witness to His salvation. Like the Philistine milk cows, they knew themselves compelled to obey.

Does this mean Peter never again wavered in his faith, never felt afraid, always obeyed perfectly from Pentecost on? Of course not. He was still just a man, subject to fear and failure as all redeemed men and women are. He, no less than we, needed to pray, "Now, Lord, consider [the enemy's] threats and enable your servants to speak your word with great boldness," so that he would not give way to fear. And though we may not experience, as did Peter and the others, that "after they prayed, the place where they were meeting was shaken," we can, like them, have it said of us, "And they were all filled with the Holy Spirit and spoke the word of God boldly," in answer to their prayer. Boldness to enter our fear and to obey God despite the threat of rejection or harm or even death—this boldness comes never from our nature but only from the nature of Jesus Himself who indwells us through the Holy Spirit.

And Peter would continue needing the Spirit's enabling, for soon he and the other apostles would be arrested again and flogged for preaching in Jesus' name, experiencing the physical pain he had fled in Gethsemane and in Caiaphas's courtyard. Only this time, Scripture says, "The apostles left the Sanhedrin, rejoicing because they had been counted worthy of suffering disgrace for the Name" (5:41). What passion the Spirit had stirred up in them to obey God in the face of suffering—even to rejoice in that very suffering!

How seldom our own passion for obedience brings us that kind of joy, though it is not beyond the reach of any believer. For Peter was no spiritual superman. He was simply a man overtaken and taken over by the Holy Spirit. "When [the Jewish leaders] saw the courage of Peter and John and realized that they were unschooled, ordinary men," Scripture tells us, "they were astonished and they took note that these men had been with Jesus" (4:13). What set Peter and John apart was not their education nor any extraordinary talent or personal charisma. What gave them courage and marked them as God's men was that they had been long with their Lord, living and listening and failing and being forgiven, and that they now had that same Lord living within them. And the Holy Spirit who emboldened them will do the same in us if we will spend time in His presence and let Him have His way with us. Obeying God without reserve is the natural expression of Jesus' life in us, for He is ever passionate to obey His Father.

Practicing Rest

How is it possible for us to live this way in our world, in our frail bodies, in our often stubborn humanness? How can we experience the kind of compelling responsiveness the Philistine milk cows experienced in obeying God's "call" on their lives, lowing all the way? What would it take for us to move even into suffering, pulled irresistibly by the gospel more and more often, and more and more willingly? How can we be more like Peter?

Surely it cannot originate in us, compromised as we are by the enemy's strongholds in our hearts. Our passion for God must come from God Himself, who is passionate for intimacy, both within the Trinity and with us. Father, Son, and Holy Spirit give and receive love and joy with utter unreservedness in their holy Oneness, and God longs to capture ever larger portions of our hearts as well. Without His Spirit's coming to knit our hearts to Him, not only would we not know what He wants us to do, but we would not have courage or power to do it.

We must listen for the Spirit's voice to our hearts and then do what He says—whether to move or to wait, to speak or to keep silence, and if to move or speak, where to go and what to say. We need not struggle to produce spiritual fruit, any more than a tree strains to bear an ample crop. All a tree has to do is stay in its place, connected to its source of nutrients and water, just as we must maintain communion with the Spirit, who is the

255

source of His own fruit in us. Our struggle is to stay rooted in God's love, quieting our souls to a place of stillness so we can hear His words of welcome and instruction. Like weaned children, we must learn to just *be* with Him, without demanding anything from Him or trying to perform well in order to win His approval. Spiritual fruitfulness requires work, but it is the work of making time to enjoy connectedness with our Lord, not the work of achieving some great accomplishment on His behalf.

And this is often a difficult struggle indeed—to stay quiet in His presence long enough to nurture our relationship with Him, to look into His eyes, and to listen for His voice. Too often we move and speak without waiting, without yielding our actions and words to the scrutiny and affirmation of the Spirit's whispered word to us. So much in our hearts and in our lives sabotages our quietness before the One who loves us. Our busyness, our fear, our perfectionism, our demandingness, our ambition, our workaholism, our besetting sins, our woundedness—our very humanness—are weapons in the enemy's arsenal to keep us from our Lover's embrace. We have become slaves to our schedules and to our terror, afraid that if we slow down He really might show up, and what would we do then? How could we bear to look into the eyes of love? What sorrow would we find there at our having run from Him for so long? What sorrow would we have to then face in our own hearts at recognizing that, compared to this love, we have lived long without having been loved well by others? Receiving His love would salt our thirst for even more of His refreshing grace, and we dread feeling thirstier than we already are.

More than that, what would have to change—in us and in our lifestyle—if we were to allow ourselves to rest in the quiet and rapture of our Savior's love? What loss of control over our own lives would occur if we were wholly His in response to His love? We would have to mourn our sin in order to grow in grace. We would have to deeply grieve our losses if our compassion is to blossom and bless others. The fruit of the Spirit springs forth from His life in us as we suffer to be like Jesus—quiet in His Father's presence and then present to the world's great sorrow.

The practice of quieting our hearts before God takes time to develop. At first the rest we find in God is sporadic, infrequent yet enticing, almost unnerving, in a glad sort of way. And immediately we find ourselves trying to hold it, to contain it, and (when it passes) to reconstruct it. But the very attempts at holding or containing or reconstructing are contrary to rest, for rest must be received and entered, not created. We cannot make it happen.

The work of God in us is so mysterious, so enigmatic, so far outside the pale of our control. The Holy Spirit changes us imperceptibly, whether we are awake or asleep, and as we are living our ordinary lives, we suddenly realize He has worked in us and we are able to obey God with a spirit we know did not and could not have initiated within our own will.

256

Moreover, our obedience then feels not so much like duty as like desire, less like obligation and more like passion. Obedience to the law of love is not even really a conscious exercise of our will but more of a welling up of spontaneous response—the response Christ Himself would have had—that seems impossible to *not* do. Like Peter and John we declare without apology, "We must obey God rather than men!" (5:29). We are able to forgive not grudgingly but gladly and we are surprised at the grace we have available to offer others. Offenses against us, which earlier had enraged or stung or at least annoyed us, now feel less dangerous, less devastating, less *offensive*. It is not that we have become jaded by disappointment, or even that we have become able to wait for the other person's eventual repentance; it is that our own heart response to God has caused our love for others to flourish, and we are eager to behave kindly and lovingly whether the other person repents or not.

Does this mean we allow others to harm us with impunity? Perhaps yes, perhaps no. It depends on whether it is more loving to deal with the other person regarding the sin against us or to simply forgive a fellow sinner. How can we determine when to confront a spouse and when to swallow the offense out of love? And what if God's grace is not to be found at all in one's partner because of hardness of heart? Suppose our confrontation of the other's sin has been continually ignored or rebuffed—what does it mean to love such a one?

No one knows but God Himself, and that is why our intimacy with Him is so critical to our obeying Him. He offers no set of steps to govern our relationships, only the blanket command, "Be perfect, therefore, as your heavenly Father is perfect" (Matt. 5:48). What help is *that* in deciding what to do or say in any given situation?

Quiet to Listen

Perhaps one of the most important sentences given to me in my own process of learning to love my husband occurred in the early months of my coming out of denial regarding Bill's alcoholism. I was meeting weekly with other family members of substance abusers, and together we were seeking God's will for our individual situations. I remember asking the group leader one night, "How can I know what is the right thing to do about Bill's drinking? I see a lot of women taking steps that really don't seem right for me to do but I don't want to be stubborn or disobedient toward God in this."

His answer—which was really a question—frustrated me before it comforted me. "Who is living inside you?" he asked. At first I was angry, because reminding me of the Holy Spirit's presence in me did not provide me with the step-by-step plan I was hoping could guide me and put an end to my confusion and fear. Later, however, I was able to find rest in knowing that, because the Spirit was living in me, He would guide me if only I would listen to Him.

And that, at last, leaves us with the question we all must answer: Are we connected to God in such a way that His Spirit not only has more and more room to work in changing our hearts, but that He is speaking to us in ways we can understand so that we can obey Him? In other words, is God at home in our hearts, and are we prepared to do what He says? Unless we can answer positively regarding our willingness to obey, why should He tell us what to do? And if we are not on speaking terms with Him, how can we hear what He wants us to do? The Spirit always pushes us beyond our sin and our fear to see our deepest heart. Will we go wherever God leads us, whatever the cost?

This kind of living is impossible for me if I do not have a great capacity for humility, repentance, and confession. To the degree I must be right or flawless, I will be unable to hear the Holy Spirit's words to my heart. If I am not so eager for His voice that I will accept words of rebuke from Him as openheartedly as words of affirmation, I will never be at rest with Him. I must allow Him perfect freedom to say whatever He wishes to say to me in any given moment, letting Him decide what I need most—whether to receive His delight or to hear His words of discipline. I must approach Him without being demanding, lest I insist that my own perception of what I need is more accurate than His. I must approach Him also with honesty about my heart, whether there is within me adoration, anger, disinterest, worship, confusion—whatever—lest I hinder the oneness of reciprocal love I so desire with Him.

This same availability and freedom I must offer to others, especially to Bill—the willingness to spend time being nourished by his love, and the freedom to speak my own heart honestly and to listen to his heart humbly enough to hear and reciprocate. If I come demanding a certain attitude or behavior, I refuse him the choice of being who and where he is at that moment. If my fear of a wrong or hurtful response from him keeps me from risking his disapproval, our relationship will never deepen to anything more than a surface and ultimately dissatisfying connection. Genuine intimacy requires mutual freedom to be present to our hearts in the other's presence, both partners open to each other and to God, each one sorrowing if the other is absent (physically, emotionally, or spiritually) but willing to wait for reunion (in time or eternity).

Sometimes the wait is long, and often dreams must die and be released, with only God's presence to compensate the loneliness. There will be times when His presence does not feel like enough, and we will need friends who will sustain us then and pray with us and for us through the dark hours. And even if we occasionally find ourselves alone in the pit of excrement like Jeremiah, cursing the day we were born (so great is our sense of abandonment by God and others), then may our memory of intimacy with God be such that we, like Jeremiah, remind ourselves in the midst of our despair, "[Even] if I say, 'I will not mention [God] or speak any more in his name,' his word is in my heart like a fire, a fire shut up in my bones. I am weary of holding it in; indeed, I cannot" (see Jer. 20:7–18).

How many of us can say that God's words make us feel like we have a fire in our bones, so much a part of who we are that we cannot hold it in— we *must* do what He has said, whatever the cost? And if we do have that kind of relationship with God, would we call this "entering His rest"?

For that is exactly what His rest is like. Jesus said, "Take my yoke upon you and learn from me, for I am gentle and humble in heart, and you will find rest for your souls" (Matt. 11:29). Jesus' rest in His Father would lead Him to "loud cries and tears" in Gethsemane (Heb. 5:7), and to being forsaken by His Father on Calvary before entering the eternal rest of His Father's embrace (see Matt. 27:46). If we enter Jesus' rest and learn from Him, our being yoked to Him may require that we follow Him into places we do not want to go, so that we can live, like Him, with gentleness and humility, especially toward husband or wife. It's not just that He never promised us a rose garden. It is that He promised us *nothing* except His presence with us in this life ("Never will I leave you; never will I forsake you"— Heb. 13:5), and His final victory over death ("In this world you will have trouble. But take heart! I have overcome the world"—John 16:33). Anything else He gives us in this life is a bonus.

Struggling to Trust

Meanwhile, we must do what the writer of Hebrews bids us do—to "make every effort to enter [God's] rest" (Heb. 4:11)—not perfecting our perfectionism but continually giving our lives back into His hands. All too often our focus in living the Christian life is on the externals—the oughts and ought nots, the do's and don'ts, the burden of never failing God. These are the kinds of things that have become the determined hallmarks of today's Christian community. Is it any wonder a multitude of discouraged and fed-up people are abandoning our churches and shunning our friendships? Who can measure up to that kind of standard? Who can achieve that level of spiritual "success"? Who needs that kind of pressure?

Why are we not, as yokefellows of Jesus, proclaiming instead the good news of His invitation, "Come to me, all you who are weary and burdened, and I will give you rest" (Matt. 11:28)? Why do we preach effort instead of grace? Why do we demand of ourselves and of others the perfection only Christ can accomplish—His perfect obedience to His Father—before we can be satisfied? Why do we lay on ourselves and on others the burden the Pharisees of Jesus' day laid on themselves and others? Those Pharisees refused grace because they were so good at religion. We tend to believe they were merely reprimanded by Jesus as loyal but somewhat misguided believers. But Jesus' sorrow is evident in His words, "O Jerusalem, Jerusalem, you who kill the prophets and stone those sent to you, how often I have longed to gather your children together, as a hen gathers her chicks under her wings, but you were not willing. Look, your house is left to you desolate" (23:37–38). Having refused the King, the Pharisees would not enter God's Kingdom unless they repented. What was at stake was the destiny of their souls. "Desolate" is a terrible thing to be.

We too want to believe our good deeds and respectable religion count for something to make us accepted by and acceptable to God. We have learned to follow the rules, but our "goodness" is not what brings us into relationship with the God who set things up according to His own standard of perfection. Jesus knew that good religion (i.e., doggedly following the rules) could never draw us close to His Father. In fact the greater our expertise at religion, the less we will experience of God's presence. Our competence will make us brash, vain, even foolhardy in our approach to the Holy One.

Only Christ's atoning death can bring us to know the joy of being cleansed and at rest with God's guidance in our lives.

The yoke Jesus invites us to wear is easy—it fits comfortably and does not chafe—because it is a yoke of grace, of boundless love, of a compassionate knowledge regarding our very finite limitations. "As a father has compassion on his children, so the LORD has compassion on those who fear him; for he knows how we are formed, he remembers that we are dust" (Ps. 103:13–14).

Our heavenly Father knows our heart's desire to please Him is easily undermined by the enemy's schemes to lure us away from obedience. He knows how easily we yield to worry instead of trusting Him. Worry is what moves our focus from God to our circumstances, from Yahweh to the giants in the land, from Jesus to the waves beneath our feet. "Is anything too hard for Me?" God asks, and our heads say no but our hearts cry out maybe! Fear raises its ugly head to block our view of God, and we cannot imagine how He can bring good out of the particular evil confronting our lives, because our imagination is too small, as is our faith, as is our perception of God Himself.

A. W. Tozer writes:

> To know that love is of God, and to enter into the secret place leaning upon the arm of the Beloved—this and only this can cast out fear. Let a man become convinced that nothing can harm him and instantly for him all fear goes out of the universe. The nervous reflex, the natural revulsion to physical pain may be felt sometimes, but the deep torment of fear is gone forever. God is love and God is sovereign. His love disposes Him to desire our ever-

lasting welfare, and His sovereignty enables Him to secure it. Nothing can hurt a good man.[1]

In this confidence we all have much growing to do.

For we must always remind ourselves that the enemy of our souls has been dethroned. He may go on harassing us with his temptations and accusations, but Satan is a defeated foe and has no power over us except as we yield it to him. He may terrorize but he cannot keep us from Christ's rest unless we choose not to enter it. Christ's life in us makes us able to obey Him every time we submit ourselves to Him in the moment at hand, and this reality can bring us into rest and can also sustain us in our resting.

How then can we overcome the terror that occasionally breaks in to discomfit us? The answer is that we cannot overcome terror but only enter it. We will not find rest by avoiding our fear nor even by moving past our fear. We must simply enter it time and again, for it is in the midst of our fear that Jesus comes to us with His "Be not afraid." We must accept rather than try to overcome our terror. It is, after all, a terror of grace, a terror of love.

For both grace and love put us out of control, out of the driver's seat and into the back of the limousine with Jesus wearing the servant cap of chauffeur. Can we trust Him, knowing He'll sometimes take us places we don't know about and may not even want to go?

Several years ago the research for a book I was writing required that I fly from Colorado to Miami, spend a too-short time in the airport with my husband, Bill, and then take off again the same evening, this time for Chicago. It was the middle of December, and I arrived in the cold of a Midwest snowstorm long after dark.

The woman I was to interview had advised me to hire a limousine for the ride from the airport to her home, where I was to spend the night. It was snowing as I waited for the limo to come, and when it appeared, I climbed gratefully into its delicious warmth and collapsed against the leather of its spacious backseat.

The chauffeur had the address, and I leaned back to enjoy watching the snow fall. Trusting him to navigate the whitening streets, I began to feel the tension flow from my exhausted body. Even when he had to call the dispatcher because he wasn't quite sure where he was, I remained unconcerned. It was his job to get me to my destination, and I was off duty. What a rare and precious gift, this rest, this reprieve. I was almost sorry to reach my friend's house. I could have spent the night in that limousine.

Resting is always a trust issue, and it is often—perhaps always—most appealing when we are weary and heavy laden. Sometimes only our realization that we are unable to control our lives gives incentive to our going off duty with God. I don't normally rest when I am out of control, of course. I struggle to *avoid* helplessness, not *enter* it. But therein lies my restlessness, for only when I accept my helplessness will I find the rest that grace alone can provide. I had to trust the limo driver because I knew nothing of the streets in that Chicago suburb. But I was also glad to trust him because I was bone weary and well beyond my own resources for doing anything but settling farther down in the blessed comfort of that luxurious conveyance. I was out of control and I rested and I realized how much I wanted to rest more and more in my heavenly Father's care.

ENTERING FEAR, FINDING REST

For when we are surrounded by the chaos of living in a fallen world and can move beyond our fear of being out of control and find our rest in God, we receive rich tastes of being bound to Him with a betrothal that is binding and cannot be broken. Someday we will see His face, but now we have work to do in preparation for our wedding day, when He will take us to His Father's Home at last. We must invite guests to be with us there; we must fill our processional torches with oil to celebrate His coming; we must create those things that will adorn our eternal Home; we must prepare our hearts to receive Christ's love. And as we wait to see His face, we can celebrate every coming of His Spirit to our spirits as a betrothal token of His coming in glory. Having received His life and resting now in His sufficiency, we can show forth who He is to a broken and dying world.

And we can keep practicing rest, keep quieting ourselves, keep doing whatever God tells us to do. There is no list of "results" to look for, but perhaps a picture of what is going on for Bill and me in the past few years will be helpful. We are ordinary people whose hearts have been broken by sin—our own and others'—and who in our sorrow have been drawn close to the heart of God. Yet we struggle (sometimes successfully, sometimes not) to remain close to Him and to rest in His sufficiency. And in spite of our weakness, God is producing fruit through our life with Him and through our life together.

That is why, as I pursue God's call on my life to communicate what He is teaching me from His Word and from our marriage, Bill makes a way for me to write and to speak around the country. Especially in his sobriety he has been present to me and has lived as kind ambassador of Christ's love toward me—not just in taking over the burden of household duties so I can birth the books the Spirit urges me to write but also in continually affirming my value and leading me into God's Word and worship. Moreover, the comfort of his prayers for me is a sustaining force in my life, especially whenever I abandon myself to God in my teaching. Because this good man takes time to quiet his own heart before God, seeking the Holy Spirit's direction for his life one day at a time, he knows how and when to sacrifice his own agenda to God's better plan for him. Thus are we learning how to be fruitful together for the extending of Christ's Kingdom in our own little corner of the earth.

And when I watch the husband I love, I see more and more evidence of God's work in him. Bill invites me to rest by doing things for me that comfort my heart and open the door for me to pursue God's call. He repents when he sins, not just in action or word, but within his heart and mind. I observe his integrity and I marvel at the risks he is willing to take in moving openly toward others because of the Holy Spirit's compelling. My relationship with him brings me peace, for he is more and more a man at peace within himself. This regenerated and repentant man is alive to God, living increasingly out of the power of the Holy Spirit in him. Am I at rest in Bill Groom? I am at rest in the presence of Jesus Christ in Bill Groom. The distinction, I have discovered, is profound.

When can a wife best rest in her husband? When she sees and experiences both his Christ-like movement into sacrificial love, and his repentance when he fails to love her well. When does a husband rest in his wife? When he sees and experiences both her Christ-like submission regarding his leadership, and her repentance when she fails to respect him well. This rest is not in each other but in the grace of God they experience in one another and within themselves.

The Joy of Obedience

Entering Christ's rest is worth whatever it might cost in obedience and repentance. For we find that, no matter what we may have had to sacrifice to give His Spirit free rein in us, His presence (which now becomes our very life, without which we cannot go on) eclipses any benefits we may have enjoyed from our striving or self-centeredness. What matters now is not our ease but our intimacy with Him, not our goodness but our redemption, not even our usefulness to the kingdom, but our oneness with the One who is love.

We no longer, like Peter, beg God to leave us because He is so holy; we plead with Him to stay because, like Moses, we cannot go on without Him. God will produce the Spirit's fruit in us without our striving, for if we will listen for His voice and obey what He says, His leading will come in ways we could never have imagined or accomplished. Central to Christ's daily, hourly "coming" into our world is the willingness of the saints to be so joined with Him in love and mind that what they do is what He Himself would do if He were incarnate among us again today.

Not long ago Bill and I had the opportunity to live out what we perceived to be God's call on us in a way we never expected. We received a call one night from a Virginia physician who had visited Haiti on a missions trip and had made arrangements for Yanick Leo, a young Haitian mother, to come to Miami for surgery to correct a crippling tumor in her back. This doctor had been unable to confirm with his Miami contact that someone would meet Yanick at the airport and he asked if we would be willing to be backup so she would not arrive in a strange city completely alone. We agreed; it seemed a small enough favor. We would go to the airport and make certain she got in the cab to be taken to the Ronald McDonald House near Jackson Memorial Hospital.

But if we had had eyes to see, we would have seen God smiling in that knowing way of His. For we had no idea as we stood in Miami International Airport the next night, watching for a young black woman to come through customs in a wheelchair, that we would fall in love with her, that Yanick would become like a daughter to us, that we would spend the next six months of our lives visiting her almost every day, receiving with her the news that her spinal tumor was cancerous, overseeing her nursing care in the hospital, taking her to physical therapy and then radiation therapy, making meals for her in the wonderful cancer facility near the hospital, bringing her to the zoo and to our home on the weekends, buying her phone cards and stuffed dolls and plane tickets and clothes and food, praying daily that God would miraculously heal her, and finally sending her back home to her husband and two-year-old little boy. All this because we had heard God telling us to be backup for a task someone else was supposed to do.

How inscrutable are God's ways and how wondrous His provision! It had not been easy for Bill and me to watch our precious "daughter" suffer, but unlike Mama's living and dying with us, we faced this loved one's cancer together. Somehow entering the grief of having a daughter with a terminal illness brought us the intimacy in sorrow we had missed in facing Mama's cancer. God is indeed the God of second chances.

But Bill and I also came to see that this experience was not intended to bless only Yanick. The path of suffering is also the path of joy, and we tasted the joy of being poured out for her, the Holy Spirit in us joining with the Holy Spirit in her as we walked a difficult path side by side. Together we knew sorrow and laughter, pain and achievement, and together we gave praise to our marvelous God for His unceasing presence with us. Besides, not only have Bill and I met many wonderful Haitian Christians here in Miami whom we otherwise may never have known, but we also have a beautiful daughter in Haiti, along with a son-in-law and a grandson we hope to meet someday. God is always up to something far bigger than we can imagine.

THE LARGER STORY

And we must never forget the greater story of God's purposes in His universe. The prophet Isaiah, prophesying about the Messiah Yahweh would one day send to redeem Abraham's descendants, records these amazing words from God to the Servant of the Lord (i.e., to Christ): "*It is too small a thing* for you to be my servant to restore the tribes of Jacob and bring back those of Israel I have kept. I will also make you a light for the Gentiles, that you may bring my salvation to the ends of the earth" (Isa. 49:6, emphasis added). That is to say, Messiah's salvation would not be limited to the Jewish nation, for God's story would be much larger than that. Centuries before Jesus was born, Yahweh announced He intended to paint His glorious plan in cosmic strokes, sketching His tales of the kingdom on a canvas far bigger than the narrow nationalism of the ancient Israelites. God's intention from eternity was to spread His love abroad to all the earth. Had He not said to Abraham, "All peoples on earth will be blessed through you" (Gen. 12:3)? Jesus Himself informed Nicodemus that "God so loved *the world* that he gave his one and only Son, that whoever believes in him shall not perish but have eternal life" (John 3:16, emphasis added).

It is said that people flourish when they have something bigger than themselves to live for and to be willing to die for. What inconceivable condescension and kindness that our awesome God invites each of us to be a part of a story so epic we cannot imagine it. Our lives can contribute to the drama of His wonderful and intricately woven kingdom saga—not because we are famous but because we are faithful, not because we are brilliant but because we are His, not because we are good but because we are precious to Him. The sweep of that kingdom plan is breathtaking in its scope, stunning in its beauty, brilliant in its intricacy, overwhelming in its sheer magnitude. How can we apprehend even a fraction of its glory, how fathom the depths of His wisdom and love in conceiving and bringing it to fruition? It is a story so large, so magnificent, so wonderful, so satisfying we will spend eternity learning it, and like children we will always be begging, "Tell it again! Tell it again!"

And also like children we will never tire of hearing our own part in it. For our story will surely be found in God's larger story. The everlasting Book of God will leave out no time period, no character, no detail of any life touched by the transforming power of His love. He has counted every hair, caught every tear, read every heart, and He has copied down the name of every believer from Eden to Apocalypse in His grace-written Book of Life. If we will receive Jesus' yoke and pursue with passion the adventure of becoming one with Him, even our most inconsequential deeds and most mundane days will have the fragrance of eternity about them, and in His perfect coming kingdom God's people beyond number will enjoy the aroma, for it will glorify the One we have all come to love with His own passionate trinitarian desire.

When we are willing to enter our terror (of death, of failure, of aloneness, of intimacy), trusting God to keep our souls from being destroyed, we

265

will find the rest Christ offers. It will not keep us from disappointment or danger or even death, for He Himself tasted all those things as He rested in His Father's will. But yoked to Him in love and obedience, we can live out our own individual role, large or small, on whatever stage He chooses for us, participating with Him in creating our life's script by listening to His quiet voice within.

Meanwhile, we wait impatiently as Christ's Bride-elect. In joy and hope we long for our promised reunion with Him, when we will see Him face-to-face and be like Him, our hearts and countenances radiant with the knowledge of being loved and of being at last in our Lover's presence. Though we sometimes suffer now in being yoked to Him in identity and purpose, in that day we will know not merely tastes of joy unspeakable but a full wedding feast of everlasting delight.

For Christ knows by experience that His suffering was and is the very doorway to freedom and joy. Scripture tells us that "for the joy set before him [Christ] endured the cross, scorning its shame" (Heb. 12:2). What was that joy? It was the joyous anticipation of having His Bride in His Home at last, of consummating His love for her. We, the church, had nothing to recommend us—no beauty, no moral uprightness, no pedigree of any kind, for it was "while we were still sinners, Christ died for us" (Rom. 5:8). Yet the "joy set before him" was Christ's joy of wedding Himself to us. Because of the cross, He gets the Bride. Is not this grace most amazing?

How hard it is to believe He loves us that much, desires us that passionately, delights in us that joyfully. Yet it is true, for He has said it is true. No suffering was too much to keep Him from securing through His death the rapture of seeing our faces and showing us His eyes dancing with pleasure.

Perhaps that is why those in whom His Spirit dwells can "rejoice and be glad" even when they are persecuted because of Him (Matt. 5:12). Maybe that is the reason Peter and the other apostles after their flogging "left the Sanhedrin, rejoicing because they had been counted worthy of suffering disgrace for the Name" of Jesus (Acts 5:41). It may account for the words of the apostle Paul: "I want to know Christ and the power of his resurrection and the fellowship of sharing in his sufferings" (Phil. 3:10).

And even if identity with Jesus means we too will suffer loss, even if sorrow is intrinsic to joy, even if love is a death sentence, our passionate desire for Him can make us declare with Paul, "I consider that our present sufferings are not worth comparing with the glory that will be revealed in us" (Rom. 8:18). For our longing to see Jesus and to be like Him will one day be fulfilled, and our resurrected faces will shine with the glory the Israelites saw on Moses' face when he descended Mount Sinai, even that same glory the three disciples saw when Moses and Elijah joined Jesus on the Mount of Transfiguration.

266

Passion from Rest

But how do we live in the now and the not yet, how enter the rest of passionate abandon to Christ even today, how respond to the inner compelling to do a particular thing that God shows us to do? It is by entering His presence again and again, standing on the holy ground of His coming to us and finding it is all we need.

Rest is about passion, the passion of yielding our hearts to Him and listening ever more closely for His voice to our hearts. It takes time to listen with our hearts, and it takes commitment to set apart the time to listen. Often I find myself too busy, and the truth is, that is what I am—*too* busy. For if I am not hearing God, it is because I have chosen not to listen. He desires to have my attention. And if sometimes I listen long and still do not hear Him, it may be because He wants me to trust Him in the silence.

For even in the silence I can hear Him, remembering the sound of His earlier speaking—though it is not always the words I remember but the fact of His having spoken to me. This is what will encourage my heart when God is trusting me with His silence. I cannot begin to understand the purposes of God in His silence to me or anyone else. I just know that when He speaks I am overjoyed, and when He does not speak, I am consumed with desire for His voice.

If God were to appear before us in all His glory right now, we would have no choice—we would fall on our faces. Worship would be our only option. Are we willing to be smitten and then lifted up and sent out? Will we be like the sinful woman who used up her precious ointment on the feet of Jesus, "wasting" it without regret? Will we be broken bread and spilled out wine in our fervor and love for Him? Will we keep our hair respectably tied up, or will we let it down in passionate worship and complete adoration? What are we withholding from God? More to the point, how much of ourselves are we willing to give over to Him? What precious part of our hearts will we pour out for Him in an abject abandon of love?

The mystery bush Moses saw as an eighty-year-old nomadic shepherd was burned but not consumed on the ground sanctified by God's presence. God burns us too when we stand in His presence, but our deepest essence is never consumed. In fact, the longer we stand on holy ground, the more we become who we most truly are. He overtakes us anew every time with His relentless love, and we know ourselves passionate to be one with Him in an ever deeper way, barely able to wait to see our Bridegroom face-to-face.

"Show us Your glory!" we implore. "Here I am. Send me!" we cry out. "How long, O Lord, before You come?" we lament with tears. It is a most sacred and exquisite longing, this passion of ours to be with Him and to be like Him at last. Any wait seems too long, any cloud between us too painful.

Perhaps that is why there are no tents on the Mount of Transfiguration. The Father knows that until He sends His Son again in glorious splendor, we will have to leave the mountaintop glory of each of His comings, taking only His presence with us into the valley, where there are those whose demons cannot be cast out without prayer and fasting. (See Mark 9:2–29 for this story.)

For as much as Christ Himself longs for us to be eternally in His presence, He also has other sheep to be drawn into His fold, other ewes to gently lead, other wayward lambs whose legs need to be broken so He can carry them on His shoulder until they love Him too much to stray anymore. "Feed my sheep," He told the fisherman/shepherd. "Unbind Lazarus so he can go home," He enjoined the stunned witnesses to the dead man's resurrection. "I have a Haitian daughter who needs you," He whispered to Bill and me. Until we are Home at last, He will not stop inviting our passion, asking that for love of Him we show love to His own. How can we refuse?

Home at Last

Each day we must live with the seeming incongruity of Jesus' words regarding our struggle to wait patiently and productively for His promised return. For He said that to find life we must give it up. He said that to be at rest we must struggle against our self-sufficiency and receive His grace. He said if we are to live as children of the King, we must become servant to all, in imitation of Him. In order to obey these hard words, we will need Christ desperately, for the forces of evil—not only in the heavenlies but in our own hearts as well—are pitted against us as we struggle to rest in abandonment to Jesus' love.

Not until we are captivated by the passionate pursuing love of our Bridegroom will we dare to face our terrified longing to be yoked to Him in identity and extravagant obedience. But bound to Him by His strong cords of love, we can commit ourselves to stop at nothing in our passion for Him and in our desire to obey Him. And when in our responsive love for Him we become willing to go wherever He tells us to go and to do whatever He bids us do, no matter what the cost or the outcome—then we can savor the nothing-to-hide, nothing-to-prove, nothing-to-lose rest of being the Bride of Christ, our Bridegroom's own man or woman, willing to follow Him into death itself.

I cannot always sustain that level of submissive rest for long periods of time without wavering in my faith. But each time I stray from Christ's rest, He draws me back again and again to His quiet presence. If I attend to His still voice and do not quench the burning of His fire within, I will hear more and more of what He wishes to tell me, and I can rest more and more quietly in His grace and in His sovereign rule over my life, even when I don't understand or like what He is doing. Each taste of His presence is also rich incentive to enjoy Him even more. This is the intoxication of holy love, God's seductive elixir offering joy unspeakable and full of glory to those who will risk the suffering of oneness with Him.

Come let us drink of His wine. Come let us rest in His love. Come let us take His yoke on our shoulders and join ourselves to His purposes. For even our reverent fear is part of the dread wonder of worshiping the One who is our coming Bridegroom.

Fear not, He says, *for you are My beloved, called to bear My name and to share My life.*

Enter My rest, His words still invite. *Come to Me, My bride, My joy. As you wait for Me, rest your heart in Me.*

I am coming soon.

Rest.

QUESTIONS TO CONSIDER

1. What has God been teaching you about rest?

2. What would you like to say to God right now?

3. What might the Lord want to say to you in response?

4. What are you willing to do to deepen your intimacy with Christ?

5. What are you willing to do to enlarge your experience of intimacy with someone you love?

6. What experiences in the past year have offered you opportunity to be part of God's larger kingdom story?

Regarding the opening story:

Todd learned an invaluable lesson as he tenderly entered suffering on Lynne's behalf, his passion for her purified in the fire of sorrow.

7. How did Todd's grieving lead him into greater rest in his intimacy with God and with Lynne?

NOTES

INTRODUCTION

1. *Webster's New Collegiate Dictionary*, 9th ed. (1985), 634.

CHAPTER 1: AMBIVALENCE

1. Walter Wangerin, *As for Me and My House* (Nashville: Thomas Nelson, 1990), 22–23.
2. Walter Wangerin, *Mourning into Dancing* (Grand Rapids: Zondervan, 1992), 94.

CHAPTER 2: DAMAGE

1. Judith Herman, *Trauma and Recovery* (New York: Basic Books, 1997), 51.
2. Ibid., 90.
3. Ibid.
4. Ibid., 89.

CHAPTER 3: DISOBEDIENCE

1. *NIV Study Bible* (Grand Rapids: Zondervan, 1995), footnote for Exodus 28:35.
2. Quoted in M. G. Lord, "Sleeping Beauty of the 90s," *Miami Herald*, 13 November 1995, p. 11A.

CHAPTER 4: CHOICE

1. Bryan Chapell, *Each for the Other* (Grand Rapids: Baker, 1998), 89–90.

CHAPTER 5: HUMILITY

1. Oswald Chambers, *My Utmost for His Highest* (Westwood, N.J.: Barbour and Co., Inc., 1963), 247.
2. See also my books *Married without Masks* (Grand Rapids: Baker, 1996) and *Heart to Heart about Men* (Colorado Springs: NavPress, 1995) for a more in-depth discussion of these issues.

CHAPTER 6: OBEDIENCE

1. *NIV Study Bible*, footnote for Joshua 3:10.
2. Ibid., note for Joshua 5:9.

CHAPTER 7: MOVEMENT

1. A. W. Tozer, *The Knowledge of the Holy* (San Francisco: Harper & Row, 1961), 111.
2. Ibid., 112.

3. Ibid., 113.
4. *NIV Study Bible*, note for Joshua 6:17.
5. Larry Crabb, Al Andrews, and Don Hudson, *The Silence of Adam* (Grand Rapids: Zondervan, 1995), 74.
6. Lawrence O. Richards, ed., *The Revell Bible Dictionary* (Grand Rapids: Revell, 1990), 189.
7. Ibid., 190.
8. Ibid.
9. Ibid., 1010.
10. Crabb, Andrews, and Hudson, *Silence of Adam*, 21.
11. Ibid., 32.
12. Ibid., 14.
13. Ibid., 110.
14. Ibid., 185.
15. Ibid., 176.
16. Ibid., 149.

CHAPTER 8: RISK

1. See *Heart to Heart about* Men, especially section 2.
2. Kenneth E. Bailey, *Poet and Peasant* and *Through Peasant Eyes* (Grand Rapids: Eerdmans, 1983), 4.
3. Ibid., 5.
4. Ibid., 9.
5. Henri J. M. Nouwen, "The Fatherhood of Compassion," from *The Return of the Prodigal*, reprinted in *Key Life Network* 11, no. 3 (July–September 1996): 10.
6. Chambers, My *Utmost for His Highest*, 6–7.

CHAPTER 9: GRACE

1. Richards, *Revell Bible Dictionary*, 855.
2. Bailey, *Through Peasant Eyes*, 12.
3. Ibid., 16.
4. Ibid., 18–19.
5. David and Karen Mains, *Tales of the Kingdom* (Elgin, Ill.: Chariot Books, 1983), 74–94.
6. *Webster's New Collegiate Dictionary*, 999.
7. Chambers, *My Utmost for His Highest*, 137.

CHAPTER 10: SACRIFICE

1. Crabb, Andrews, and Hudson, *Silence of Adam*, 183.
2. Richards, *Revell Bible Dictionary*, 1043.
3. Crabb, Andrews, and Hudson, *Silence of Adam*, 121.
4. Ana Veciana-Suarez, "Life without Father," *Miami Herald*, 15 June 1997, *Tropic* magazine, p. 4.
5. Crabb, Andrews, and Hudson, *Silence of Adam*, 179.

CHAPTER 11: TRUST

1. See Groom, *Married without Masks*, for an in-depth exploration of this important concept.

CHAPTER 12: REST

1. Tozer, *Knowledge of the Holy*, 106.

ABOUT THE AUTHOR

Nancy Groom is a popular speaker and the author of several books on marriage and relationships. She graduated from Calvin College and now lives with her husband, Bill, in Hudsonville, Michigan.